BURMA
VICTORY

*Donated
In Memory of*

MELVIN PFEIFFER

By

Marilyn Moore

BURMA VICTORY

Imphal, Kohima and the Chindit issue,
March 1944 to May 1945

DAVID ROONEY

ARMS AND
ARMOUR

Arms and Armour Press
A Cassell Imprint
Villiers House, 41–47 Strand, London WC2N 5JE.

Distributed in the USA by Sterling Publishing Co. Inc., 387 Park
Avenue South, New York, NY 10016-8810.

Distributed in Australia by Capricorn Link (Australia) Pty. Ltd, P.O.
Box 665, Lane Cove, New South Wales 2066.

British Library Cataloguing in Publication Data: a catalogue record
for this book is available from the British Library

ISBN 1-85409-109-3

Jacket illustration: *The Battle of the Tennis Court* by Terence
Cuneo.

Designed and edited by DAG Publications Ltd. Designed by David
Gibbons; edited by Michael Boxall; typeset by Ronset Typesetters,
Darwen, Lancashire; camerawork by M&E Reproductions, North
Fambridge, Essex; printed and bound in Great Britain by
by Hartnolls Ltd, Bodmin, Cornwall.

CONTENTS

LIST OF MAPS

INTRODUCTION

THIS BOOK aims to tell the story of the campaign of Fourteenth Army in Burma and, in particular, the two great battles of Imphal and Kohima, in which the Japanese forces suffered the greatest defeat in their history. The book is intended, not for the military history expert, but rather for the general reader, for a younger generation, perhaps the grandchildren of the veterans who fought there, so that this story of bravery and suffering will not be lost. In Britain the memory of this campaign has been kept alive by the admirable work of the Burma Star Association, but it must be remembered that these victories belong above all to the fighting soldiers of the Indian Army, the members of so many proud Indian divisions – 5th, 17th, 20th, 23rd and others – and their unique blend of Indian regiments with British county regiments.

A number of excellent books have been written about the Burma campaign, but many of them are extremely detailed and rather confusing to the beginner. I should like to pay tribute to these books and to the work of their authors, and to say that I have drawn heavily on them in obtaining material for this story, which I hope may act as an introduction to the study of the Burma campaign and may encourage the reader, having been given a clear outline, to study these other books in greater detail.

The battles of Imphal and Kohima were extremely complex, and the terrain in Burma is confusing. To prevent the reader from getting lost, therefore, a sketch map appears at the beginning of each chapter or section of a chapter, and every place-name occurring in the text can be found on the relevant map. Similarly, some books are difficult to follow; out of the blue a name is mentioned – British, Indian, Japanese or Gurkha – but the unfortunate reader is given no indication as to the who and why.

So a brief biographical note on almost all the principal characters has been provided. When a name first appears in the text, the rank is given, but thereafter just the surname. The list is alphabetical and is thus quite easy to refer to. The notes have been deliberately kept brief, and refer to the rank of the person at the time. This is not in disrespect of men who subsequently gained higher rank, but is intended simply to assist in the swift identification of those who took part in these battles. Full details of ranks, honours and awards are readily available in the books listed in the Bibliography.

Similarly, in some chapters where the name of a regiment appears frequently, the full title has been abbreviated so as to assist the flow of the narrative; I hope this will not offend the sticklers for correct titles, whose views I entirely understand. Occasionally the term 'British forces' is used, and is meant to include British, Indian, Gurkha and African units.

The Bibliography contains a short list of the main books dealing with the Burma campaign, together with a brief comment which may be useful to those readers not familiar with this area of military history.

My research into the battles of Imphal and Kohima led inevitably to the Chindit campaign and its eccentric leader, Major-General Orde Wingate. This is a highly controversial field which I have only touched on briefly, but it raises serious issues which deserve further study; notably how far the Chindits in Operation 'Thursday' influenced the outcome of the two battles and, even more importantly, the attempt by the official establishment to denigrate Wingate and all that he did.

Here I should like to pay tribute to Louis Allen, who kindly offered me help and advice, and to his outstanding book *Burma, The Longest War*, which has changed everyone's perception of the Burma campaign. The result of a lifetime of dedicated study, his book is a mine of information which enables readers to understand the campaign from both the Japanese and British angles. I should also like to express my gratitude to all those who have helped and advised me during the preparation of this book: my former colleague at RMA Sandhurst, David Chandler, now Head of the Department of War Studies; the staff at the Cambridge University Library; the Public Record Office, Kew; the Imperial War Museum; the National Army Museum. Most of all I wish to thank my good friend, the Reverend Peter Kane, former Lieutenant-Colonel in the Gurkhas, and a loyal Chindit, whose knowledge and help was invaluable. Phil Dewey, The Royal Norfolk Regiment, generously provided photographs taken during a recent pilgrimage to Kohima and Imphal; Tony Mills, former editor of *Dekho*, kindly helped in the initial stages of this project; Douglas Williams, author of *194 Squadron, The Friendly Firm*, provided valuable information on the role of the RAF; Bill Clarke of the Cambridge Burma Star Association, gave early encouragement. Finally, I am grateful to our daughter Kathy Rooney for her help with the script, and to my wife for her endless help and support. I have received much assistance in this project, but the responsibility for any mistakes is entirely mine.

THE BURMA STAR ASSOCIATION

In 1990, Tony Mills, then the editor of *Dekho,* offered to put a note about my book in the next issue of *Dekho*, and this brought a gratifying response, which provided much valuable detail and assisted me in presenting the view of the fighting soldiers and airmen. The name of all those who contacted me are listed below, and I express my gratitude to them and my apologies to those who sent me information which has not been included in the text. Several correspondents pointed out that the part played by small units – e.g., The Recce Regiment – is often overlooked in books about the campaign. I sympathize with that point of view, but unfortunately in a general book of this type and, much to my regret, it has not proved possible to rectify that criticism.

I greatly admire the work of the Burma Star Association, and I am pleased that the Publisher, Arms and Armour Press, has agreed to enable the Association to benefit from sales of the book. The following members kindly wrote to me: Allen, Louis, Durham; Atkins, D., Pulborough; Baker, H., Clacton; Barnett, A., Camberley; Braybrooke, D., Bourn End; Brooman, G., London; Cammack, A., East Preston; Cane, P., Cambridge; Child, W., Falmouth; Clarke, W., Cambridge; Clarke, W., Oakington; Collins, L., Plymouth; Conroy, P., Sandown; Delaney, A., Queensland, Australia; Dewey, P., Littleport; Gammons, J., Huntingdon; Gibson, J., Cheam; Gorman, W., Dalry, Ayrshire; Hunter, C., Elgin; Ingham, K., Bristol; Jones, G., Belfast; King-Clarke, R., Shandon, Dunbarton; Kirk, H., Hull; Maillard, H., Sheffield; Marsh, E., Eastbourne; Maurice, Dr R., Marlborough; McCarthy, Miss M., Wimborne; Mills, A., Totnes; Mountstephen, P., Melbourne, Australia; O'Driscoll, Dr M., Finchley; Peattie, D., Plymouth; Pendred, N. Rye; Pollock, E., Dulwich; Roy, A., Putney; Sampson, A., Surbiton; Skene, J., Bristol; Still, E., Southampton; Swanston, W., Jedburgh; Weiler, T., Isleworth; White, Miss M., St Albans; Williams, D., London; Wood, Mrs M., Lincoln; Wright, J. H., Lincoln.

David Rooney, Cambridge, 1992

CHAPTER I
BACKGROUND

AFTER CHRISTMAS 1943 a visitor who had spent the holiday with friends in Imphal described the area as idyllic – like Shangri La – a wonderful climate, beautiful scenery, a happy smiling people, a profusion of the most wonderful plants and trees, with endless flights of wild fowl, and with the rivers and streams teeming with fish. Yet, within the space of a few weeks, Imphal and neighbouring Kohima were to witness some of the most savage fighting of the Second World War, and afterwards the two small towns were to resemble the battlefields of the Somme.

RETREAT, 1942

The backdrop to these battles lay in the humiliating defeat and retreat of the British forces when the Japanese invaded Burma in January 1942, and also in the strategic situation in southern China where the Japanese faced the corrupt regime of Chiang Kai-shek. The Japanese had been fighting in China since 1931 and they had driven the Chinese defenders into the west and north. By 1939 Japan held the whole of the Chinese coast, with Chiang Kai-shek bottled-up in Chungking in the far south-west, and Mao Tse-tung, after the Long March, similarly beleaguered in north-west China where he was actively indoctrinating the peasants in the theory and practice of Communism.

The Burma road, from Rangoon, through Mandalay and Lashio to Kunming provided Chiang Kai-shek with his only link to the outside world. He depended substantially on American help, and he had an effective lobby in Washington which cultivated the idea of China as a valiant ally fighting against the Japanese. He succeeded to the extent that a strong faction among the American Chiefs of Staff put support for Chiang among their highest priorities. They were prepared to provide large sums of money and millions of dollars worth of equipment to keep China in the war and, further, to develop south-west China as a base from which US aircraft could bomb Japan, and Chinese forces with American backing could eventually defeat the Japanese ground forces. Thus the overland route – the Burma Road – and, equally, the airlift from 1942–1944 by American airmen over the mountains to Chungking, known as 'The Hump', remained a major factor in US policy and was to have a direct impact on the battles at Imphal and Kohima.

The Japanese occupation of Indo-China in July 1941 prompted
America to increase its Lease Lend aid for China through Rangoon and up
the Burma Road. Inefficiency, theft and corruption accounted for the
two-thirds of those supplies that failed to reach Chungking, and the vast
stocks which built up at Rangoon proved to be a tempting target for the

Burma: The 1942 Retreat

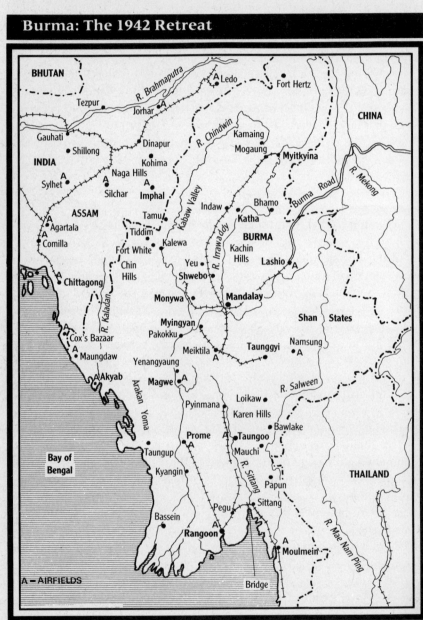

A = AIRFIELDS

Japanese when, after their lightning strikes at Pearl Harbor, Hong Kong, Singapore and Malaya, they invaded Burma in January 1942.

Burma was ill-prepared in every way for the Japanese assault. Administratively it was linked to India, but during the 1930s it had been granted a new constitution and a legislature in response to Burmese demands for more political progress. These measures did little to satisfy Burmese demands, and the Japanese had no difficulty in gaining support for their underground movement led by Colonel Suzuki. He organized the Burma Independence Army which gave considerable help to the Japanese during their advance.

In Burma, almost impenetrable mountains in the north dominate the country, and from this bastion, formidable ranges sweep southwards penning in the great Irrawaddy and Chindwin rivers which join just south of Mandalay, and flow southwards past Prome to the sea near Rangoon. The rivers dominated the strategy of the Burma campaign and provided the main highways and lines of communication – the primitive railway and the few metalled roads merely following the river valleys.

Partly because of the terrain, defence had been gravely neglected. The government had no overall defence plan, few properly trained troops, and few aircraft, tanks or guns. The 1st Burma Division, prepared for little more than internal security activities, proved to be quite inadequate against experienced and battle-hardened Japanese divisions. Similarly, 17th Indian Light Division was rushed into the breach in January 1942, having been trained and equipped for rapid movement in the western desert of north Africa. At the last moment – 20 February – 7 Armoured Brigade arrived, and though ill-equipped for jungle warfare, fought all the way to the borders of India. Wavell and Alexander, like their troops, were thrown into an almost impossible situation. Against such inadequate defences the Japanese attacked initially with two experienced divisions, 33rd and 55th, and later added three more.

British forces were rapidly driven out of Burma in 1942, but it should be remembered that although it was a major defeat and a country bigger than France and Belgium was lost to the enemy, the British troops involved were two small and inadequate divisions, not trained or equipped for the task that faced them. It was from such a situation that the myth of the invincible Japanese arose.

General Slim, who had fought in Africa and the Middle East, arrived in Burma from Iraq on 13 March 1942, to take command of the two battered divisions, which were given the title Burma Corps, though he was provided with no proper headquarters and just had to do his best in a hopeless situation. Slim suffered with his men in the retreat, but won their respect and affection. Later, he was to rebuild their confidence and prowess, and lead them to victory at Imphal and Kohima. Initially he had the advantage that he was in no way responsible for the disgraceful inadequacies of the Burma defences.

On his arrival he reported to General Alexander at Prome, nearly 150 miles north of Rangoon which had already fallen. Slim had been charged by General Wavell in India, to ensure that his forces were not cut off completely by the Japanese, to protect the road from Assam into Burma via Imphal, and to keep contact with the Chinese forces in north-eastern Burma. The Chinese constituted a new factor which Slim had to grasp very rapidly.

As the Japanese advance continued Slim became closely involved with the Chinese forces under their colourful commander General 'Vinegar Joe' Stilwell. He had been US Military Attaché in China up to 1939, and in January 1942 became Chief of Staff to Chiang Kai-shek, and commander of the Chinese forces in north Burma. On his appointment, Stilwell arranged that the supplies from the USA for the proposed thirty Chinese divisions should be under his control, and should be diverted through Calcutta when Rangoon fell. He also arranged for enough aircraft to lift this huge volume of supplies to China over 'The Hump'.

Slim and Stilwell arrived in Burma at about the same time and faced similar daunting problems. By the middle of March the Japanese had inflicted a crushing defeat on 17th Division at the Sittang Bridge, had taken Rangoon and were driving rapidly north. At the eastern end of the front a Chinese division was bravely attempting to hold the Japanese at Taungoo. Stilwell, who nominally had other divisions under his command, tried to get two more divisions to come forward and support the Taungoo defence, but, as he was to discover over the next two years, the divisional commanders often frustrated his orders or dragged their feet on the secret instructions of Chiang Kai-shek. There is little doubt that three Chinese divisions could have held the Japanese at Taungoo, but Chiang's duplicity made this impossible and Stilwell's forces were bundled northwards alongside the British.

Alexander and Slim, though to their own disadvantage, accepted the directive that they should maintain contact with the Chinese forces. Slim generously sent a strong force drawn from 17th Division and 7 Armoured Brigade to try to rescue the Chinese at Taungoo. This proved to be a disaster; the British force was itself surrounded and suffered heavy casualties in men, guns and tanks, without being able to do anything to help the Chinese. The Japanese advance rolled relentlessly forward, and there were several occasions when they were known to have used their British and Indian prisoners for bayonet practice.

During April Burma Corps retreated further north, and Slim had the unenviable task of destroying the great oil wells at Yenangyaung. In the battle here, Stilwell repaid to some extent the help he had received during the incident at Taungoo, and sent the Chinese 38th Division under General Sun to help Slim during the battle for the oilfields. This was a generous move because 38th Division under Sun was about the only Chinese division that was properly led and prepared to fight. It did well at Yenangyaung and helped to extricate the forces of Burma Division.

Before the end of April decisions had to be made about the future withdrawal strategy, both of Burma Corps and of the Chinese forces under Stilwell. Wavell, sitting in Delhi, appeared to be dangerously out of touch with the reality of the situation, although he continued to give detailed orders. He even suggested that part of 7 Armoured Brigade should retreat with the Chinese forces up to Chungking. Alexander and Slim felt this to be unwise, and on 25 April Alexander gave the order for the British forces to cross the Irrawaddy near Mandalay and to retreat north and north-west in the general direction of Kalewa at the southern end of the Kabaw valley. Great relief was felt by all that there was no further suggestion that they be sent to China.

As the retreat continued during April 1942 the Japanese sent off a division to the eastern flank to make a swift dash towards Lashio on the Burma Road. Several Chinese divisions just disintegrated and fled when the Japanese approached. Stilwell, continuing to work closely with Slim and Alexander, was nearly demented because, although Chiang Kai-shek had ordered all officers to accept Stilwell's commands, frequently Chinese divisions refused to attack or to defend key points. Similarly, Chiang Kai-shek would give his agreement to an attack and then change his mind a few days later and order a division to withdraw – without any reference to Stilwell. On the eastern front the Japanese advanced 80 miles in three days simply because the Chinese would not fight. In this shambles, Stilwell took command of a Chinese division and personally led a counter-attack which halted the Japanese and drove them back near Taungyi, to the east of Meiktila, which showed that with determined leadership the enemy could be defeated.

Towards the end of April Alexander, Slim and Stilwell met for a final conference just north of Mandalay. The Chinese divisions had just crumpled up and the Japanese were approaching Lashio. The three generals agreed on an overall withdrawal north of Mandalay. Their remaining tasks were to get their forces safely out of Burma without being cut off by the Japanese; to decide on their route for withdrawal; and to consider how to keep contact between the British and Chinese forces. While they were conferring, two Japanese battalions with some tanks attacked and captured Lashio, from which 3,000 Chinese troops withdrew without fighting. The fall of Lashio seriously affected the decisions that had to be made about the line of retreat for the different armies. After further discussion it was agreed that Stilwell and the

Chinese divisions should go north from Mandalay along the railway route
to Myitkyina. Slim, with Burma Corps, now aimed to get his forces from
Monywa to Kalewa and over the Chindwin to Imphal. Movement for all
military units was made more difficult by panic-stricken masses of
refugees among whom were criminals as well as some Burmese and
Japanese agents who mingled with the crowds to loot, rob and murder.

On 1 May Slim faced a severe test of his leadership when the
Japanese, using their usual hook tactics of getting behind retreating
troops and establishing road-blocks, captured Monywa. This could have
been a disaster for Burma Corps, but Slim quickly reorganized his forces,
drove out the Japanese and by 3 May had established both divisions and 7
Armoured Brigade at Yeu. By 9 May the majority of Burma Corps,
though gravely hindered by the continuing mass of refugees, had reached
Kalewa and had crossed the Chindwin. The Corps rearguard had a
difficult time at Shwegyin where the road crossed the Chindwin. Here the
Japanese put in a strong attack, so that hundreds of tanks, guns and
vehicles had to be destroyed. Despite this, Burma Corps were able to save
30 jeeps, 50 trucks and nearly 30 guns as they started out on the last stage
of their retreat.

After Kalewa they faced the unhealthy Kabaw valley. Here, when
most were already sick or exhausted and their resistance at its lowest ebb,
thousands fell victim to the ravages of the malarial mosquito for which
the valley was notorious. To add to their discomfort the monsoon broke.
Malaria, cerebral malaria, dysentery and other tropical diseases took a
heavy toll as the exhausted and emaciated troops struggled along the
Kabaw valley and up the 7,000-foot climb to the Shenam Pass, where at
last they were able to look down to the Imphal plain.

Then, when the worst of their suffering should have been over, they
found that their bitterest moments were still to come. They had fought
bravely and had conducted themselves with honour, but instead of being
welcomed into a safe haven they were treated with scorn and derision.
Even Slim was greeted with harsh contempt by General Irwin, the tense
and arrogant Corps Commander at Imphal, who was responsible for
arranging their reception. Slim complained about Irwin's rudeness and
was told by Irwin, 'I can't be rude. I'm senior.' One incident can illustrate
the suffering of all. General Cowan, who had taken charge of 17th Indian
Division during the retreat, was conducted to a bare hillside with the
monsoon rain cascading down it, and was told that this was the area for
his division to encamp. He refused, and had a blazing row with Irwin, in
which he was stoutly supported by Slim. His troops were eventually
billeted in empty buildings in Imphal, but they felt a deep and bitter anger
at the way they had been treated. Irwin and Slim were to clash again.

Stilwell, leading the tattered remnant of his forces, also went through a gruelling retreat. In early May he reached Indaw with a small group of his American and Chinese staff. Here he learned that the Japanese had outdistanced him and had already captured Myitkyina, thus blocking his route north. He therefore changed his plan. Instead of moving north to reach China, from Indaw he led a party, including the staff and nurses of a mission hospital, westwards over daunting hills towards the Chindwin valley, and from there on to Imphal. He set out on 6 May.

The survival of his party depended very much on his own determination and leadership. He was disgusted with the Chinese generals who were only interested in saving their own skins. As the retreat progressed his anti-British criticism became fiercer. 'Dumb Limeys sitting around.' Later he commented, 'Two-thirds of the Limeys on ponies but none of our people.' [i.e., American.] Although the first storms of the monsoon were upon them, as his group approached the Chindwin they found the going easier, and were often welcomed in the prosperous Naga villages where there was food and help available. They trekked past Homalin, which was completely deserted, and then, while still some way from Imphal, they were met by the British 'With food, doctor, ponies, everything.' Stilwell's party finally arrived at Imphal on 22 May by which time Slim had completed his hand-over to Irwin and had left for Ranchi. Perhaps his fierce clash with Irwin achieved some good, for Stilwell, instead of his usual acid comments, noted, 'Cordial reception from the Limeys.' Two days later he flew to Delhi, and from India, China and Washington received high praise for his efforts in Burma. Slim commented, 'Stilwell had a dogged courage beyond praise.'

While Slim and Burma Corps were struggling towards Imphal, the Chinese forces were faring little better. Chiang Kai-shek ordered two divisions to continue marching north towards the area of Fort Hertz, but discipline in these divisions broke down completely and they became little more than marauding groups of bandits. In contrast, 38th Chinese Division under General Sun, which had co-operated with Slim during the retreat, received no orders from Chiang Kai-shek. Under Sun's positive leadership, the division conducted a skilful rearguard action against the Japanese and came out into northern Assam. Here, like the British, they received a cool reception.

Farther east the Japanese, after their capture of Lashio, advanced swiftly up the Burma Road, but the Chinese destroyed the bridge over the Salween gorge, and here they finally held the Japanese advance. At Lungling the Chinese at last showed some determination and in a major battle they defeated a strong Japanese force.

At the end of May 1942 the Japanese held a dominating strategic position. They had captured all their objectives and, although temporarily halted by the monsoon, they were in a position where they could attack either India or China, and they could bomb Calcutta. More importantly, they had cut the Burma Road and had effectively isolated China.

FORGING THE WEAPON, 1942–4

From the black days of May 1942, when there was little except the monsoon to stop a Japanese advance into India, the forging of a weapon which could halt the Japanese and defeat them, centred increasingly on the character, ability and drive of General Slim.

Some thought for the future had been given even during the retreat. Many men of the Burma Division were given a rifle, 50 rounds of ammunition and three months' pay, and told to go back to their village and await the return of the British. During the retreat Burma Corps had suffered 13,000 casualties in killed, wounded and missing. Those who survived were not fit to fight, and most had to be sent to the hospitals of eastern India which were not prepared for such a large influx of sick and dying. Slim's first task was to visit these hospitals and do what he could for his men.

In June 1942 Slim took over as Commander of XV Corps at Barrackpore outside Calcutta. Here he had two divisions under his command: 14th Division under General Lloyd, based on Chittagong and facing the Japanese in the Arakan; and 26th Indian Division, based on Calcutta, which had the difficult task of ensuring internal security in Bengal and Bihar, i.e., most of north-east India. Before Slim could start building up an effective striking force he had to oversee the defence of northern India and its very long coastline against the possibility of a Japanese attack from the sea, either to effect a landing on the coast, or to sail up the delta of the River Brahmaputra – the Sunderbans – and to attack Calcutta. There were few aircraft and virtually no naval defences to secure this huge area.

Fortunately, the Japanese made no attacks, but Slim soon faced serious problems of internal security, which started in August 1942. In forcing his demands for political independence, Gandhi started a campaign of Non-Violent Protest to force the British to 'Quit India'. In practice the campaign soon became extremely violent and threatened the forces at their most vulnerable point. All the railways and roads for the Burma front centred on Calcutta, and passed through Bengal where the most serious acts of violence took place. Supporters of the campaign made frequent vicious attacks on the railways, on stations, on signals and points, and on the trains themselves. Often trains were stopped and

Europeans were taken out and hacked to death. The outbreak in Calcutta, where there were plenty of troops, was easy to contain, but it was far more difficult to defend the entire railway system over the vast distances of Bengal and Bihar. Slim had to deploy 57 battalions on internal security instead of giving them urgent training for jungle warfare. He had the added worry as to whether, with the strong anti-British feeling which Gandhi had whipped up, the campaign of sabotage against the railways was being co-ordinated with plans for an attack by the Japanese.

The danger to the Burma forces from the campaign of railway sabotage can be illustrated by the fragile rail link from Calcutta. It travelled north-eastwards to Dimapur (the rail junction for Imphal) and on to Ledo, the rail centre for Stilwell's forces in North Burma and the supply base for the flights over 'The Hump' to Chiang Kai-shek in China. From Calcutta the railway went on normal gauge for 200 miles. Then all supplies had to be unloaded and re-loaded on to a 1-metre gauge railway for another 250 miles. At the end of this stretch of line the wagons had to be shunted on to barges to cross the River Brahmaputra, and were then put back on the railway to travel 150 miles to Dimapur, and beyond that another 200 miles to Ledo. This was the precarious supply route for all the

*_enough for 6+ infantry divisions._

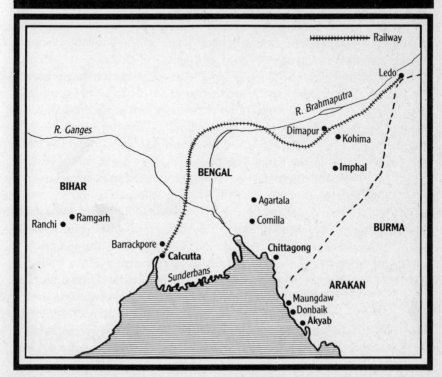

North-East India

Railway

Ledo

R. Brahmaputra

R. Ganges   Dimapur

Kohima

BENGAL

Imphal

BIHAR

Agartala

Ranchi   Ramgarh   Comilla

BURMA

Barrackpore

Calcutta   Chittagong

Sunderbans

ARAKAN

Maungdaw
Donbaik
Akyab

future operations to drive the Japanese out of Burma. In 1939 the railway could carry 600 tons a day; by the end of 1943 the capacity had been increased to 2,500 tons, and then six American railway battalions with highly trained staff and modern equipment lifted it to well over 4,000 tons a day. Fortunately the Indian protesters did not realize the damage they could cause by sabotaging this particular line, and they were not in touch with the Japanese.

At the same time as the railway route was being built-up, a substantial road construction programme was proceeding. The achievements of the Indian, British and American engineers in building three strategic roads have rightly received the highest praise. The first went eastwards into the Arakan where, because there was no stone, brick kilns were built to supply the road base; the second led up to Dimapur and then onwards past Kohima and Imphal to Tiddim; finally the Americans were building a spur going north from Dimapur to Ledo and thence southwards towards Myitkyina.

During the crisis over internal security, XV Corps Headquarters was moved to Ranchi where Slim was at last able to start on serious military training for his divisions. Gradually his strength increased. First, British 70th Division and 50 Armoured Brigade came under his command, then Indian 7th, 5th and 20th Divisions. All these were to play a distinguished part in the great battles of Kohima and Imphal.

As part of the build-up at Ranchi, Slim also had close links with General Sun and the two Chinese divisions which had come out to India in the 1942 retreat. Slim paid tribute to Stilwell's work in preparing these divisions for battle. 'Stilwell was magnificent,' he said, 'because he got Chiang Kai-shek to agree to supply the troops, India to accept them, the British to pay and equip them, and the Americans to fly an additional 13,000 over The Hump to be trained in India.'

Slim now had the chance to use his experience and his ideas to forge a victory weapon. He had learnt the lessons of the retreat, when Burma Corps had been tactically outclassed at every level by the Japanese who, instead of fearing the 'impenetrable' jungle, used it as a welcome means of concealed manoeuvre and surprise, especially in their hook tactics which they used to get behind retreating British forces and set up well-defended road-blocks. Slim's training brief started with the jungle: use the jungle; patrol actively; form a defensive box if surrounded; do not make frontal attacks on a narrow front; tanks can be used anywhere except in swamps but should be used in strength. Finally, he trained all units to keep the initiative, for then the enemy were easier to kill. Although Slim was already establishing close liaison with the RAF and USAAF, he did not at this stage mention air supply because he did not have the resources to provide it.

Active and successful attempts to build a confident and well-trained
new army, and to provide a sound infrastructure to support it, received a
dangerous setback when, under pressure from Churchill, Wavell ordered
the Eastern Army under General Irwin to move forward and attack in the
Arakan. This campaign, initially aiming to achieve a land advance
together with a combined operations attack on the island of Akyab, was
undertaken by 14th Division under General Lloyd, supervised directly by
Irwin at Eastern Army HQ. The operation started quite well in September
1942, and 14th Division advanced to Donbaik. Then, disastrously, it
paused, and this gave the Japanese time to bring up reinforcements and
to build defensive bunkers. The British advance then ground to a halt in
front of these well-sited bunkers which the Japanese defended strongly,
while Irwin sent more and more troops – five brigades in all – to reinforce
the failure of 14th Division – and to suffer grievous casualties. A few
tanks were thrown into the battle, but were quickly knocked out.

Slim, at XV Corps HQ at Ranchi, had no responsibility for this
operation and, while completely ignored by Irwin, he watched the
débâcle with increasing alarm. Eventually, in March 1943, Irwin ordered
Slim to go and assess the battle in the Arakan, but gave him no
responsibility for taking any action. Slim found morale at rock bottom
and most units scared and jittery. On one occasion while he was there
two Indian units started firing at each other, and an observer said, 'At
least we won that battle.' On 18 March Lloyd, who rejected Slim's advice
because he considered the jungle to be impenetrable, put in a final attack.
This failed, with very heavy casualties, but very soon afterwards the
Japanese advanced rapidly through the impenetrable jungle, cut behind
one brigade, cut behind another which just disintegrated (47 Brigade),
and overran a third (6 Brigade).

The retreat continued and at the end of April Irwin replaced Lloyd
with General Lomax, and at last appointed Slim to take over as Corps
Commander of the forces in the Arakan. He and Lomax organized a
withdrawal to an area north of Maungdaw where, with the start of the
monsoon in May, they felt they could hold the Japanese. The Arakan
defeat destroyed much of the confidence which had been built up in XV
Corps, reinforced the old fears of the Japanese fighters in the jungle, and
again brought morale to a dangerously low ebb.

The Arakan incident illustrates another aspect of modern war – the
intense and sometimes bitter rivalry between commanders – bad among
the Allied forces but more than matched by the Japanese. Irwin, who
commanded the Eastern Army, had deliberately kept Slim out of the
Arakan operation even though Lloyd with nine brigades in his division
badly needed the support of a Corps HQ. Then when the Japanese had
already won a substantial victory, Irwin ordered Slim to take command.

Just a few weeks later Irwin cabled Slim to tell him that he was relieved of his command. In a black moment Slim said he would go home and join the Home Guard. Later, in *Defeat into Victory*, Slim, in his honourable way, makes no mention of this incident, and merely records that on 21 May 1943 he heard that General Giffard had replaced General Irwin. Slim's biographer Ronald Lewin gives more details of this remarkable incident. He describes how Irwin – having already cabled Slim's dismissal – was visiting Imphal when he received a cable relieving him of his own command. He then cabled to Slim, 'You are not sacked. I am.' In fact Slim was called to Delhi for urgent consultations with General Giffard, with whom he continued to have an excellent relationship throughout the rest of the Burma campaign. The question still remains, had Irwin tried to involve Slim at the end of a disastrous campaign just in order to get rid of him?

Slim's sound and successful work in building up XV Corp's morale and expertise had not gone unnoticed and on 15 October 1943 he was called to Delhi and given command of Fourteenth Army. Wavell, who became Viceroy of India, had been succeeded by General Auchinleck who immediately summoned Slim to a conference about supplies for Fourteenth Army. Slim pays generous tribute to Auchinleck for his achievement in galvanizing an inefficient and moribund supply system into something that was able, within a few months, to provide all the necessary food, ammunition, weapons, vehicles and aircraft in sufficient quantities to make possible the successful campaign at Kohima and Imphal, and the advance to Rangoon.

The situation in November 1943 was difficult. Food supplies were totally inadequate for a force of half a million men requiring many different types of rations. Lack of fresh vegetables created another hazard. Shortages of weapons and ammunition – from .303in rounds for rifle and Brens to shells for howitzers – and the problems of transporting them seemed likely to undermine any chance of military success. Problems of health loomed even larger. In 1943, for every man evacuated with wounds, 120 were evacuated with sickness. The incidence of malaria came to 84 per cent per annum, and to this had to be added the depredations of dysentery, typhus and other tropical diseases. Slim took a tough line. The new drug Mepacrine effectively prevented malaria, but often men did not take it because a dose of malaria could mean evacuation to hospitals in India, with a chance of never rejoining your front-line unit. Slim's method worked quickly. He had sudden checks made to see if troops had taken their Mepacrine, and in units which dropped below 95 per cent he sacked the CO. He only had to do this three times and the message got through.

Medical services established Forward Treatment Units which meant that men could be treated just behind the lines and quickly returned to their units. This also discouraged malingerers. The Forward Treatment Units and the knowledge that wounded men would be flown out to good hospitals rapidly improved morale.

Slim's views on morale were clear, pungent and effective, and he rapidly imbued the whole of Fourteenth Army with a positive sense of purpose.

STRATEGIC ISSUES

By the middle of 1943, despite the setback in the Arakan, a substantial build-up of Indian and British forces was taking place in and around Imphal, but decisions taken elsewhere were to decide the pattern of events which shaped the actual battle. The Quebec Conference of August 1943, attended by Roosevelt, Churchill and their chiefs of staff, discussed the war situation and made some crucial decisions.

In their discussions the Americans gave priority to support for Chiang Kai-shek and the re-establishment of the Burma Road, which remained the objective of Stilwell's forces. Although Stilwell had informed Washington of the duplicity, deceit and dishonesty of Chiang Kai-shek, the Americans were continuing to send millions of dollars' worth of money, supplies and equipment over The Hump to Chungking. Chiang Kai-shek used this, not to pursue the war against the Japanese in Burma, but rather to bribe the local warlords to stay on his side and, more particularly, to build up his forces ready to attack Mao Tse-tung and the Communists as soon as the Americans had defeated Japan. The demands of air transport over The Hump were soon to clash severely with the urgent need to bring help to the beleaguered garrisons of Imphal and Kohima.

In contrast, the British gave priority to the concept of a series of amphibious assaults leading via Rangoon to Singapore. A land battle in Burma was no one's absolute priority. Perhaps the most important decision made at Quebec was the establishment of South East Asia Command, and the imaginative idea of Churchill to suggest Lord Louis Mountbatten as Supreme Commander. The more detailed Quebec plans included an advanced by XV Corps in the Arakan; IV Corps to advance from Imphal and cross the Chindwin; Stilwell to advance down the Ledo road; the Chinese to attack on the eastern flank from Yunnan; and Wingate to lead a Chindit expedition to land behind the Japanese lines, in the area of Indaw, to disrupt the lines of communication to the Japanese forces facing Stilwell.

Mountbatten arrived in Delhi in October 1943 and quickly established his authority over some older commanders who resented his promotion. His most important decision was to appoint Slim to command Fourteenth Army, and from that moment Mountbatten and Slim, those two outstanding commanders, worked in harmony – complementing each other ideally.

The tasks they had to tackle – before they could be ready to face the Japanese – are well illustrated by a memorandum written by Mountbatten after he had met his naval, army and air force commanders. They had explained that they could not stop the Japanese in the jungle, that air supply of forward units was not possible, that the monsoon prevented fighting and flying for five months of the year, that they disapproved of any support being given to Wingate, and that they rejected the offer of American railway battalions to work on the Dimapur railway. They concluded by rejecting the suggestion that they should visit front-line units in order to build up morale. It is a measure of the joint achievement of Mountbatten and Slim that, from this defeatist attitude, they were able in the six months before the battles of Kohima and Imphal began, to weld Fourteenth Army into an effective fighting force. Even in this their strengths were complementary. Most RAF veterans remember the terrific impact of Mountbatten's impromptu talks, while some West Yorks, with perhaps a more down-to-earth approach, preferred Slim, considering Mountbatten a bit of a 'Flash Harry'.

Mountbatten gained an immediate response from Slim and Air Marshal Baldwin, the RAF Commander, but his ideas of continuing to fight through the monsoon and, when necessary, supplying all units by air so as to prevent any more retreats, were at first rejected with disdain by many subordinate commanders. Although Mountbatten gave Slim unstinting support, it must be remembered that as late as November 1943 the strategic plans of the Chiefs of Staff pointed towards amphibious assaults on Rangoon, Singapore or Sumatra, rather than a major battle at Imphal. There also remained the problem of Churchill's reaction to the unrest in Bengal, his distrust of the Indian Army, and his fear of another Indian Mutiny – a fear which persisted even when the Indian Army had won more than twenty VCs during the Burma campaign. A fundamental change of emphasis from amphibious landings to a land battle came about because all the ships and equipment which Mountbatten had expected for his operations were suddenly transferred to support the Second Front in Europe – and so the spotlight returned to Burma. The decision not to proceed with amphibious landings also gave the opportunity for Chiang Kai-shek to wriggle out of his commitment – made at Quebec – to launch a major attack with his armies from Yunnan, in co-ordination with attacks by Stilwell and by Fourteenth Army.

While the Allies were implementing the decisions of the Quebec Conference, the Japanese were planning their strategy. Early in 1943 they established the Burma Area Army with its Headquarters in Rangoon. Within this command General Mutaguchi, who was to be the key figure on the Japanese side in the Burma campaign, commanded 15th Army. From his HQ at Maymyo he directed three divisions – approximately 100,000 men all told: 56th Division faced the Chinese in Yunnan; 18th Division faced Stilwell in north Burma; and 33rd Division guarded the Chindwin. Mutaguchi, a powerful and aggressive commander, had been shaken by Wingate's first expedition (11 February–April 1943). Mutaguchi later wrote that his entire strategic thinking had been changed by Wingate's expedition which had convinced him that he must attack Imphal to pre-empt an Allied offensive. It also gave him the idea that he could send off divisions into the jungle with minimal rations and supplies – an idea which cost the Japanese dear in the months to come. Mutaguchi quickly worked out a plan of attack, but it was not finally approved by Burma Area Army and by the High Command in Tokyo until September 1943.

He planned to use three divisions for his main assault on Kohima and Imphal: 33rd Division under General Yanagida, to attack the Tiddim area, destroy 17th Indian Division and advance up the road to Imphal; 15th Division under General Yamauchi together with the main force of the Indian National Army (recruited from Indian prisoners of war), to make two pincer movements towards Imphal from the east; and 31st Division under General Sato, to capture Kohima and drive forward rapidly to capture the strategic rail, road and supply centre at Dimapur. From there, Mutaguchi intended to embark on his triumphal 'March on Delhi' accompanied by Subhas Chandra Bose leading the Indian National Army.

The main attack by these three divisions was due to start on 15 March, but an essential part of the plan was an aggressive advance by 55th Division under General Hanaya against 5th and 7th Indian Divisions, and 81st West African Division in the Arakan. The purpose and careful timing of this attack was to force Slim to commit his reserves to the defence of the Arakan before the main Japanese attack on Imphal took place.

All Mutaguchi's plans depended on a rapid advance which would sweep aside the Indian and British opposition, as had been done in 1942. Assuming, wrongly, that he had learnt the lesson of Wingate's first expedition, he sent off all his units with one month's supply of food and ammunition, which was to be supplemented by what could be captured at the great supply bases around Imphal which he knew the British had been assiduously building up. Some units in the Japanese 31st Division deployed for the advance from the northern Chindwin front were provided with additional mules and herds of bullocks, which could be used later on to supplement rations, but this idea did not work well in practice.

The Japanese 55th Division, a unit of about 8,000 men, started the 'Ha Go' offensive in the Arakan on 3 February 1944, by a swift advance against 5th and 7th Indian Divisions – an advance which seemed to take the defenders completely by surprise. After several days of fairly swift Japanese advance, the two divisions rallied and held their positions, and Slim gave the order that they were to be supplied by air. On 6 February, in face of further Japanese advances, the defending forces formed the 'Administrative Box' – a new defensive tactic by which a unit of any size would assume all-round defence, while being supplied by air.

The Admin. Box successfully held out from 6 to 24 February. At the beginning the Japanese were able to disrupt some of the air supplies, but for most of the time the new Spitfire squadrons were able to establish air superiority and ensure the safety of air supplies to the Box. As the 'Ha Go' offensive and siege of the Admin. Box continued, Slim brought two more divisions into the Arakan – 26th Indian Division and the British 36th Division.

On 24 February Hanaya suddenly ordered 55th Division to with-draw. His men were short of ammunition, many were starving and he had sustained 5,000 casualties, but on the other hand he had caused considerable disruption to two enemy divisions and had caused Slim to commit two additional reserve divisions to the Arakan, just when the main Japanese attack on Imphal was about to start. This is exactly what Mutaguchi wanted.

On the British side, the Battle of the Admin. Box was a considerable success. A motley assembly of ancillary troops – cooks, clerks and drivers – strengthened only by two highly trained fighting units, 25th Dragoons and 2nd West Yorks, had held out and had beaten one of the best Japanese divisions, inflicting more than 5,000 casualties. This was an excellent boost to morale at a critical time. Slim, certainly, had to use some of his reserves, but soon afterwards it was the Japanese who had to rush reinforcements into the Arakan to oppose the firm advance of XV Corps, and Slim, through the excellent work of the RAF and USAAF, was able rapidly to transfer divisions back to the Imphal and Kohima theatre before the battle.

With the Imphal battles fast approaching, Mutaguchi had not assimilated certain significant lessons from the campaign in the Arakan. He had failed to recognize the significant new dimensions to jungle fighting that had been demonstrated at the battle of the Admin. Box – namely, that, with air superiority, a unit surrounded by the enemy can defend itself quite easily while being supplied by air. He had failed to realize that the Indian and British units in 5th and 7th Indian Divisions – notably 25th Dragoons and 2nd West Yorks – had shown a tough and determined fighting quality, and did not quickly succumb to Japanese pressure. Finally, Mutaguchi had failed to notice that one reason for the collapse of 55th Division at the end of the 'Ha Go' campaign was that the men were starving – one month's rations were not enough.

CHAPTER 2

THE TIDDIM ROAD BATTLES

B Y CHRISTMAS 1943 17th Indian Light Division had firmly established itself in the Chin Hills lying south and west of the small town of Tiddim. Commanded by General 'Punch' Cowan, who had brought the division out of Burma in the retreat of 1942, it had been re-equipped, brought up to strength and trained to a high pitch of excellence. As a 'Light Division' it consisted of only two brigades: 48 Brigade made up of 9th Battalion the Border Regiment, 2/5th Gurkhas and 1/7th Gurkhas; and 63 Indian Infantry Brigade with 1/3rd Gurkhas, 1/4th Gurkhas and 1/10th Gurkhas. The 9th Border Battalion had not been in action before, and was quietly blooded in the high hills and deep valleys lying south of Tiddim in the Chin Hills.

Those infantry units within striking distance of the Japanese had had sharp clashes with enemy patrols and, over a period of several months, had built up a series of formidable and well-sited defences. Normal bunkers were deep enough for two men to fire from, they were roofed with substantial logs and were sufficiently spacious for one man to sleep during the two-hours-on two-hours-off duty rota. Each trench had a wire or string to communicate with the neighbouring trench and all trenches were linked in a defensive fire plan.

Several units had been sufficiently static to have time to build bamboo messes and even a bamboo chapel. Many of these positions lay at a height of more than 8,000 feet and were frequently covered in cloud and mist. The height meant that all water had to be carried up, usually by mule, and having a bath necessitated a descent of several thousand feet to

Units Involved in the Tiddim Road Battles

British	Japanese
17th Indian Light Division	33rd Division
General Cowan	General Yanagida
48 Indian Infantry Brigade	214th Regiment
63 Indian Infantry Brigade	215th Regiment
	(A Japanese regiment had
	three battalions)

The Tiddim Road Battles, March to April 1944

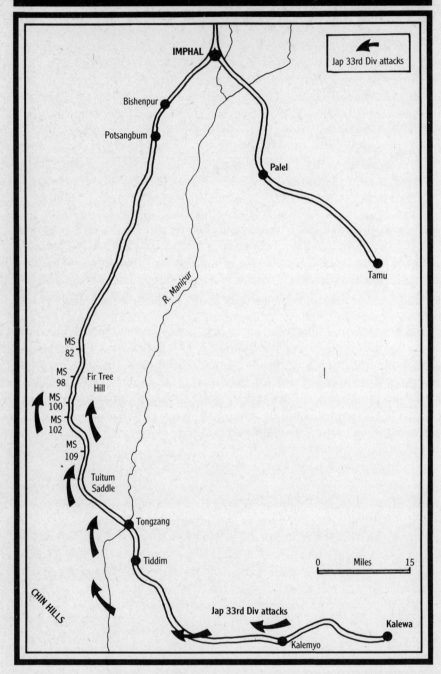

IMPHAL

Jap 33rd Div attacks

Bishenpur

Potsangbum

Palel

R. Manipur

Tamu

MS
82

MS
98

Fir Tree
Hill

MS
100

MS
102

MS
109

Tuitum
Saddle

Tongzang

Tiddim

0   Miles   15

CHIN HILLS

Jap 33rd Div attacks

Kalewa

Kalemyo

the River Manipur, and a climb back up equivalent to ascending Ben Nevis.

A steady routine had been established. The units stood down at 0600 hours, checked weapons and had breakfast. The cooks made a mixture like porridge which was served with bread and a mug of tea. Sometimes bacon or soya link sausage and baked beans were added to vary the monotonous diet. Lunch consisted of sardines and biscuits; for tea, bully beef or occasionally fresh meat if a mule had been killed. Platoons and sections not on patrol spent their days improving defences, checking weapons and studying every available Intelligence detail brought back by previous patrols.

On Christmas Day 1943 a patrol from the Border Regiment had a sharp clash with a Japanese patrol while in the chapel others were singing Christmas carols. 'Death as well as birth was in the air that morning.' After the carol singing a Christmas dinner was served, with turkey or chicken and an extra ration of beer or rum.

The relatively fortunate situation of 17th Division at this time had been made possible by the outstanding achievement of the engineer, transport and technical units which had laboured since September 1942 to build the road southwards from Imphal to Tiddim. At that time there had been seventeen miles of shingle leading south from Imphal, then a few miles of cart track which petered out into a rough path. To build 130 miles of road over that country with limited equipment was an engineering tour de force and reflected the greatest credit on the Indian and British engineers and other units involved. Much of the labour on the road came from local Chin villagers who gave up their farming in return for cash payments, and who had established good relations with most units. The road had been built to make possible a major advance against the Japanese, so by Christmas 1943 the units strung out along the road could reasonably celebrate a job well done. At Christmas most units organized parties for Indian and British troops, with extra goats, turkeys and chicken, Christmas puddings and plenty of rum at one shilling a bottle. Some units even brought up dancing girls from Imphal.

Some parts of the road were healthier than others; while some units had a good health record others had nearly 90 per cent down with malaria. Outbreaks of cholera and scrub typhus were more serious and caused frequent casualties. The men in some units that had remained in fairly static positions on the road had taken local Manipuri girls to live with them, and venereal disease proved quite a problem. The Japanese tackled this difficulty more realistically by having an establishment of Korean 'comfort girls' on the basis of one girl to forty men. The girls could earn their release but often stayed on loyally with their unit.

static positions, food quality, disease – all are enemies of trained, motivated troops.

Fourteenth Army, extremely conscious of health problems in the jungle, had encouraged units to grow vegetables. This was the idea of General Snelling, a senior staff officer, and his name was linked in rude rhymes about radishes – the only vegetable that grew – and the soya link sausage which no one liked. By the end of 1943 morale in both the forward fighting units and the support units was high, but there were still the usual grumbles about bad decisions and bungling. One unit which lost its CO in an early skirmish recorded, 'This translated the CO to a higher sphere and one in which he could do less damage. The second in command took over amid general rejoicing.' Another officer, as the Japanese moved in, commented that, 'The Japanese have caught us short again.' In the same unit, the CO who had refused to recommend a VCO for a King's Commission found a cobra in his thunderbox.* The phrase 'SNAFU' (Situation normal all fouled up), which was popular at the time, tells its own story (see D. Atkins *The Reluctant Major* and *The Forgotten Major*).   * portable privy.

The Tiddim Road – a road strong enough to take two-way traffic for thousands of heavy military vehicles, including tanks and the huge Matador trucks that brought up the heavier guns and howitzers – was to play an important part in the events of the next months. The men who had built the road and constructed the bridges ready for a major attack, had to take part not in a triumphal advance, but in a hurried and hard-fought withdrawal, sometimes even having to blow up the very bridges they had sweated and laboured to build.

In the weeks after Christmas the level of fighting and reconnaissance patrols substantially increased. A reconnaissance patrol could consist of perhaps two men armed with tommy guns and a few grenades, but the more usual type of patrol would be of platoon strength. A platoon would take its 2in mortars and Bren guns with extra ammunition carried by a couple of mules. Food for several days would include bully beef, cheese, sardines, biscuits, tea, sugar and milk with a Tommy cooker. All units maintained a very high level of readiness both in static positions and on patrol. Aggressive patrolling had established a confident domination over the whole battle area, and morale remained high as the division prepared for a large-scale attack on the Japanese. This confidence explains to some extent the reluctance and tardiness of General Cowan to act on the order he received on 12 March to withdraw as rapidly as possible up the road to Imphal.

This withdrawal was part of General Slim's plan to entice the Japanese divisions forward from their positions in the Chindwin valley to the plain of Imphal. At Imphal the Japanese would have very long and vulnerable lines of communication, and the British would have the advantage of open country where their superiority in both armour and

* two usually mutually exclusive concepts.

artillery could be used to best effect, and where if necessary the whole of IV Corps could be supplied by air. This plan was not fully communicated to the fighting men of 17th Division, and it did not work out at all as expected.

To comply with the order of 12 March, Cowan faced a difficult task. He had to move 16,000 troops, 2,500 vehicles and 3,500 mules for about 150 miles, up a precarious road through jungle-covered mountains. What was worse, by the time Cowan started to move (14 March) the advanced troops of Yanagida's 33rd Division had swept round to the south and west of Tiddim and were already in a position to cut Cowan's line of retreat. So, instead of the swift and uncontested withdrawal that Slim had intended, 17th Division was fighting for its life every inch of the way northward from Tiddim.

A major clash took place at Tongzang (16 March) where the Imphal road crossed the River Manipur. This bridge, so crucial to the entire withdrawal, was defended by 1st Battalion West Yorks, which Cowan reinforced with the major part of 63 Brigade. Fighting lasted several days, but a Japanese battalion slipped past the defenders and established another road-block farther north. This created another crisis for Cowan, but he assembled all the available artillery – 129 Field Regiment, 29 Light Mountain Regiment, and 82 Indian Field Regiment. With the combined fire power of these units, together with an air strike by Hurricanes, he brought down a powerful bombardment on the Japanese positions and followed this immediately with an attack by a Gurkha battalion with bayonet and kukri. The attack succeeded and the Japanese withdrew.

The jungle-covered mountains bereft of human habitation made recognition very difficult, and many hard-fought battles can be identified only by the number of the milestone on the Imphal road. Milestone 109, where a large supply dump had been established ready for an advance, was the scene of several fiercely fought engagements. High hills overlooked the rare flat ground which had been chosen for the supply dump, and by 17 March these had been occupied by the advanced units of Japanese 33rd Division. Just before the Japanese attacked, 5,000 porters and labourers were led out to safety down a jungle track, but there were few fighting troops to defend the depot and the Japanese rapidly took it over – delighted to find enough food and stores to last a division for two months.

48 Brigade (9th Borders, 2/5th Gurkhas, 1/7th Gurkhas) now set about recapturing the depot and the surrounding positions. The Borders attacked first and were thrown back, but the follow-up attack by 2/5th Gurkhas succeeded in retaking the hill overlooking the depot. From there they could see that the Japanese had fled in haste. Here was discovered another instance where two Indian soldiers had been tied up and had

The Japanese Attack, March 1944

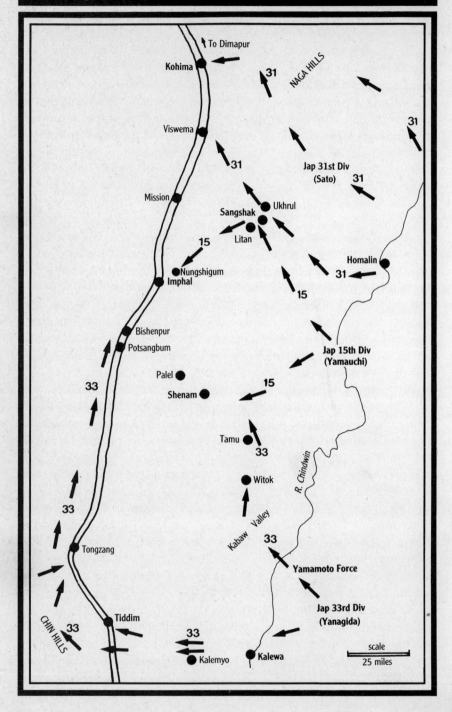

To Dimapur

Kohima

31

NAGA HILLS

31

Viswema

31

Jap 31st Div
(Sato)

31

Mission

31

Sangshak   Ukhrul

Litan

15

Homalin

Nungshigum

31

Imphal

15

Jap 15th Div
(Yamauchi)

Bishenpur

Potsangbum

Palel

15

33

Shenam

Tamu

33

R. Chindwin

Witok

33

Kabaw Valley

Yamamoto Force

33

Tongzang

Jap 33rd Div
(Yanagida)

CHIN HILLS

33

Tiddim

33

scale

Kalemyo   Kalewa

25 miles

been used for bayonet practice. A witness said it was the most horrifying sight that he had seen during the entire war.

Next the Gurkhas had to attack a ridge which overlooked the road and the depot. Two companies set off on a long march round the flank, but were delayed by almost vertical cliffs which they could only surmount by driving their bayonets into the ground to make a ladder. They scaled this obstacle and took the Japanese by surprise, but in a further attack the Gurkhas suffered heavy casualties in killed and wounded. They held their position overnight on 24 March even though they had no food and hardly any ammunition. The next morning a commando group of two platoons attacked along the ridge and the Japanese finally withdrew. On 26 March, 1st West Yorks regained the depot and recovered much of the equipment and stores. Many trucks had been saved because the Indian drivers had removed the contact-breakers from the engines.

While 48 Brigade fought to recover the depot at MS 109, 63 Brigade at Tuitum Saddle were still fighting a strong rearguard action against the Japanese 214th Regiment which was supported by tanks and artillery. The Japanese attacked for seven successive days and nights. On 24 March they made three attacks, but the defenders, with mines, barbed wire, medium machine-guns and artillery, repulsed every attack, inflicting 600 casualties and destroying four out of five tanks with mines prepared by the sappers. The exhausted Gurkhas, before they moved north, finally blew up the bridge over the River Manipur.

In his book *Defeat into Victory* Slim honourably maintains that the delay in ordering 17th Division to withdraw northwards to Imphal was his responsibility. In fact he had left the decision to the Corps Commander, General G. A. P. Scoones, to make as soon as he received firm evidence of large-scale Japanese movement west of the River Chindwin (wags said that he left too many gaps in his defences). There is considerable evidence that Scoones made several errors at this stage. After the battle Cowan disputed Scoones' report on the timing and detail of the orders which were given to 17th Division to move north, but whatever the reason, because of the delay, from the moment the division set out on 13 March it was fighting for its life. On the same day, Scoones ordered General Roberts' 23rd Indian Infantry Division – the only reserve division in Imphal – to send a brigade down the Tiddim Road to help Cowan's men. In fact, twelve hours before this, Roberts had already sent off 37 Indian Brigade, clearly suggesting that he thought Scoones was acting too slowly. Similarly, Evans and Brett-James' comment, 'Had there been less secrecy, less vagueness, such a sudden move could have been better organized and supplied.' (Evans and Brett-James, *Imphal*, p. 122.) At almost the same time, 50 Indian Parachute Brigade was in danger of being overwhelmed at Sangshak, its position also endangered by blunders at Corps Headquarters (*see* Chapter 4).

37 Brigade, consisting of 3/3rd Gurkhas, 3/5th Gurkhas, and 3/10th Gurkhas, moved quickly south and reached Milestone 82 where there was a small transport camp. By 14 March the Japanese were attacking in strength at MS 100 against a Jat machine-gun company which had been hurriedly sent to defend a critical section of the Road. The Jats, a fine fighting regiment, were very seriously threatened by a Japanese attack, and the 3/5 Gurkhas were sent forward to help. They quickly became involved in confused fighting with the Japanese, who had already established some prepared positions which they defended effectively. The Gurkhas eventually reached the Jat defenders, who were nearly out of ammunition, but two companies of Gurkhas suffered heavy casualties in driving out the Japanese. During the night the Japanese threw in attack after attack, and by morning both Jats and Gurkhas were seriously short of food and ammunition.

On 17 March the Japanese put in a fierce and prolonged attack on 3/5th Gurkhas which lasted all day. Positions were taken, held, lost and retaken in hand-to-hand fighting, with heavy casualties on both sides, until suddenly the Japanese withdrew. The Gurkhas' CO realized that, having sustained very heavy losses, with forty stretcher cases, and with all his troops short of food, water and ammunition, he could no longer defend their positions. He was aware how vulnerable his men would be if the enemy attacked while they were moving off, but he took that risk. So, during the night, the defenders slipped silently away, carrying their wounded on stretchers as they climbed up and down 2,000-foot hills and eventually staggered exhausted into the rear HQ near Fir Tree Hill.

After this encounter the Gurkhas enjoyed only the briefest respite. Almost at once they were ordered to advance south towards MS 109 where they were due to meet the forward units of 17th Division on or about 20 March. In fact, on 20 March they were still held up near MS 98. The action here is a good illustration of the fighting which continued day after day. On Fir Tree Hill the Japanese had built some well-defended bunkers. The Gurkhas attacked and took part of the position, but the Japanese remained in their bunkers. The artillery shelled them — unfortunately killing some Gurkhas in the forward trenches. Next the RAF dive-bombed the bunkers, then tanks came forward and fired over open sights straight at them. Still the Japanese held on and even counter-attacked, making a suicide assault on the leading Indian tank. The Gurkhas advanced again and got to within ten yards of the bunkers. They threw in grenades, but still the Japanese held on and again forced the Gurkhas off the hilltop.

The next day, 22 March, the Gurkhas made three major attacks on the bunker without success, and again the Japanese counter-attacked. By this time the Gurkhas were themselves cut off and had to be supplied by air drop. Fierce, close and confused fighting continued for three more days until the Japanese showed the first signs of withdrawing. Finally, on 27 March, Fir Tree Hill at MS 98, which had cost so many lives on both sides, was occupied by the Gurkhas, and the next day at MS 102 they made contact with the first units of 17th Division.

The Japanese 33rd Division under General Yanagida had come very close to destroying 17th Division during its withdrawal from Tiddim, and had been prevented largely by the stout fighting qualities of the Gurkha battalions. Few divisions had been under such intense pressure over such a long period. They had sustained more than 1,200 casualties in the three weeks of fighting, in a withdrawal which should have been swift and uncontested. Thus many lives were lost because of decision-making errors at a higher level. While British descriptions of these battles give an impression that the Japanese were everywhere making confident and aggressive attacks or stubbornly defending well-sited bunkers, the view from the Japanese is very different.

Initially the Japanese were lucky. Their forces moving to the south and west of Tiddim were seen by a small Gurkha patrol, but its report of seeing 2,000 Japanese troops was not believed by British Intelligence, and the Japanese reached MS 108, very close to the supply dump, virtually unmolested. The Japanese, from the Army Commander Mutaguchi downwards, expected to sweep all opposition aside in a matter of days, as they had done in the 1942 advance. They were therefore severely shaken when their leading unit, 214th Regiment, was seriously mauled at the first main clash at Tongzang. There the leading battalion lost three company commanders and half its men. They then sent in tanks, but these were destroyed by mines. Yanagida, the divisional commander, who had not hitherto commanded a unit in action, received a message from a forward battalion saying that they were burning their code-books and would fight to the last man. Yanagida misunderstood this message and promptly cabled to Mutaguchi to say that there was no possibility of taking Imphal in three weeks, and with the imminent start of the monsoon they were inviting a tragedy by continuing with the advance. He also referred to the serious effect of the Chindit landings on the supply situation for the forward divisions. (The Chindit landings took place on 5 March near Indaw. *See* Chapter 7.) Mutaguchi sent Yanagida an immediate and furious reprimand, which became known at divisional headquarters.One of Yanagida's officers noticed that he was visibly upset when they walked past some bloated corpses with maggots coming out of their eyeballs. Yanagida's chief of staff was openly critical of him, and, from then onwards he was regarded with suspicion and even contempt by some of his own officers and certainly by Mutaguchi.

As the fight went on the Japanese continued to suffer heavy casualties. Provided with food and ammunition for only three weeks, on the assumption that after that they would be using the large dumps of weapons, food and ammunition which they would have captured at Imphal, they were already facing severe shortages. Their morale was low, and several committed suicide. Subsequently Mutaguchi blamed Yanagida for poor leadership, and argued that 33rd Division should have stormed ahead and attacked Bishenpur in the Imphal plain before the British could reorganize. In practice, because of the opposition from 17th Division, this was never remotely possible. The gravest mistake on the Japanese side, which stemmed from Mutaguchi himself, was an attitude of contempt for the Indian, Gurkha and British troops, and an assumption that they could be easily defeated. Significantly, the Japanese commanders failed to learn the lessons of the 1944 campaign in the Arakan where the British forces had repelled the Japanese attacks, and even when surrounded they had stayed in defended boxes where they were supplied by air. These factors more than any other led eventually to the Japanese defeat.

By the end of March 1944 17th Division, although at heavy cost, had fought its way up the road from Tiddim and reached the southern section of the Imphal perimeter. In spite of its casualties its morale was high because it realized that it had inflicted much higher casualties on the enemy, and had seriously blunted his attacking edge. In the subsequent battles at Bishenpur and Potsangbum – so bitterly and closely fought – the Japanese might well have been victorious if it had not been for the serious damage inflicted on them by 17th Division on the Tiddim road. By the time his forces reached the British positions at Bishenpur, Yanagida was not the only Japanese officer who had serious doubts about Mutaguchi's whole plan of campaign.

CHAPTER 3

20TH DIVISION'S WITHDRAWAL TO SHENAM

WHILE 17TH DIVISION had confidently established itself around Tiddim, 20th Indian Infantry Division under General Gracey were even more firmly entrenched in an area which stretched from the high pass of the Shenam Saddle down into the Kabaw Valley and eastwards to the River Chindwin.

The Divisional Headquarters lay in the lower Kabaw valley near Tamu which, after a prolonged effort by Fourteenth Army engineers, was now connected to Shenam by a metalled road which climbed 3,000 feet up to the pass. The road had been planned and constructed ready for a major advance by 20th Division, as had a huge store dump at Moreh, a few miles from Tamu. This dump had enough stores to feed and equip two divisions for several weeks during the proposed advance.

100 Indian Infantry Brigade, centred on Witok, guarded the southern outpost of 20th Division's area, with the particular task of stopping any Japanese advance northwards up the Kabaw valley towards Tamu. The brigade had worked hard to improve a track over the mountains to Mombi, and had patrolled energetically southwards from Witok, through Htinzin, and even as far south as Yazagyo where there was a fairly substantial Japanese garrison. The brigade had the support of a squadron of sixteen Lee tanks from the Carabiniers; a Jungle Field Regiment being used as infantry; and a battery of 9 Field Regiment with 25-pounder guns. Successful patrolling had brought confidence and high morale to the entire brigade. One reconnaissance patrol, with orders not to engage the enemy, passed through a village where Japanese soldiers

Units Involved in 20th Division's Withdrawal to Shenam

British	Japanese
20th Indian Infantry Division	33rd Division Yamamoto Force
Major-General Gracey	General Yamamoto
32 Indian Infantry Brigade	213th Infantry Regiment
80 Indian Infantry Brigade	215th Infantry Regiment
100 Indian Infantry Brigade	Two battalions from 15th Division
	Thirty tanks

20th Division's Withdrawal to Shenam, March 1944

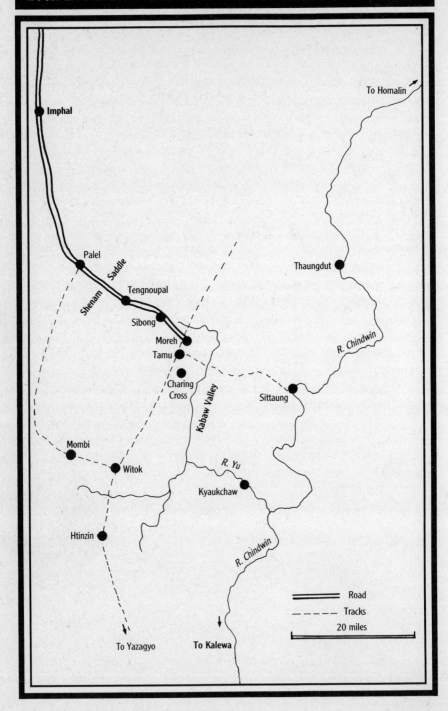

were busily occupied in the bamboo houses with their comfort girls. With remarkable discipline, the recce. patrol refrained from attacking.

As 20th Division waited for the first Japanese moves, an important source of Intelligence about the enemy came from the V Force units which were scattered along the front. These small units, often two or three strong, and living well behind the enemy lines, were made up from former tea planters, forestry officers, or the staff of timber companies, who had stayed behind after the 1942 withdrawal. Most had received some basic training in handling weapons and radios, and they were backed up by a skeleton force of British officers. All units kept in touch by radio with a headquarters in Imphal. The V Force was particularly valuable in the area east of the Chindwin where the Japanese were forming up for their attack. The task of the V Force units was made easier because the Japanese troops, both officers and men, appeared to have received no training on Intelligence matters. Japanese soldiers did not expect to be captured, but when they were they passed on a lot of useful information. Similarly, their officers frequently carried detailed copies of future plans which gave valuable information to British Intelligence, though they rarely had any grasp of the overall situation outside their immediate area. The best known V Force leader – though not from this area – was Miss Ursula Graham Bower, who lived and worked among the Naga people in the mountains west of Imphal, and was noted for her brave Intelligence work. V Force agents worked closely with the advanced reconnaissance patrols along the banks of the Chindwin. In one small action a corporal from the Border Regiment, leading a patrol of three men, suddenly came upon a Japanese staff car parked by the roadside. He shot the occupants, grabbed all available documents and disappeared into the jungle. He had obtained the detailed plans for the whole advance of Yamamoto Force up the Kabaw valley. This powerful Japanese force, forming the right wing of 33rd Division, included 213th Infantry Regiment, part of 215th Regiment, some infantry from 15th Division, as well as artillery and thirty light tanks.

By the beginning of March 1944 Intelligence from patrolling, from aerial reconnaissance and from V Force units had built up a valuable picture of Japanese activity. A large number of rafts had been seen on the Chindwin, though attempts to bomb them had not been successful. The locations of 31st, 15th and 33rd Divisions were clearly established, and some units which had been in the Arakan were identified. The volume of traffic up the road to Homalin – the base of 33rd Division – had substantially increased, and it was recorded that huge herds of cattle were collecting near the banks of the Chindwin.

Gathering Intelligence was not always easy. One agent travelled fifty miles behind the Japanese lines to carry out a reconnaissance for an

airstrip for the proposed Chindit landings at Indaw. He obtained the
information and had nearly reached the banks of the Chindwin on his
way back when he was attacked by a wild buffalo. Although badly injured
he reached the river and at gun point forced some enemy soldiers to build
a raft. He set off on the raft, but half-way across the river it sank.
Fortunately the current carried him to the farther shore and he was able
to stagger on until he met a friendly unit and was able to pass on his
information.

Similarly, during the early months of 1944, although the front along
the Chindwin was relatively quiet, certainly compared to the battles
which were to follow in March and April, there were some fierce
exchanges when rival patrols clashed. In January the 1st Northamptons,
as part of 32 Brigade, put in an attack at Kyaukchaw on the River Yu,
against a Japanese defensive position – illustrating that at this part of the
front the Japanese were well forward of the Chindwin. The Northamptons had obtained considerable information about the Japanese from
frequent reconnaissance and standing patrols. One patrol had established
the daily pattern of Japanese activity from reveille, breakfast, washing
and so on throughout the day. On the basis of this information an attack
was planned. On 20 January, after a strike by Hurribombers (Hurricane
fighters adapted to carry bombs), the attack went in. One platoon was
pushed back by a shower of grenades thrown from the bunkers by the
Japanese defenders. At this point Lieutenant Horwood organized and led
another attack which included his own platoon of Northamptons, with
some Gurkhas and some Sappers from 93 Field Company. This attack was
repulsed and he was killed; he was awarded a posthumous VC. In
succeeding weeks many Gurkha, Indian and British units were to
discover, as the Northamptons had done, that the Japanese defended
their positions with skill and bravery.

South of Witok, 100 Brigade had left a small standing patrol near
Htinzin to give warning of any Japanese advance, and the first action
came on 4 March when this patrol, from 14/13th Frontier Force Rifles,
were attacked by an infantry unit supported by tanks – the Yamamoto
Force. This alerted 100 Brigade to the presence of tanks, and strong
fighting patrols were sent out to harass and delay the Japanese advance
during the following week. These spirited actions succeeded in delaying
Yamamoto Force and also gained valuable information from another
captured document which gave further information about the route and
timetable of the Japanese advance to Tamu and Shenam.

After several days' confused fighting, the Japanese had pressed
forward as far as Witok where, on 14 March, there was a major battle
between the Gurkhas and the Border Regiment on the one hand, and
213th Regiment, the leading unit of Yamamoto Force supported by tanks

on the other. As the battle progressed, six tanks from the Carabiniers came to the assistance of the Gurkhas and the Borders. The jungle here was so dense and the fighting so confused that at one stage Japanese tanks unknowingly pulled up for the night within a hundred yards of the Gurkha positions.

During the course of the battle the British Divisional Commander sent the code-word 'Wellington', which was a pre-arranged signal for an immediate withdrawal to Tamu and the supply depot at Moreh. 100 Brigade disengaged successfully and started the withdrawal, but on 17 March were ambushed by the Japanese who had cut rapidly round to a flank through the jungle – reminiscent of their hook tactics of 1942. As a result, several more days of heavy fighting followed, during which both sides suffered casualties. The British had the added problem of withdrawing with a fairly large number of wounded on makeshift stretchers which had to be carried along precipitous jungle paths. In this mêlée the doctor of the Borders was killed, and the CO of the Gurkhas was bundled over by a stampeding mule and ended up head first in a ditch full of water, but by 19 March the Borders, the Gurkhas and other units had reassembled near the supply base at Moreh. Their efforts had not been in vain, for the carefully timed advance of Yamamoto Force – of which 20th Division now had full details – had been delayed for more than a week.

While 100 Brigade had held the southern defences around Witok, 80 Brigade had been deployed farther north near Sittaung to watch for any Japanese units crossing the Chindwin there. Another brigade, 1 Indian Infantry Brigade in 23rd Division – the reserve division in Imphal – had in similar fashion been sent forward to an area yet farther north at Thaungdut. Initially their role was to make a feint crossing of the Chindwin to mislead the Japanese and distract their attention from the fly-in of Wingate's Chindit forces which on 5 March embarked on Operation 'Thursday': the landing of two brigades at Indaw to cut supplies and communications to the advancing Japanese divisions.

1 Brigade remained in the Thaungdut area and on the night of 15 March observed major enemy movements across the Chindwin. The Japanese had very cleverly built pontoon bridges which were kept concealed during the day and floated across the river in the dark. At dawn they were towed back and hidden from Allied bombers under the bank. All 1 Brigade units were in touch by field telephone, and during the night evidence came from many points of a substantial Japanese advance. Infantry, tanks, guns, equipment and mules all crossed the pontoon bridges and advanced rapidly westwards. At one crossing alone, near Thaungdut, more than 500 men and their accompanying mules crossed the river.

The Indian units were well prepared, and by skilful defensive actions ensured that the Japanese advance was delayed. The delaying tactics were valuable, but more important was the efficient relay of information which was passed swiftly to Gracey at 20th Division Headquarters. Having engaged in heavy defensive fighting for five days, the brigade then under the 'Wellington' Plan withdrew to positions on the Tamu road. This careful and controlled withdrawal with few casualties, was in stark contrast to the bloody struggle endured by 17th Division in its withdrawal up the Tiddim road at about the same time.

While many sites, even of major battles, could only be identified by the milestone number on the road, others were given a nickname by the soldiers who fought and died there. One such came from 32 Brigade, which earlier had been engaged in the fighting at Kyaukchaw when Horwood won the VC. By the middle of March the brigade was defending an area north of Witok, roughly between the other two brigades. 32 Brigade realized that Yamamoto Force was advancing rapidly, and with the help of a squadron of the Carabiniers, prepared a clever ambush. They called it Charing Cross. It lay a few miles south of Tamu on the track to Kalewa, and here they hoped to inflict a serious defeat on the leading tanks and infantry of Yamamoto Force.

The Japanese advanced rapidly with their tanks towards the position carefully prepared by the 9/14th Punjabis and 3/8th Gurkhas. On the given signal all the infantry weapons, supported by anti-tank guns, mortars and 25-pounders, opened up on the unsuspecting Japanese. This furious encounter lasted about half an hour, and inflicted on the Japanese a serious defeat with heavy casualties. The Japanese then withdrew and 32 Brigade moved off to pre-arranged positions at Moreh.

General Gracey and 20th Division had planned and were carrying out a skilful withdrawal from the Kabaw valley up to the heights of Shenam, but the withdrawal caused serious tension between Gracey and the Corps Commander, General Scoones. Gracey had fashioned a well-trained and confident division which in the Kabaw valley and along the Chindwin had established effective domination over the enemy. After months of hard fighting and active patrolling, he and his division were extremely reluctant to hand over to the Japanese all they had fought so hard to gain.

In a bitter message to Scoones, Gracey asked what was the point of building roads and building-up a colossal supply base at Moreh just to withdraw and hand it over to the Japanese without a fight. Gracey's comment raises a significant issue which has never been adequately explained. If Slim's strategy was to withdraw to the Imphal Plain and fight the Japanese in the open country there, when did he make that decision, and why did Fourteenth Army continue to pour supplies forward to the Moreh base? On the day it was finally evacuated, as the last convoy of trucks, loaded with petrol, left for Shenam, another convoy of trucks arrived *from* Shenam – loaded with petrol. It certainly appears that Slim's decision to withdraw was not effectively communicated to the Quartermaster branch at Corps Headquarters. Did the fault lie at Army or Corps HQ?

Gracey protested, but knew that he would have to carry out his orders. Indeed, while his brigades were coming back to Tamu, he had already sent off all the support units and civilian labour – more than 20,000 personnel – including Elephant Bill (Colonel Bill Williams) and all his elephants which had been invaluable in transporting heavy loads over difficult country. This large movement of men, animals and vehicles from the Kabaw valley, up the road to Shenam, and on into the Imphal Plain, had been carefully rehearsed and took only four days, thus leaving the road clear for when the fighting units would need it.

Gracey's plans for 20th Division had all worked well, and by 20 March his brigades were moving to pre-planned positions where the road from Moreh climbed the hills up to the Shenam Saddle. As this operation was progressing, Gracey received an urgent message from Scoones saying that 20th Division would be called on to send units to help in the dangerous situation at the north end of the Imphal Plain. Gracey again sent an angry reply to Scoones, pointing out how well the division had performed, and adding that they would feel badly let down if they were forced to send units elsewhere. He reminded Scoones again that he and his troops strongly objected to giving up Moreh which had supplies enough for two divisions.

The depot at Moreh measured two and a half miles by one and a half, and contained vast stores of food, ammunition and petrol. After the first Japanese advance, some stores had been removed, but on 31 March, when most of the stores still remained, 32 Brigade had the miserable task of destroying the whole dump. This brigade also begged to be allowed to stop at Moreh and make a fight of it, but they too were overruled. They slaughtered more than 200 cattle and destroyed more than £1m worth of supplies and equipment. The Northamptons, 3/8th Gurkhas and 9/14th Punjabis took part in the final exit from Moreh, but the most important role fell to the sappers who booby-trapped the entire camp and then had the final task of firing the oil. The brigade had worked most efficiently and did not lose a single man in their retreat from Moreh to their positions on the road to Shenam.

Although 20th Division's withdrawal was a model of careful planning and anticipation, the Japanese attackers were still able to cause disruption and confusion by their 'Jitter Raids' (quick strikes by small groups to keep the defence jittery). One of these came close to success when Gracey and his small headquarters staff were attacked during the night by a group of Japanese firing automatic weapons. Bullets flew everywhere. Gracey had to rush to his slit trench in his pyjamas, not even having time to put on his dressing-gown. When the attack was over, the General's driver appeared quite casually and explained that he had got a group together and had driven off the attackers.

A more serious threat to 20th Division's withdrawal came from a special Japanese patrol which had set out to blow up the bridge at Sibong, seven miles north of Moreh, where the road from Moreh up to Shenam crossed a fast-flowing river. This fighting patrol, from Japanese 213th Regiment, was more than forty strong and was supported by a group of specially trained engineers. This part of the road was defended by 80 Brigade which, realizing how important the bridge would be to the passage of the two remaining brigades, had sent 3/1st Gurkhas to hold the bridge. The Gurkhas had time to prepare sound defences, with pre-arranged defensive fire plans for artillery and 3-inch mortars. On 22 March the Japanese attacked. They had assembled in a thickly wooded area which had been carefully targeted, and as they prepared to attack, a terrifying bombardment fell upon them. The high-explosive shells set fire to the trees, and those Japanese who were not killed were driven out by the blazing jungle into the small-arms fire of the waiting Gurkhas. This destructive clash provided valuable Intelligence including full details of plans to attack the road. The Japanese patrol included some unusually large and strong men, each of whom had carried 100 pounds of explosives. This unit did not reappear, but others continued to attack the road without much success.

Yamamoto Force, which by the time it reached Tamu and Moreh, had been joined by units detached from Japanese 15th Division, had the shortest and most direct approach to the Imphal Plain. Tamu itself was only twenty miles from the Japanese base on the Chindwin; from Tamu it was only eighteen miles up to Shenam, and a further five miles to the forward RAF airstrip at Palel – altogether a far shorter route than the Tiddim–Imphal road, up which the rest of Japanese 33rd Division were attacking. The fighting soldiers of 20th Division had been as reluctant as those of 17th Division at Tiddim to give up hard-won territory, but 20th Division had planned the withdrawal carefully and were able to reach their positions at Shenam in good order and with few casualties.

While 80 Brigade defended the road, including the bridge at Sibong, 100 Brigade passed through their lines to take up defensive positions at Tengnoupal, at the crest of the steep ascent. 32 Brigade, after destroying the dump at Moreh, moved rapidly up the road through the other brigades and went into a reserve position at Palel. By 1 April 100 Brigade

* That quick! There'll always be an England

were already in position at Tengnoupal, but the Japanese had reached there too, and were established on Nippon Hill. Here again in a wilderness with no identifiable names, the British soldiers distributed nicknames. Nippon Hill, named in grim recognition of the Japanese bravery, was held by the enemy throughout the months of fighting which lay ahead. Most of the other names in this area came from the Mediterranean – Gibraltar, Malta and Crete. Other hills were named after units which had fought a particularly heroic action at the spot, e.g., Punjab Hill. On their side the Japanese tended to name places after the CO of the unit which captured it – brief immortality.

20th Division successfully reached the Shenam Saddle, chosen as the best place to defend the approach to the Imphal Plain, and chosen by the Japanese as best route for their advance – helped by the fine road which had just been built by the British. 20th Division realized that the Japanese had to be held there at all costs. The Shenam Saddle overlooked the Palel airstrip nearly five miles away, and beyond that the plain itself, and if the Saddle were lost, all the other defences of Imphal would be placed in jeopardy. The withdrawal of 20th Division to Shenam was the prelude to months of closely fought actions along this bleak and inhospitable ridge, surrounded by thick jungle, with dramatic precipices falling away hundreds of feet to the narrow valleys below, and, throughout most of this time, under the deluge of the full monsoon.

CHAPTER 4

THE BATTLE OF SANGSHAK

T HE NAGAS were a friendly people living in the hills around Kohima, and Sangshak was one of their small hilltop villages lying about 25 miles north-east of Imphal. It became the site of one of the first encounters that, together with Shenam, Bishenpur, Nungshigum and others, make up the Imphal–Kohima battle.

The rapid Japanese advance to Sangshak was part of a clever plan by General Mutaguchi, the commander of Japanese 15th Army. He had three divisions, 33rd (Yanagida), 15th (Yamauchi) and ?t (Sato), with which he planned to attack Imphal and Kohima, and to advance on the road, rail and supply base at Dimapur. That was to be his springboard for a triumphant 'March on Delhi'.

From its base in the Chindwin valley, Mutaguchi sent part of 33rd Division from its position near Kalewa, on a wide sweep to the south-west to outflank Tiddim where 17th Indian Division under General Cowan was firmly established, and to cut off its retreat northwards to the Imphal plain. The remainder of 33rd Division under General Yamamoto, accompanied by armour and artillery, moved north-eastwards to attack Witok and Timu, and to advance out of the Kabaw valley up to Shenam, where a pass through the mountains led down to the Imphal plain.

Mutaguchi's next step was to use 15th Division to deceive Slim, and to make him think that the major Japanese attack would be on the south

Units Involved in the Battle of Sangshak

British	Japanese
50 Indian Parachute Brigade	31st Division (Sato)
152nd Battalion (Indian)	58th Regiment
153rd Battalion (Gurkha)	124th Regiment
4/5th Mahrattas	138th Regiment
Field Squadron of Engineers	Mountain Battery
Medium Machine-Gun Company	Engineer and Medical unit
	15th Division (Yamauchi)
	60th Regiment
	51st Regiment

of the Imphal front towards Shenam. Mutaguchi directed one battalion of 15th Division to cross the Chindwin and ostentatiously move south-west towards Tamu, in order to give the impression that the whole of 15th Division was moving in that direction. At the same time, and in total secrecy, the remainder of 15th Division also crossed the Chindwin but moved north-west towards Sangshak, in order to enter the Imphal plain from the north.

Simultaneously, 31st Division under General Sato advanced westwards with three groups. The southernmost group under General Miyazaki, an experienced and aggressive infantry leader, had been ordered to advance rapidly via Ukhrul to Kohima. The other two groups moved with remarkable speed through the Naga Hills towards Kohima and Dimapur. If the Japanese could secure this vital base the whole of the British position in Assam would be threatened.

In the area west of the Chindwin both sides had engaged in active patrolling and Intelligence gathering. A young Japanese officer, Captain Nishida, with a small patrol had reconnoitred jungle paths leading westwards out of the Chindwin valley. His meticulous work made possible the subsequent swift advance of Sato's 31st Division towards Kohima. The leading units even carried prefabricated bridges which Nishida had measured up correctly, and which prevented any delay at the many river crossings.

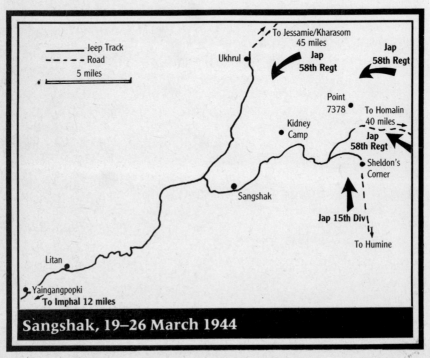

Sangshak, 19–26 March 1944

British Intelligence also enjoyed its successes. V Force (small groups of Naga or Kuki people led by a few British officers with radio transmitters) covered the whole area down to the Chindwin and beyond. The Kukis betrayed many V-Force units to the Japanese, but the Nagas remained steadfastly loyal throughout. One unit under an officer of the Royal Engineers questioned a captured Japanese agent and discovered the exact location of a large concentration of the troops of 15th Division. Early in February 1944 an attack by Mitchell bombers on what appeared to be an innocent strip of jungle resulted in an estimated 4,000 Japanese soldiers being killed or wounded – a serious setback for 15th Division before it had even started. The RAF caused further problems and delays by bombing bridges, roads and railways.

The attack on Tiddim at the south of the front had started on 8 March and progressed well. Then, according to a carefully pre-planned time-table, Japanese 15th and 31st Divisions crossed the Chindwin on 16 March. They chose a moonless night to move thousands of men with cattle, oxen, mules and elephants across the river. This huge force moved rapidly westwards – not unobserved but initially unopposed.

Mutaguchi watched the swift progress of his troops and, to his delight, learnt that 23rd Indian Division – the reserve division for IV Corps at Imphal – had been pulled out to go to the assistance of 17th Division which was under severe attack at Tiddim, and on the road leading north was being heavily ambushed by units of 33rd Division. Mutaguchi's timing seemed to be working perfectly. One of the units of 23rd Indian Division to be sent south was 49 Brigade which, without any great urgency, had been settling into the Ukhrul and Sangshak area. Their failure to fortify the area with dugouts, barbed wire, mutually supporting bunkers and defensive artillery fire tasks, was to cost the lives of many defenders when the Japanese attacked.

50 Indian Parachute Brigade, which was to play the leading role in the Sangshak battle, had spent most of 1943 on intensive airborne training for combined operations, but these never took place, usually because the necessary landing craft were needed more urgently in other theatres. After these disappointments the brigade, which had been trained by Brigadier Hope Thompson, was posted to the Kohima area in February 1944 to undertake some more advanced jungle training. It arrived at Kohima with only two battalions, 152nd and 153rd. The brigade's third battalion was still completing its parachute training.

On 16 March, the day the main Japanese forces crossed the Chindwin, 50 Brigade was hurriedly sent forward to take over the positions just vacated by 49 Brigade. Their positions lay across a road, from Kohima via Ukhrul and Sangshak down to the Chindwin, which had been constructed by the engineers of IV Corps ready for a British advance. It had been formally opened in early March by General Roberts (GOC 23rd Division).

50 Brigade, posted to Kohima for jungle training, were not geared for action. They had, for example, brought the Mess silver but had no steel helmets. They quickly established themselves in the Sangshak area, but although 152nd battalion had drawn stores and ammunition at Litan as they moved up to Sangshak, the brigade received no further supplies or ammunition – and above all no further information from Corps or Division HQ about the Japanese advance. No operational orders at all were received until the Japanese had put in their first attack. The inertia and incompetence at Corps HQ in its dealings with 50 Brigade has caused deep resentment among the survivors of this hard-fought battle, with even the war diaries of Corps HQ 16–20 March showing chaos and confusion, and confirming that no directions or orders were sent to 50 Brigade. This situation seems even more extraordinary as the Brigade had a land line to 23rd Division HQ at Litan, and even after Sangshak had been cut off an effective radio link was maintained. Thus the valuable information about Japanese movements, which the V Force agents had risked their lives to obtain, because of failure in Corps or Division HQ, never reached the very unit which was about to be attacked. ⓥ

50 Brigade had further cause for complaint; 153rd battalion had been left in Kohima and, despite signals from Brigadier Hope Thomson, was told that there was no transport available to bring the battalion up to Sangshak – this at a time when 30,000 non-combatants had been taken from Imphal to Dimapur, and much of the transport had returned empty. The Gurkhas of 153rd Battalion eventually arrived at Imphal and were eager to rejoin the brigade at Sangshak. In Imphal they found they were not expected, they received no food, no ammunition and no information. After a long wait they were given a few old lorries. Finally, in dribs and drabs, they reached Sangshak. Fewer than 400 men arrived in time for the battle. The rest stayed in Litan where they reported to the garrison commander who was drunk.ⓧ

The lapses at Corps and Divisional HQ over information, transport and supplies were serious enough, but even worse was the lack of barbed wire for defensive positions. Although frequent and urgent demands were sent through by 50 Brigade, no barbed wire ever reached Sangshak and this cost countless lives. When the survivors of the battle eventually reached Imphal, nothing angered them so much as seeing triple bands of wire around every headquarters building.

On 18 March, when Hope Thomson had been considering a new brigade training programme, he received the first information from his leading company that the Japanese were approaching. This Company of 152nd Battalion was already forward on Point 7378, a good hill position

* For officers only.
ⓥ what about Slim? - he had overall responsibility.
ⓧ Ditto.

overlooking tracks to Ukhrul and Imphal. The Company had a section of 3-inch mortars and two medium machine-guns, but no artillery was far enough forward to give them support.

At 0930 on 19 March, having had no warning of an approaching enemy, the Company sighted about 900 Japanese – the advanced guard of 58th Regiment. By 1400 the Company was completely surrounded, but beat off frequent attacks which continued all day and throughout the night. Suddenly, during the following morning, the Japanese attackers noticed the defenders' fire had ceased – they had run out of ammunition. Then about twenty survivors made a hurried counter-attack, but unfortunately they had been unable to see a deep ravine to their front and many fell into this and were killed. The rest were captured. 'C' Company were completely eliminated, but the Japanese suffered 160 casualties including seven officers. By midday on 20 March the engagement was over – a tragic sacrifice of a fine fighting unit because of incompetence in providing supplies, barbed wire, ammunition and, above all, up-to-date Intelligence. Hope Thomson, still unaware of the size of the forces attacking him, and lacking any support from his superior headquarters, decided to concentrate his available forces and to prepare defences.

As the Japanese forces approached, Hope Thomson had under his command 152nd Indian Parachute Battalion; a part of 153rd Battalion (less those left behind at Litan); a battalion of Mahratta Light Infantry (detached from 49 Brigade when it moved off towards Tiddim); a mountain battery; a mortar troop; a parachute field ambulance; a small engineer unit – all told, just about 2,000 men and mules.

On 20 March, the day that 'C' Company was overrun, he decided to concentrate at Sheldon's Corner. The two units there called for an air drop and then were ordered to move again. They were about to move when the air drop, which should have been cancelled, arrived. They had to delay and destroy the stores, but it did mislead the Japanese who, seeing the air drop, assumed the units were staying put. The Japanese always welcomed those supplies which fell on them – they called them 'Churchill rations'.

On 23 March, after three days of constant Japanese attacks, the two forward battalions reached Kidney Camp, only to receive another urgent message to move towards Sangshak. They eventually arrived totally exhausted, and realized that the Battle of Sangshak had already begun.

50 Brigade, though unaware of it at the time, was to influence one of the most crucial decisions of the whole Burma campaign. General Miyazaki, an experienced and ambitious leader, was forward with the leading regiment of Sato's 31st Division, and was aiming to advance as rapidly as possible towards Kohima, but Sangshak lay in his path.

Miyazaki had to weigh up many factors. Although proud of the swift advance he had led from Homalin on the Chindwin, he realized that 60th Regiment, the leading unit of 15th Division on his left flank, had advanced more slowly, but he was ambitious to prove himself superior and to grab the glory and prestige from a spectacular advance. Like Mutaguchi, he still tended to despite the British and to assume that any British force could be rapidly swept aside. None the less, a full enemy brigade group astride his main supply line was a real danger. Technically Sangshak lay in the operational area of 15th Division, but Miyazaki could claim with some justification, that since Sangshak threatened his flank, and since he had reached it first, he was justified in attacking it. He therefore took what proved to be a momentous decision. He ordered his leading unit, which had already reached Ukhrul, to turn south and attack Sangshak, intending it to overrun Sangshak immediately and then advance swiftly to Kohima. This decision probably cost thousands of lives, and could have cost the Japanese the prize of Kohima, Dimapur and a victorious advance into India.

The retreating troops of 50 Brigade had fought a series of clever delaying actions in their move from Sheldon's Corner to Sangshak, and they arrived thirsty, hungry and exhausted. They dispersed at once and started to dig in. It was then they discovered to their horror that there was no barbed wire. As Harry Seaman, who fought there as a young subaltern, has written, 'Sangshak was most certainly lost for the lack of a few rolls of barbed wire.' (*The Battle at Sangshak*, p. 82.)

The village of Sangshak lay on a fairly bare hill. It had twenty or thirty houses and an American mission church at the highest part of the village. As the defenders started to dig in they made two more unpleasant discoveries. The hill was a volcanic outcrop and just a few feet below the surface was solid rock which made digging impossible. Secondly, there was virtually no water.

The rearguards had arrived during the afternoon of 22 March, and the Japanese attacked at dusk. From West Hill, the leading company of 58th Regiment attacked the Gurkhas on the western edge of the perimeter. They had had time to organize the 3-inch mortar section and some machine-guns into their defensive fire plan when the attack came in. The Gurkhas held their fire as the Japanese advanced over fairly open ground and a rough football pitch, then opened fire, killing 90 of the 120 men in the leading company. Despite this setback the Japanese put in another attack and lost a further twenty men before being repulsed.

By 23 March the Japanese, who had used elephants to bring up their heavier guns and ammunition, started shelling Sangshak, which from that day was completely surrounded. The narrow perimeter and crowded troop positions meant that every bombardment caused some damage or casualties. As the siege wore on, because of the very shallow trenches in the rocky ground, the decomposing bodies of men and mules were constantly blown up and scattered over the defenders with a nauseating stench.

The success of the Gurkhas in repelling the first attack encouraged the garrison to resist the frequent attacks which followed. On the second day a Japanese officer was killed within the perimeter, and it was discovered that he was carrying the detailed battle plans for both 31st and 15th Divisions, together with the proposed routes and timetables for their advance to Imphal, Kohima and Dimapur. Hope Thomson realized how valuable this information was. He had copies made of the documents and Captain Allen, the Brigade Intelligence Officer, slipped through the Japanese lines and delivered his precious message to Corps HQ in Imphal on 25 March.

This incident raises some interesting issues. General Slim had a conference at Imphal with his two Corps Commanders, Scoones and Stopford, on 28 March. At this conference he decided to defend Kohima. It has been forcefully argued that the vital information which Allen risked his life to deliver to Corps HQ, never reached Slim. If he had received it and knew the details of Mutaguchi's plan for an entire division to attack Kohima (not a battalion or a brigade as Slim had assumed), surely Slim would never have sacrificed the Royal West Kents and other units which were pushed into Kohima as late as 5 April. Nor would he have allowed the brave garrisons at Jessami and Kharasom to be overwhelmed. This

The Battle of Sangshak, 19–26 March 1944

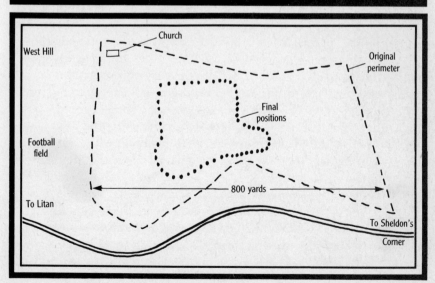

telling argument is backed up by IV Corps' War Diary, which has no record of the message delivered by Captain Allen on 25 March.

The battle continued day and night, and as the attacks were pressed home there was fierce hand-to-hand fighting. One Indian gun crew was nearly overwhelmed when a havildar (sergeant) who had been stunned, suddenly came to, seized the steel ramrod of the gun and killed four attackers with it. After several days of fighting, nearly three hundred wounded were lying in the shallow slit trenches, where 80 Indian Field Ambulance did excellent work. The brigade, which was highly trained in air supply, had great hopes of support by air drop, but because the perimeter was so small, much of the urgently needed water and ammunition fell into the hands of the Japanese.

By 25 March the Japanese had captured the church at the high point of the perimeter and were using it as an observation post to bring accurate fire on to every position. On 26 March Miyazaki, frustrated by the dogged resistance of the Sangshak defenders, encouraged the now depleted units of 58th Regiment to make a final attempt to overrun the hill. At the same time the Gurkhas, even more depleted in numbers, mounted a counter-attack which succeeded in burning down the church and depriving the Japanese of their observation post. Throughout the day fierce hand-to-hand fighting continued from before dawn to late afternoon. A brief lull in the fighting at midday enabled the enterprising cooks to take round to each surviving trench, past piles of decomposing Indian, Japanese and British corpses, a gruesome meal of curried mule and apple.

In the late afternoon the Japanese withdrew once more, their assault having failed to overwhelm the defence. Japanese records pay tribute to the Indian, Gurkha and British defenders, and admit the very heavy price paid by 58th Regiment. It lost six of its eight company commanders, and when it moved on to Kohima it had been reduced to less than half of its strength. After the engagement one of its 120-strong companies had eight men left and all of them were wounded.

At dusk on 26 March Hope Thomson received the remarkable radio message from Corps HQ, 'Fight your way out. Go south and west.' This order presented him with severe problems, particularly over the fate of the hundreds of wounded, but he made a clear plan. At 2200 hours all the guns opened up – in order to expend their ammunition. More than 100 wounded, too ill to move, were left by their slit trenches. The rest of the wounded were allocated able-bodied colleagues to help them. At 2230 the whole garrison moved off silently through the positions held by the Mahrattas. To their amazement they were able to slip through the enemy lines without being discovered, and moved silently on their way.

At almost the same time, Colonel Fukunaga of 58th Regiment was preparing himself to make a final suicide attack. He wrapped himself in his flag and strode bravely up the hill. It was empty. He immediately stood down his regiment and they slept where they fell.

The brave but tattered remnant of 50 Indian Parachute Brigade and the 4/5th Mahrattas broke up into small groups as soon as they got into the jungle. They had more than thirty miles of jungle-covered hills to cross, many rising to over 4,000 feet. They had a few tins of cheese and some raisins, and had to rely on mountain streams for water. One incident illustrates the privations these men suffered. An officer, too badly wounded to be moved, woke up to find a Japanese soldier going through his kit. The officer killed the intruder and staggered off into the jungle. Shortly after he found a corpse and took a grenade from a pocket. Later he threw this into a stream and killed some fish. He staggered on and days later reached Imphal. He eventually made a complete recovery.

General Miyazaki, upset at the carnage as he surveyed the battle-ground at Sangshak, found a young Japanese officer who had been buried with his sword. Profoundly moved by this, he ensured that prisoners were properly cared for, and later when his unit was retreating and unable to guard prisoners properly, many were released – in their underpants.

Of the two parachute battalions, 152nd lost 80 per cent of its strength, 153rd lost 30 per cent and a remarkable number of survivors reached Imphal and were then evacuated to hospital in India. These gallant soldiers, who had survived one of the worst ordeals of the campaign, were to suffer from a disgraceful aftermath. Very soon, rumours began to circulate that they had run away in the face of the enemy. This rumour spread all over India. Later, the Corps report gave the impression that Hope Thomson had mishandled the whole situation. In fact he had received no information about the enemy until 900 Japanese were seen approaching his forward unit. Forty years later – the bitterness still apparent – Harry Seaman in his excellent book *The Battle of Sangshak* wrote, 'It is impossible to avoid the conclusion that 50 Indian Parachute Brigade and its commander had been made the scapegoats for the errors and omissions of those above them.' Having researched the Japanese resources which pay tribute to the outstanding bravery of the Parachute Brigade, Seaman adds, 'The enemy's military history makes a total contrast to the scenes later etched by the poisonous pens and tongues on the British side.' This extremely unfortunate dispute was further exacerbated by a tendentious description of Sangshak which appears in *The Fighting Cock*, the official history of the 23rd Indian Division, published in 1951.

Mutaguchi, in his overall plan for his March on Delhi, expected to capture the Imphal plain and Kohima by the first week in April 1944, and then to advance swiftly to Dimapur before its defences could be organized. These plans would clearly have been affected by the swift response of Mountbatten and Slim in flying 5th Indian Division to Imphal (completed by 24 March), and 2nd British Division to Dimapur (completed by 1 April). However, the greatest actual delay and disruption to the Japanese strategy came from the defence of Sangshak by 50 Indian Parachute Brigade. Sangshak also had a major effect on the Battle of Kohima. The defence of Kohima by The Royal West Kents, who came so close to being overwhelmed, could have had a very different outcome if the leading Japanese unit, 58th Regiment, which carried out the attack, had not lost two-thirds of its officers and half its men during the mauling at Sangshak, before it marched on to Kohima.

CHAPTER 5

THE ROLE OF
THE AIR FORCES

MUTAGUCHI'S carefully planned attacks in February and March 1944 achieved remarkable early success. The attack in the Arakan – code-name 'Ha Go' – which started on 3 February, took the British by surprise and, because of the Japanese impetus, forced Slim to move his reserve divisions into the Arakan – exactly as Mutaguchi wanted him to do. Keeping to his pre-planned timetable, Mutaguchi then dispatched 33rd Division on their encircling move to by-pass Tiddim and cut off 17th Indian Division at the southern bastion of the Imphal defences. Here again Mutaguchi's plans succeeded, and Slim had to use 23rd Indian Division – his reserve division in Imphal – to come to the rescue of 17th Division as it struggled back up the road to Imphal. On the northern wing of the Japanese attack, 31st Division under General Sato made rapid progress towards Kohima, so that by 17 March 1944 Mutaguchi's hopes of overrunning Imphal and Kohima, and advancing on the rail and supply centre at Dimapur, appeared to be going like clockwork. He had high hopes that from Dimapur his victorious forces, using the large supply of weapons, ammunition and food he knew had been built up there, would be able to make a victorious 'March on Delhi'. With him would march Subhas Chandra Bose and the Indian National Army, whom the down-trodden peoples of Bengal, who had already risen against the British, would enthusiastically support. Such a scenario appeared quite feasible.

In contrast to the clear and carefully devised plans of the Japanese, British strategic thinking seemed to be muddled. By February 1944 there had been a large build-up of roads, airstrips, camps, and hospitals, together with stores of weapons, ammunition and food at Imphal, Kohima and Dimapur, ready to support an advance across the Chindwin. Subsidiary bases had been established at Moreh, Kanglatongbi and elsewhere. From Intelligence reports Slim and Scoones (IV Corps Commander in Imphal) realized that the Japanese were preparing to advance westwards over the Chindwin. From information in captured documents Slim estimated that the major offensive would start on or about 15 March, but expected the main attack to be launched against Imphal. He made a serious mistake, which he openly admitted, in expecting that only one Japanese regiment – the equivalent of a British brigade – would make the attack on Kohima and Dimapur. At the same time, he realized that if the Japanese made a serious attack, both 17th and 20th Divisions were too spread out and were dangerously exposed. He considered that he had three possibilities: to attack the Japanese before they attacked him; to fight on the line of the Chindwin; or to let the Japanese advance across the Chindwin towards Imphal, and then fight the main battle at Imphal where Fourteenth Army would have the advantage.

On 13 March, when Imphal, Kohima and Dimapur were in peril from Mutaguchi's assault, Mountbatten and Slim had a crucial meeting with Air Marshal Baldwin who commanded Third Tactical Air Force. In view of the crisis in Imphal, Baldwin and Slim supported Mountbatten who, far exceeding his authority, transferred thirty Dakotas from The Hump forces, in order to fly 5th Indian Division from the Arakan to bring reinforcement to the defences of Imphal.

Troop Carrier Command, which had been heavily involved in the Arakan campaign, then carried out the operation in which, from a base near Chittagong, an entire infantry division, with all their men, guns, vehicles, equipment and mules, without any prior practice, were bundled into Dakotas and flown off to Imphal, to face the enemy almost as soon as they disembarked. The airlift started on 17 March and by the 27th two brigades had reached Imphal and a third had reached Dimapur. 194 Squadron of Dakotas, which had just completed the fly-in of the Chindit's Operation 'Thursday', flew three sorties a day from Chittagong to Imphal to transport 5th Indian Division. This operation, which saved both Imphal and Kohima, has been described by the historian of the Air Battle of Imphal, N. L. R. Franks (p. 37): 'We are going to see the eighth wonder of the world tonight. The Daks are going to bring in the 5th Division by air . . . These Daks were stacked up one behind the other, quarter of a mile apart, touching down and those with troops were simply taxiing along and the soldiers rolling out and then the Dak was straight off again. Then the others came in on the other side of the runway with mules, guns, etc. A half-hour before dawn the larger part of the division was in Imphal. It was the most magnificent piece of air transport I have ever seen. The logistics were unbelievable. They were literally coming in, rolling along and then taking off again back to Chittagong.'

At this juncture there is no doubt that without the determined actions of the crews and ground staffs of the RAF and USAAF the battles of Imphal and Kohima would have been lost, and Dimapur would have fallen.

From 27 March onwards, the troops at Imphal and Kohima relied on the tireless determination of the pilots and ground crew with their Dakotas. Later, Mountbatten, who as Supreme Commander of SEAC had his own private Dakota, said that if one piece of equipment more than any other could be said to have won the Burma War, it was the Dakota. The crisis at Imphal and Kohima, eased by the arrival of 5th Indian Division, continued into April, but by then Slim began to feel more confident because, under the wings of the air forces, reinforcements were flowing in.

The RAF had been active in preparing for the showdown at Imphal. The Headquarters of 221 Group RAF under Air Vice Marshal Vincent was established beside the main airstrip at Imphal. This and Palel were all-weather strips, supported by fair weather strips at Kangla, Tulihal, Wanjing and Sapam. These airstrips relied on interlocking ground cover material called Meccano, and on Bithess, a hessian strip covered by bitumen, which worked well until the main monsoon rains started. In 1943 the RAF had set up radar posts and observer units well forward of Imphal towards the Chindwin valley. One very important observation point and radar station had been established near Tamu in 20th Division's area. This was connected by land line to headquarters, and gave advanced warning of any attacking aircraft. The land line link was vital because radar and radio communication was so unreliable in such mountainous country. The withdrawal from Tamu by 20th Division (4 March–1 April) created severe problems for the RAF which thereby lost one of its most valuable warning systems, just at a time when the Japanese were developing the technique of low-flying attacks by just a few aircraft in order to avoid detection.

During the weeks before the battle actually started, the RAF had set up an impressive defensive system, but the Japanese with their Sally bombers and Oscar fighters had made a number of damaging attacks, since the Oscars were able to outmanoeuvre the Hurricanes. The tables began to turn in November 1943 when squadrons of Mk 8 Spitfires flew in to the base. During the next three months Spitfires destroyed or damaged more than 100 Japanese aircraft for the loss of five pilots. At the same time, American Mustangs and Lightnings attacked forward Japanese airfields which had ineffective warning systems, destroying more than 100 aircraft on the ground, and forcing the Japanese to withdraw their aircraft to bases more than 500 miles away near Rangoon.

These preliminary air battles established Allied air superiority which made possible the whole concept of large-scale air supply to military units, as well as enabling the second Wingate expedition, Operation 'Thursday', to proceed. As the military battles developed, the fighters and fighter-bombers – Hurribombers, Vultee Vengeance dive-bombers, Mustangs and Lightnings – evolved close and effective air support for the troops on the ground, often acting as an additional arm of artillery in attacking Japanese strongpoints.

By the beginning of 1944 the RAF and the Indian Air Force had four squadrons of Hurricanes at Imphal and Palel (1, 28, 34 and 42 Squadrons), two squadrons of Spitfires and later a squadron of Beaufighters at Kangla and Sapam (81, 136 and 176 Squadrons). In addition to these forces, Wellingtons, Liberators and Vengeances flew in from India and from the advanced bases lying to the west of Imphal at Silchar and Khumbirgram. The Dakota squadrons, 194 and 117, based at Agartala, were moved forward to Tulihal to fly in the Chindits for Operation 'Thursday' starting on 5 March.

While the Japanese forces were advancing rapidly on the ground, they also made some determined air attacks on the airstrips at Palel, Tulihal and Imphal, where twenty men from Corps HQ were killed. Although the Japanese had lost overall control of the air, they continued to attack Imphal throughout the siege. The Japanese 5th Air Division, its HQ back at Maymyo under General Tazoe, kept up sporadic attacks on Imphal, but gave hardly any support to the three advancing divisions,

Airstrips during the Imphal Siege

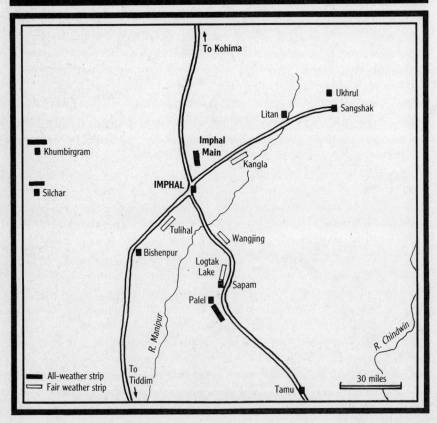

even though they needed it badly. The reason for this was the fault of Mutaguchi who, perhaps forgetting the domination of the Japanese air force in the 1942 advance, decided that air support was not necessary for infantry divisions. This caused deep resentment, as can be seen from the diaries of captured Japanese soldiers, which spoke of the frightfulness of the enemy air attacks and the hundreds of burnt-out vehicles that crashed down into the valleys, their drivers riddled with bullets. In spite of the general Allied air superiority, Japanese air attacks enjoyed some success during March and April 1944. On 25 April, while flying to Imphal, five Dakotas and their crews were destroyed by a Japanese attack, but the RAF quickly countered this tactic by establishing a corridor from Silchar over the hills to Imphal, which was regularly patrolled by Spitfires.

On 29 March units of the Japanese 31st Division, in making their sweep towards Kohima, cut the Imphal–Kohima road so that Imphal was completely cut off. This created a totally new supply situation because the garrison numbered more than 150,000 men, and Troop Carrier Command was already heavily involved in supplying the Chindits behind the Japanese lines, as well as carrying out very difficult air drops into the narrow perimeter of Kohima – now also surrounded by the Japanese. If Spitfires and Hurricanes were the heroes of the Battle of Britain, and Lancasters of the bombing offensive against Germany, there is no doubt that the heroes of the Imphal siege were the Dakotas whose ground crews enabled the pilots to fly their unarmed aircraft day after day in appalling weather, into the dangerous airspace of Imphal.

As soon as the siege started, a conference of air and military staff agreed to keep the garrison going with food, ammunition, fuel, vehicles and all types of replacements; this meant that more than 500 tons a day would have to be flown in – the equivalent of 150 aircraft loads.

Bombs for the Hurribombers operating out of Imphal, shells, mortar bombs, aviation fuel, trucks and tanks, general supplies and food, and even fodder for the ubiquitous mules, formed the bulk of the cargo to be flown in. Sometimes the supply squadrons were flying five sorties a day to the hard-pressed garrison. The daunting supply problem was made more manageable by flying out some headquarters staff – e.g., 221 Group Headquarters moved out to Silchar. Similarly, many non-combatants went out on the returning Dakotas, as did all wounded. For the men fighting around Imphal, the knowledge that if they were wounded they would be rapidly flown out to safety boosted their morale.

Within the perimeter of Imphal, an area nearly 30 miles from north to south and surrounded on all sides by mountain ranges, cut off by the Japanese from 29 March onwards, RAF and army units alike prepared defensive 'boxes', and these were given code-names of fish, e.g., Salmon, Trout or Kipper. Squadrons dug slit trenches and covered them with tarpaulins or corrugated iron, and further defended them with trip wires. Some aircrew thought it a bit off having to dig their own trenches, but most rallied round and even took their turn at nightly guard duty.

The supply system became so efficient that everything the fighting divisions and the combat squadrons needed could be flown in. It was off-loaded or dropped by parachute, or just dropped. The phrase 'death by flying fruit', coined when someone was killed by a crate of tinned fruit dropped from a Dakota, shows that this method did have its dangers. There was such a huge demand for parachutes that Slim's staff, with the help of Calcutta jute merchants, invented a cheaper parachute made of jute (nicknamed parajute) which was used for dropping stores and equipment. Thus guns, jeeps, engines for vehicles, 44-gallon petrol drums, mules, sheep, goats and chickens were all delivered safely. As the weather deteriorated towards the start of the monsoon in May, when flights often had to be aborted, the staging posts at Silchar and Khumbirgram, a relatively short distance west of Imphal, were built up so that aircraft already loaded could quickly fly over the intervening hills as soon as the weather cleared.

It nearly always happened that units close to the enemy achieved much closer co-operation than those behind the lines. In the supply system it was agreed that priority should go to the unit with the most urgent need – be it fuel for a Spitfire squadron or shells for a battery, and there were rarely any disputes. After weeks of the closest co-operation during the siege, and the warmest relations with the army units they were supporting, one squadron wanted to adopt the IV Corps badge. Their application had to go to GHQ in Delhi – who turned down the request!

Some idea of the achievement of the air supply squadrons is given by the official record of the siege, which shows the tonnage carried:

423 tons of sugar	919 tons of grain
5,000 live chickens	27,000 eggs
5 million vitamin tablets	12,000 bags of mail
1,300 tons of animal food	43 million cigarettes
800,000 gallons of fuel	

In addition to this and to all the guns, ammunition, vehicles and replacements, 12,000 reinforcements were flown in, and 10,000 sick and wounded were flown out. The Imphal garrison might have survived the siege without the Spitfires and Hurricanes, but all the valour of the fighting soldiers would have come to nothing without the Dakota.

The battle of Imphal saw some of the most savage hand-to-hand fighting of the war, but within the garrison the experiences of men in different parts of the perimeter varied dramatically. The Battle of

Nungshigum (Chapter 8), one of the key battles on the northern front of Imphal, in which both sides sustained very heavy casualties, was observed in fascination by men of the RAF Regiment who were guarding and supplying a vital radio post at a height of more than 5,000 feet in the surrounding mountains. They could see the Vengeance dive-bombers and Hurricanes going into the attack on the Japanese positions, and see the men moving on the ground. On other occasions they were able to see Dakotas going in to land, or dropping parachute-loads of supplies. They noticed that the clusters of eight jerricans of petrol were always dropped by parachute, but large bags of rice, since they could come to little harm, were dropped free. Some of the more static units fared better than those actually in contact with the enemy. One enterprising unit constructed a double seat for their latrine and got a neighbouring Flight Commander to perform the opening ceremony – before *Clochmerle!*

Most units suffered severely from food shortages, and most people were always hungry, but there were occasions when a cook was praised for conjuring a tasty meal out of the inevitable dry biscuits, bully beef, and the much hated tinned beetroot, which nearly achieved the notoriety of the soya link sausage. Most units had to collect water from a filtration plant on the River Manipur, but others, higher up in the surrounding hills, had to rely on rain water, and in the end became unimaginably filthy. In the less fortunate units the monotonous diet consisted of hard biscuits and jam both morning and night, while the midday meal consisted of biscuits with a tin of bully beef between four men. At most meals there was a dixie of tea, made from tea, granulated sugar and tinned condensed milk, but the best moment of the day came at evening stand-to when each man had a tot of rum.

Army units all relied substantially on mules for their transport, and within Imphal the RAF units maintaining the radio posts on the higher peaks also employed mules. Each muleteer had to collect two mules from the Indian mule lines and return them at the end of the day. Most men who looked after mules became very fond of them, and found them to be highly intelligent – even refusing to eat ration biscuit – and, unlike a horse, a mule could tell whether water was safe to drink. When properly handled, mules responded well and could even be loaded into Dakotas and tethered to the side of the aircraft – though it needed a lot of cleaning out after it had taken a load of mules.

Static units and fighting units alike shared the misery of Imphal in the monsoon. In May 1944 the monsoon started early and brought 400 inches of rain. When the rains began the whole countryside steamed, everything went green, clothes rotted, men's fingers turned white and wrinkled with the damp, nearly everyone suffered from dysentery and diarrhoea, and from sores and bites inflicted by swarms of mosquitoes.

Yet morale remained high because of the challenge of the Japanese attack and the comforting thought that the condition of the Japanese was infinitely worse. Their supply lines had been cut by the Chindits and by RAF and USAAF bombing, they were running short of ammunition and were nearly starving.

Some accounts of the siege of Imphal give the impression that after the great air battles in mid March, the Japanese were swept out of the way. This was not so; they mounted quite heavy attacks throughout the siege. On 15 April a force of nine Sally bombers escorted by 40 Oscars took part in an air battle over Imphal, and when some of the bombers got through they caused heavy casualties on the ground. Encouraged by this success, they launched another attack two days later on Palel, with six Sally bombers and 50 Oscars. Attacks continued. On 21 April 28 Oscars attacked Kangla airstrip but although they took the defences by surprise they inflicted little damage. The next day they attacked Imphal Main airstrip, and destroyed three Beaufighters that were used for weather reconnaissance as well as night-fighting. In April fairly frequent and very heavy thunderstorms made flying difficult, and put an end to operations from the fair-weather strip at Wanjing because it became waterlogged. During the month, more than 5,000 attacking sorties and 1,500 defensive sorties were flown from the other strips, together with more than 800 tactical reconnaissance flights. The RAF lost thirty aircrew and 24 aircraft, with a further eight aircraft damaged.

In May the monsoon increased in intensity, adding to the difficulties. The bad weather also increased the number of accidents. In early May a Dakota skidded off the runway, wrecking four Spitfires. The Japanese kept up their jitter attacks on the ground, and air attacks on the strips, while the RAF mounted very heavy attacks on the Japanese positions at Bishenpur with Liberators, Mitchells, Wellingtons and Vengeances, which were escorted by Spitfires and Hurricanes.

At Kohima a scratch garrison, including 4th Royal West Kent Regiment, was besieged by the Japanese from 6 to 18 April. During this time RAF and USAAF pilots felt a special concern for the besieged troops, their plight being so obvious and the area they occupied so small. Aircraft flew dangerously low in attempting to deliver their loads into the defended area and not to the Japanese attackers. The progress of British forces trying to rescue Kohima from the north, forced the Japanese to step up their attacks on Imphal in an urgent bid to overrun the garrison while they still had the chance. The Japanese then brought up heavier guns to shell the airstrips from the hills surrounding Imphal and on 18 May launched a large-scale air attack with more than 40 Oscars. With the continuing pressure from the Japanese, and the deteriorating weather, losses of Spitfires, Hurricanes and Dakotas increased. Throughout May, 221 Group RAF flew more than 6,000 sorties, and engaged in frequent dog-fights with attacking Oscars. Losses for the month amounted to twelve Hurricanes lost or damaged, thirteen Spitfires lost or damaged, with several more damaged on the ground. While the dog-fights continued, the Dakotas kept up their regular supply service, and the strips at Imphal, Sapam, Palel and Tulihal were kept in constant use, even though they were officially designated fair weather strips.

The monsoon rains became even worse during June, and interrupted flying on most days. Spitfires had established effective domination over the Imphal area, and they were now fitted with additional drop tanks on their wings in order to increase their range. These had the disadvantage that they had to be jettisoned in combat, and if an aircraft met the enemy when it was at the extent of its range, and had to jettison its tanks, it sometimes did not get back to base.

The main role of the Spitfires was to scramble and defeat the invading Oscars, and to patrol the corridor for the Dakotas coming in from Silchar, but the Hurricanes were used offensively in very close co-operation with the army units on the ground. Army liaison officers were trained to give the most precise detail to the RAF squadrons, and then the Hurribombers would drop their bombs or go into the attack from as low as 50 feet. The army frequently identified a target by 2-inch mortar smoke and the Hurricanes would then close in to bomb or strafe.

Although all the airstrips lay within the Imphal perimeter, their conditions varied considerably. Palel, although it was up in the hills on the southern sector and dangerously close to the Japanese, seems to have been a more relaxed and cheerful place than, say, Tulihal or Imphal Main. At Palel, off-duty crews could often watch Hurricanes bombing the Japanese forward guns which were actually shelling the strip. With the succession of aircraft flying in and out, the RAF seemed to get those useful little extras that the military units in constant action did not receive. For example, some aircraft had been modified so that when they returned from India they could be stocked up with gin, rum or whisky.

The men were nearly always hungry, but one station had a ready supply of baked beans which were always available in the mess. Americans always seemed to have more generous rations and caused considerable envy when, having just flown in, they would cook sausages, bacon and eggs on a primus stove beside their aircraft. Some strips lay fairly close to Logtak Lake, which in pre-war days had been famous for its wild fowl shooting, and these units were able to supplement the bully beef with duck or succulent pigeon. Visitors, especially those from GHQ Delhi, unable to appreciate the difference between GHQ and the front line, often made fools of themselves by complaining about the standard of saluting, or even complaining that it was unsporting to shoot a sitting bird.

Throughout the siege the aircrews, who were themselves flying double the recommended hours, gave high praise to the ground crews and especially to the skill and dedication of the engineers and fitters. With a spanner, a pair of pliers, a screwdriver and a hammer they seemed to work miracles on damaged aircraft. If more than one Spitfire was out of action, another would be cannibalized to keep the rest going. One fitter recalled that they worked night and day during the siege, but they really had no idea where they were, and they had no idea of the destination of the aircraft they were servicing. Frequently, the aircrew felt guilty when they flew out for the night to the relative safety of Assam, leaving the ground crews to undertake the defensive sentry duties against the attacking Japanese.

Descriptions of life during the siege vary substantially. Many speak of the endless enervating damp and the cascading rain which flooded the airstrips. Others recall that most letters from home, arriving on the daily mail aircraft, only took three or four days – and recall that the weather was always fine. The sufferings and shared danger welded squadrons together in a unique way. For example, 194 Squadron, which flew Dakotas in the Imphal siege and was totally involved with the Chindits in Operation 'Thursday', still holds reunions. One veteran, recalling with great affection the original and higly respected Squadron Leader 'Fatty Pearson', recounted that watching Fatty Pearson getting into a Hurricane was like watching Mae West getting in to a girdle. Such memories and loyalty are a tribute to the achievements of all those who endured the siege of Imphal.

The bulk of the air fighting during the siege centred on the need to protect the constant stream of Dakotas. This battle continued until 22 June when 2nd Division, having driven the Japanese out of Kohima, advanced down the road to Imphal and made contact with the advanced units of 5th Indian Division, fighting its way out of Imphal northwards up the road to Kohima. From then on more and more supplies came in by truck, but the role and the responsibilities of the air forces increased, and they were to play another critical part in the pursuit of the Japanese back down the Tiddim road and onwards to Mandalay and Rangoon.

The raising of the Imphal siege on 22 June lifted some of the pressure from the squadrons within the perimeter, but their front-line role was illustrated just after the siege was lifted, when on 3 July a Japanese raiding party infiltrated the ground defences at Palel airstrip and destroyed seven aircraft on the ground before being driven off. It was fortunate that the Japanese did not realize the effectiveness of this tactic until it was almost too late. There was a tragic finale to the achievements of the RAF during the siege. In early August 615 Squadron's Mk 8 Spitfires flew off on leave to Calcutta. They hit an unpredicted monsoon storm, the Commanding Officer and three pilots were killed, three more baled out, and eight aircraft were lost.

The appalling conditions under which pilots and aircraft had to operate are illustrated by the number of aircraft lost during the siege. Of 70 lost, sixteen fell to Japanese fighters – nearly all Oscars – seventeen were lost to anti-aircraft fire and 37 to accidents, storms and bad weather. This heavy toll of experienced pilots and valuable machines was the price that the RAF and USAAF paid for playing the decisive role in one of the greatest and most significant battles of the Second World War.

Without the contribution of the air forces, in flying in the reserve divisions from the Arakan, in supporting Kohima, and in supplying 150,000 men during the siege of Imphal, there is no doubt that Kohima would have fallen, Imphal would have been lost and the war in the Far East would have taken a totally different course. Perhaps Mutaguchi would have made his triumphal 'March on Delhi'.

No assessment of the role of the air forces during the Imphal siege would be complete without reference to their continuing part in the Arakan campaign, and their critical role in the launch of Operation 'Thursday' which started on the night the Japanese made their first move against Imphal. So, throughout the siege, 194, 62 and 117 Squadrons, in addition, were flying deep into the Arakan, and were continuing their daily and nightly support for the Chindit columns operating in the area of Indaw, 200 miles south-east of Kohima.

A moving tribute to the air forces in the battles of Imphal and Kohima, and in the subsequent defeat of the Japanese, came fittingly from Mountbatten, The Supreme Commander SEAC, who wrote that in reconquering Burma, 'It was the Transport aircraft, British and American which made it possible.' (D. Williams, *194 Squadron, The Friendly Firm*, p. 59.)

CHAPTER 6

THE BATTLE OF KOHIMA

E ARLY IN 1944 4th Battalion The Royal West Kent Regiment – a
pre-war Territorial battalion – had taken part in fighting in the
Arakan as part of 5th Indian Division. They had seen action at
the Battle of the Tunnels and had sustained more than 200
casualties. They were therefore as surprised as the rest of 5th Division to
be bundled out of the Arakan and flown to Assam. On 29 March 1944,
with their vehicles, guns and mules, they were flown to Dimapur, and by
30 March had arrived in Kohima. They immediately started digging slit
trenches because rumours of the rapid advance of the Japanese
abounded. From the welter of alarms and gossip it appeared that while
the Japanese (31st Division under General Sato) had advanced with
remarkable speed, they had been held up temporarily at Jessami and
Kharasom, nearly 30 miles east of Kohima, by the action of the Assam
Regiment and the Assam Rifles – relatively untried units which were part
of the Kohima garrison.

Kohima, an attractive little town, was situated on a ridge of small
hills approximately halfway along the road from the important rail and
supply depot at Dimapur to the larger garrison town of Imphal. Although
it lay on a high ridge (about 5,000 feet) it was surrounded by massive
mountain ramparts rising, like Mount Pulebadze on the south-west, to
more than 10,000 feet. The Dimapur road, as it approached Kohima,
climbed a steep hill and passed the site of the Indian General Hospital
(IGH Spur). The Deputy Commissioner's bungalow, in its attractive,
spacious and colourful grounds, dominated the centre of the town. These
grounds, like most of Kohima, had been terraced, with a substantial drop
between each terrace – so at different levels there were the DC's
bungalow, the tennis court and the Club. The bungalow looked south
over a series of small hills which had recently been developed by the army
as a supply base: first Garrison Hill; then Kuki Piquet; then the Field
Supply Depot (FSD), where there were several more substantial bashas
(bamboo huts), with, for example, a row of large ovens; finally the Daily
Issue Store (DIS). The Deputy Commissioner, Charles Pawsey, had been
in the area for twenty years and had built up a remarkable rapport with
the local Naga people who lived in the well-defended hill-top villages in
the surrounding area. Pawsey and his loyal Nagas were to play a
significant part in the Battle of Kohima.

* The C-47 (Dakota) deserves its reputation, but
it must be said – It was not a large airplane by
todays standards, It could lift relatively few tons,
and the side cargo door strictly limited the size of
any object that could be loaded.

71

After a day's very hard digging, The Royal West Kents (RWK), were suddenly ordered to move, prompting one soldier to ask 'Why can't the top brass make up their bloody minds?' Unbeknown to the battalion they were about to become the victims of serious high-level disputes. 161 Brigade in which, with 4/7 Rajputs and 1/1st Punjabis, RWK had been trained to a high pitch of readiness for jungle warfare, was commanded by Brigadier Warren. Warren was appalled to discover that his brigade – part of the proud 5th Indian Division – was to be detached and put under the command of the Area Commander, Major-General Ranking (Area or Garrison commanders were usually men who were too old to have command in an active division). Similarly, Lieutenant-Colonel Laverty, the CO of the Royal West Kents, was horrified that his battalion had to join the Kohima garrison commanded by Colonel Richards. These personal disputes exacerbated an already serious and difficult situation.

On 28 March the deployment of the Royal West Kents was considered at a conference at Imphal where Slim expressed his view that the Japanese would reach Kohima by 3 April, and could advance to Dimapur by 10 April. Because of the speed of the Japanese advance India Command had agreed, as a matter of urgency, to send XXXIII Corps, made up of 2nd British Division, together with four separate brigades, and commanded by Lieutenant-General Montagu Stopford, to help Slim

Kohima, 6–18 April 1944

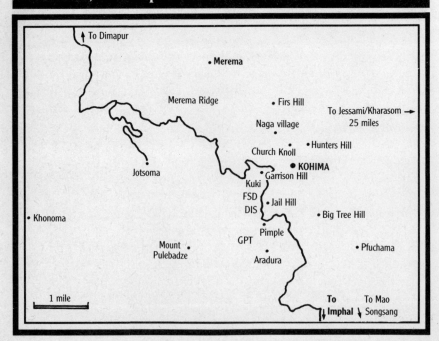

at Imphal and Kohima. Stopford reached Imphal on the day of the conference, and was immediately put in charge of operations in the Kohima and Dimapur sectors. He saw his first priority as being the defence of the base at Dimapur and the railway from there up to Ledo. With very lttle time in which to decide his strategy, he ordered Ranking, the Area Commander at Kohima, to defend Dimapur, as first priority, and to build up a strike force there — second priority, to defend Kohima. This instruction, and its order of priority, caused Ranking to make the disastrous decision that Warren should withdraw 161 Brigade (including the Royal West Kents) from Kohima and move them to Nichugard Pass, at the southern approach to Dimapur, i.e., to defend Dimapur at the cost of abandoning Kohima.

In Kohima Brigadier Warren and Colonel Richards conferred urgently with Charles Pawsey who for years past had demanded defences for Kohima, and now was to be proved right. He was astounded at the order for 161 Brigade to move to Dimapur because it would be letting down his Naga people, and would appear to be abandoning the Assam units still engaged at Jessami and Kharasom. Warren and Richards agreed with Pawsey, believing that if Kohima fell it could lead to disaster for the whole of Fourteenth Army and Stilwell's forces farther north. Warren argued that if his whole brigade were dug-in at Kohima it would be too powerful a force for the Japanese to bypass. He felt so strongly about this that he demanded to be allowed to fly and see Slim (30 March). After a vicious and bitter argument, Ranking refused his request, leaving him and Pawsey and Richards in despair at the likely fate of Kohima and the Naga people.

Slim and Stopford disagreed about withdrawing 161 Brigade from Kohima to Dimapur, but Slim allowed Stopford's decision to stand, despite protests from the local commanders. Stopford, having been given his priorities, and knowing the speed of the Japanese advance, was perhaps wise to concentrate his forces at Dimapur. Neither he nor Slim could know that Sato, for other reasons, did not intend to attack Dimapur.

The Royal West Kents moved out of Kohima on 31 March, leaving Richards with 'a few odds and sods' – a company of Gurkhas, a company of the Burma Regiment and a few other minor units. Rations and ammunition, of which fortunately there was plenty, were issued, but the supply of water was precarious. There were some large metal tanks near the DC's bungalow, but these were extremely vulnerable. Richards was told to hold Kohima for as long as possible, and was promised that the survivors of the Assam Regiment from the battles at Jessami would come to his assistance. Richards had sent urgent demands for barbed wire, essential for the defence of every type of position, but – just as at

Kohima: Dispositions at 6 April 1944

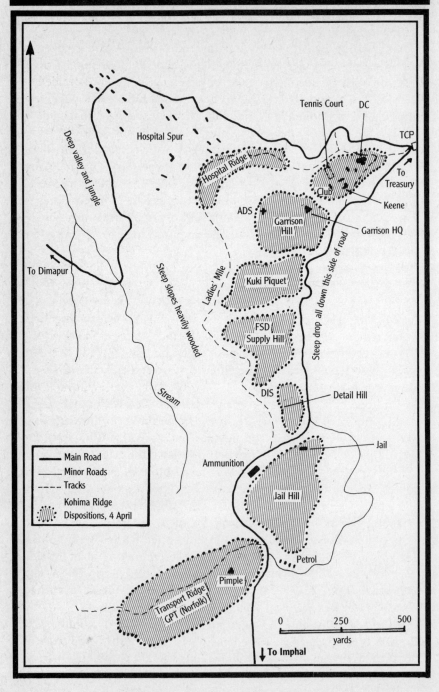

To Dimapur

Deep valley and jungle

Hospital Spur

Hospital Ridge

Tennis Court

DC

TCP

To Treasury

Club

Keene

ADS

Garrison Hill

Garrison HQ

Steep slopes heavily wooded

Ladies' Mile

Kuki Piquet

FSD Supply Hill

Steep drop all down this side of road

Stream

DIS

Detail Hill

Jail

Ammunition

Jail Hill

Main Road

Minor Roads

Tracks

Kohima Ridge
Dispositions, 4 April

Petrol

Transport Ridge
GPT (Norfolk)

Pimple

0   250   500

yards

↓ To Imphal

Sangshak – the front-line units about to be attacked received none. In desperation Charles Pawsey, who throughout the siege wore grey flannel trousers and an open-necked shirt, got his Nagas to sharpen wooden stakes to protect the bunkers.

By 4 April, when the first units of 2nd Division were arriving at Dimapur, Stopford conferred with Ranking and Major-General Grover (GOC 2nd Division). Seeing the build-up at Dimapur, Stopford decided he could afford to send 161 Brigade back to Kohima. The fury, the frustration and the language of the soldiers involved can be imagined. As the Royal West Kents advanced again up the Kohima road they met hordes of panic-stricken soldiers and civilians. They relieved them of any arms and ammunition, but allowed them to go on. Lieutenant-Colonel Laverty decided that, although the Japanese were at the outskirts of the town, his battalion would advance as rapidly as possible into Kohima. As they arrived, accurate Japanese shelling began, destroying much of their kit and most of their trucks. This was the unpromising start to one of the epic sieges of the Second World War.

During these frustrating days the Assam Regiment, which had been sent from Kohima to Jessami and Kharasom, was bearing the brunt of the attack by 138th Regiment, the leading unit of Sato's 31st Division. The first action took place on 28 March at Jessami when the Assam Regiment held their fire and then wiped out the leading Japanese platoon. The Assams had been told to hold their position to the last man, and this they prepared to do. The Japanese, after their first reverse, put in one attack after another and suffered big losses. They then brought forward 124th Regiment together with artillery and mortars. Faced by such overwhelming numbers, the Assam Regiment held grimly on, through days and nights of fierce hand-to-hand fighting, and they kept firing until the barrels of their Bren guns were red hot. One Japanese attack separated a part of the battalion from the main body, but both groups still fought on. Eventually the battalion received an order from Colonel Richards to withdraw, which they did on 31 March. However, Captain Young, commanding the minor unit, sent off his men, but stayed at his post alone, hurling grenades at the enemy until he fell riddled with bullets. Once again, as at Sangshak, the bravery and determination of an isolated unit had caused a vital delay to Sato's leading forces. From the Assam Regiment and the Assam Rifles about 250 survivors eventually reached Kohima by 3 April.

Sato and 31st Division had made good progress towards Kohima, and his HQ was now south of Jessami, but he was angry that the advance of his whole division had been held up by determined opposition. Later he complained, with considerable justification, that if his leading units had bypassed Sangshak and Jessami the outcome of the Kohima battle would have been very different.

While 161 Brigade was returning to Kohima, the advance guard of 2nd Division were arriving at Dimapur to scenes of complete chaos. They grumbled that they were arriving in a fighting zone in dribs and drabs and without weapons, guns or transport. The Dimapur stores were disposed over an area eleven miles long by one mile wide; most of the staff had fled and there was indescribable confusion. Again, the fighting units criticized the HQ staff.

The return of the Royal West Kents to Kohima on 5 April could not have been more discouraging. They noticed that bunkers and trenches had been badly sited, no good gun positions had been established and even the garrison HQ had not been properly dug in. At least the trenches they had previously dug were still there, and they rapidly dispersed to their company positions on IGH Spur, Garrison Hill, Kuki Piquet and DIS.

Already the Japanese 58th Regiment, which was in good heart despite its heavy losses at Sangshak, had moved towards Aradura Spur and had driven off some Manipur State troops. Next, at 0400 on 6 April a Japanese company entered the Naga village and rapidly took over the buildings. The defenders seemed unaware of this, and casually turned up at 0900 to draw their rations. They were quickly and quietly captured. By midday the Japanese had control of the village and had brought up their main body of troops. Sato now had three regiments – the equivalent of three British brigades – all ready to attack Kohima. Slim's assumption that the enemy would only advance to Kohima with a couple of battalions proved to be dangerously inaccurate.

For their part the Royal West Kents were incensed at being separated from their brigade and their division, with whom they had trained, and had been thrown into a serious fight with, as they saw it, a lot of odds and ends of base units. Their criticism fell, unfairly, on the garrison commander, Colonel Richards, who had himself been pitchforked into a difficult situation. Brigadier Warren (161 Brigade) made matters worse by refusing to communicate with Richards and speaking only to Laverty, the CO of RWK. Later in the siege Laverty, carrying his prejudice to absurd lengths, even refused to re-charge the wireless batteries at Richards' HQ, thus adding to already serious difficulties.

On 6 April Warren made an important decision. The remainder of his brigade, including 1/1st Punjabis, 4/7th Rajputs and 24th Indian Mountain Regiment, had reached Jotsoma, about two miles west of Kohima. He therefore established a defensive box at Jotsoma from which there was good observation of the whole of the Kohima ridge, and towards which there was a reasonably good track for the brigade transport. He quickly established the guns on a reverse slope and registered fire tasks on to likely targets on the Kohima battlefield. These guns, helped by the outstanding observation work of Major Yeo inside the garrison, achieved a high level of remarkably accurate fire which they kept up throughout the siege.

On 6 April the Japanese put in their first major attack. They took Jail Hill, and though they sustained heavy losses they continued their advance and made another attack on DIS and FSD. The defenders were helped by the guns from Jotsoma, which put down pre-arranged fire tasks and caused heavy casualties among the Japanese attackers. They, in turn, replied with 75mm guns sited on GPT Ridge. The persistent Japanese attacks gradually made inroads into the Royal West Kents' positions and began to threaten 'C' and 'D' Companies' positions on FSD and DIS. By the morning of 8 April RWK were effectively dug-in, with most of the men in slit trenches. That morning the trenches lay cold and wet under a thick mist, a mist which chilled everyone and added to the fear and uncertainty. The men stood-to and checked the fixed lines for the Bren guns. Rather to their surprise, just after stand-to, the cooks arrived with tea, porridge, sausage, bacon and biscuits.

The forward platoon on DIS faced Jail Hill which had been held briefly by a scratch group of Gurkhas, but was now held by the Japanese who, from that vantage point, could overlook most of the RWK positions. Laverty considered a counter-attack, but realized that he had not enough men to carry it out. Instead, the 3-inch mortars under their outstanding NCO, Sergeant King, were cleverly resited and then retaliated effectively. The rest of the platoons continued with their digging, studied the ground ahead, improved their field of fire where possible and waited for the regular hail of shells and mortar bombs which the Japanese normally sent over at dusk. After the bombardment the Japanese tried their old trick of shouting 'Hey! Quick, let me through, the Japs are after me!' The RWK, having met this trick in the Arakan, held their fire so as not to reveal their positions to the accurate Japanese snipers. Usually, the Japanese attacked with screams and yells and with bugles blowing, but occasionally, they crept forward in total silence to within a few yards of the forward trench. That night the Japanese threw in one attack after another and gradually infiltrated the RWK positions on FSD.

This incursion threatened the other positions and had to be removed. Laverty quickly organized a counter-attack on FSD and the bashas now occupied by the Japanese. A young sapper officer invented an ingenious pole charge with gun-cotton in ammunition boxes, to destroy the walls of the bashas and help the infantry forward. This attack was to provide an example of truly remarkable heroism by Lance-Corporal Harman of The Royal West Kents, which inspired his own platoon and strengthened the whole battalion through the grim weeks ahead. As his platoon attacked

they came under heavy automatic fire and a shower of grenades. Harman
saw two machine-guns on the flank, walked calmly towards them, used
his teeth to pull the pin from two 36 grenades, and lobbed them into the
enemy weapon pit. He jumped into the pit and soon emerged holding up
the machine-gun. Seeing this, the whole platoon charged forward and in
hand-to-hand fighting cleared the enemy from the bashas. One larger
building remained. Harman entered this and found that it had been the
bakery, and the Japanese were hiding in the large ovens. He rushed out to
fetch grenades and returned to the bakery. There were ten ovens and he
dropped a grenade into each. Afterwards, finding two Japanese still alive,
he picked them up and carried them back to his platoon lines, to a wild
round of cheering.

The following morning (8 April), after a night of shelling, jitter raids
and company attacks by the Japanese, 'D' Company Royal West Kents
had to mount another counter-attack against a machine-gun post.
Harman ordered his Bren gunner to give him covering fire and walked
calmly forward, stopped twice to kill two Japanese defenders, fixed his
bayonet and then charged the post. He finished off three men with his
rifle and bayonet, and then jumped out of the trench holding up the
machine-gun. Then, to the horror of his watching comrades, he began to
walk casually back towards his lines. They yelled to him to run, but he
kept walking and despite their covering fire was cut down by automatic
weapons. His friends rushed out and carried him back to his trench,
where he looked up and said, 'I got the lot, it was worth it.' He died a few
moments later. He was subsequently awarded a posthumous VC.

Harman's bravery saved a critical situation, but the Japanese
continued their attacks as more reinforcements – including elephants
carrying heavy guns – came up. On the same day, 8 April, the Japanese
138th Regiment had circled to the north of Kohima, and had cut the
Dimapur to Kohima road at Zubza (Milestone 36), thus cutting off
Kohima garrison as well as 161 Brigade at Jotsoma.

At this stage of the siege, there is an interesting contrast in the
conditions suffered or enjoyed by neighbouring units. While the whole of
his brigade were cut off and faced a very grave military situation,
Brigadier Warren, at Jotsoma, who had bought some chickens from a
local village, had a chicken run built near the officers' mess. He also got
his water carriers to pick wild raspberries which he had for supper; after
supper he usually played a few hands of pontoon with his brigade staff.

Inside the perimeter things were very different. In the area of the
DC's bungalow and the tennis courts, the defending troops came under
increasingly heavy artillery and mortar fire, and had to repel frequent
infantry assaults by the Japanese battalion based on the Naga village.

Initially these attacks were beaten back, but the Japanese gradually advanced and reached the end of the tennis court. From this time until the siege was lifted, the area saw some of the hardest, closest and grimmest fighting, with rifle and automatic weapons and showers of grenades being hurled across the tennis court at point-blank range. The Assam Regiment, the Burma Regiment and the Royal West Kent HQ fought off the attacks, and were helped by the remarkably accurate fire from the Jotsoma guns – guided by the indefatigable Major Yeo.

Easter Sunday fell on 9 April, and many men, from units as far apart as Dimapur and Tiddim, have recalled their thoughts at that time, of home and loved ones, and the Easter message. In many units men attended a brief service, clutching their rifles or Bren guns, but within Kohima no service was possible, though Padre Randolph, the RWK padre, was always present, comforting the fit and wounded alike, and giving moral support and Christian leadership. Other comfort came from the colour-sergeant responsible for the food. Although two of his cooks had been killed, he made a special effort on Easter Day. He crawled to the forward trenches, often only about 30 yards from the enemy, taking a dixie of tea, one of stew, one of potatoes and, as it was Easter Day, he added sardines – a real treat. He even apologized that he had not managed pink eggs for breakfast.

One RWK soldier was in a trench near the tennis court when it was overrun by the Japanese. They killed his mate and left him for dead. He lay doggo for a whole day, while the enemy stood on him and piled ammunition on him too. He waited until the following night, then rushed across the tennis court, dived into an RWK trench, and fought throughout the night.

While Padre Randolph emerged as one of the truly admirable characters during the siege, the entire unit gained inspiration from the doctor, Lieutenant-Colonel John Young. He had been near Jotsoma, but hearing that things in Kohima were getting pretty sticky he had walked in through the Japanese lines to see what he could do to help. He did excellent work coping with the casualties and the ghastly conditions of the wounded. One night, because the wounded were suffering badly from the cold, he led an unarmed patrol of stretcher-bearers to the trucks lying outside the perimeter to bring back some blankets. He silenced a sentry with his bare hands, and his party then staggered back to his hospital with more than 200 blankets.

A deep trench had been dug for the wounded, but from it they could actually see the Japanese on Jail Hill loading their mortars, and after the crack when it was fired could see and trace the mortar bomb on its trajectory until it landed nearby. On one occasion a bomb actually landed in the trench for the seriously wounded, and there were agonized screams as the stretcher-bearers and digging parties tried desperately to separate the living from shattered limbs and corpses. Gruesome incidents abounded. Men watched a young surgeon, helped by an orderly, work for an hour and a half to amputate the leg of a wounded man, and just as he had finished, a bomb fell in the trench and all three were blown to pieces.

On 9 April, while the Japanese were strengthening their grip on Kohima, General Stopford, XXXIII Corps Commander, conferred with General Grover (2nd Division). They both realized that the whole of Sato's 31st Division were attacking Kohima, and Grover undertook the task of clearing the road to Kohima as quickly as possible; he planned an attack with two brigades.

At Jotsoma, the Japanese put in constant attacks on the brigade box, but were repelled by well-directed automatic fire and by well-aimed 36 grenades. After five days of battle the whole area was littered with bloated corpses, and inside Kohima the defenders hoped every day that the battalions in Jotsoma would break through and raise the siege, but the troops in the Jotsoma Box were now themselves surrounded and fighting for their lives.

On 10 April Grover ordered Brigadier Hawkins and 5 Brigade (Worcesters, Dorsets and Cameron Highlanders) to lead the advance towards Kohima from their position near Zubza where there was a Japanese road-block. Things were not easy and for his part Warren even considered withdrawing the whole Kohima garrison to Jotsoma. Grover forbade this. The following day 5 Brigade, in their first real action, sustained a fair number of casualties by milling about in the open and failing to adapt quickly enough to the harsh realities of battle. Grover and Hawkins went forward near Zubza, and when they saw the height and steepness of the hills and the depth of the jungle realized that their original plans – made without having reconnoitred the ground – were absurdly optimistic. The danger and the dilemma of commanders giving orders without having seen the ground over which the troops must operate, was frequently illustrated at this stage of the Kohima battle. Stopford thought Grover was slow; Grover thought Hawkins and 5 Brigade were slow; and Hawkins thought his leading battalion was slow – until he saw the ground.

Many of the battles at Kohima and Imphal were not really battles for divisions or brigades, but rather for companies or even platoons, confined to narrow jungle tracks. 2nd Division not only had to adapt to totally new terrain and a new type of warfare, but at the same time adapt to mule transport, 400 mules having arrived just when 5 Brigade reached Zubza.

Inside Kohima the Royal West Kents, in a spirited attack, had driven the Japanese out of the DC's bungalow, but they were running dangerously short of supplies of all kinds: water, medical supplies, 2-inch and 3-inch mortar ammunition, rifle and Bren ammunition and 36 grenades. Because of their urgent plight they asked for an air drop. Their tiny dropping zone, less than 300 yards long, lay between Garrison Hill and Kuki Piquet. At the same time, the beleaguered Jotsoma troops asked for an air drop. Shortly afterwards the aircraft arrived over the Kohima dropping zone and responded correctly to the signals. Then the tense defenders, knowing that their lives depended on getting water, ammunition and supplies, watched with mounting horror as these vital supplies floated off into the Japanese positions. Then a new flight came in. The men's spirits rose when the parachutes landed safely, but when they opened the cases they found that they contained the 3.7 ammunition for the howitzers in the Jotsoma Box. The final straw came when the Japanese began, with devastating effect, to fire the mortar bombs which had just been dropped, from British 3-inch mortars which they had captured previously.

The Japanese continued to press forward around the whole perimeter. Some of the heaviest clashes took place in the FSD area, where the Japanese held on despite counter-attacks by the Royal West Kents, Rajputs and Assam Rifles. Wherever men were fighting, they could see the appalling condition of the wounded, who lay in the open and were often hit by shell and mortar fire. Morale was not helped by the knowledge that no one was getting out. On 13 April Colonel Richards, the garrison commander, issued a special order of the day, congratulating the whole garrison on their magnificent effort and appealing to everyone to stand firm because help was on its way. In fact he conferred with Laverty and Warren next day, and they all agreed that unless they were rescued soon it would be too late. They knew that 2nd Division was advancing towards them, but the beleaguered garrison began to wonder if they would ever arrive. The Royal West Kents continued to defend the FSD area against wave after wave of Japanese attacks. The sections often held their fire until the enemy were only fifteen yards away, and then slaughtered them with Bren and rifle fire. If a few got through they fought hand-to-hand. One man in the RWK passed out, but regained consciousness later to find a Japanese officer in his trench. He waited for a suitable moment, killed the officer with his bare hands and returned to his Bren gun. If the Dakota was the hero of the Burma war as a whole, the Bren gun was the saviour of the infantry soldier in close-quarter fighting in the jungle.

Inside the Kohima garrison, under constant pressure from the whole of 31st Division, the defenders came close to despair as day after day help failed to appear. For their part, the leading troops of 2nd Division were finding to their cost the effectiveness of the well-sited Japanese bunkers. The Japanese too were suffering appalling casualties. Attacking at Zubza on 13 April, they lost 96 out of 100 men, and they suffered similar losses elsewhere. In spite of the delay 5 Brigade was making some progress, and on 14 April was ready to attack Zubza with mortars, artillery and tanks. At 1230 the artillery started a bombardment and the 3-inch mortars joined in. The tanks moved forward, the Camerons mounted the ridge and the Japanese fled – a complete Japanese Company had been wiped out. Later that day another battalion of 5 Brigade, the Dorsets, pressed forward and made the first contact with the defenders of the Jotsoma Box. Even then, Warren expressed his grave fears about the remaining troops inside Kohima – especially RWK who, out of a total of 600 men had more than 250 wounded waiting to be brought out.

While Warren understood the plight of the Kohima defenders, he realized too the danger from the Japanese artillery on Merema Ridge which dominated the road into Kohima. He therefore decided that the final rescue operation would have to be postponed from 16 to 17 April. What Warren could not have appreciated was the intensity of the attacks and counter-attacks and the savage hand-to-hand fighting which was continuing in every part of the shrinking area inside the garrison. On 16 April, near the DC's bungalow and the tennis court, a mixed unit of the Assam Regiment and the Assam Rifles put in another attack. On FSD the Royal West Kents still held out, but were slowly driven back in hand-to-hand fighting. Then when Warren again postponed the assault designed to rescue them, the troops began to wonder how much more flesh and blood could stand.

On the night of 17 April, the forward positions on Kuki Piquet were taken over by the Assam Regiment and Assam Rifles, all of whom had fought valiantly during the siege. Soon after taking up their positions they were subjected to a prolonged and severe bombardment and at last, after twelve days of shelling, sniping and bloody hand-to-hand fighting, they gave way. They rushed back through the defending lines, but the weary West Kents, helped by Sergeant-Major Haines who had been blinded but stayed with his unit to steady them, held firm. Colonel Laverty heard on his battalion 48 wireless set what had happened, realized that he did not have the men to keep the whole perimeter safe now the Assam soldiers had broken, and decided to withdraw from Kuki Piquet. At that moment Sergeant King, who throughout the siege had used his 3-inch mortars with great accuracy, and who already had a severe wound to his face and jaw, carefully resited his mortars to fire on Kuki Piquet and plastered the Japanese who had just taken it over. Thus in the final stages, the perimeter defended by the Royal West Kents and the Assams had been reduced to a few hundred yards, from the area of the DC's bungalow to Garrison Hill.

Kohima: Dispositions at dawn, 18 April 1944

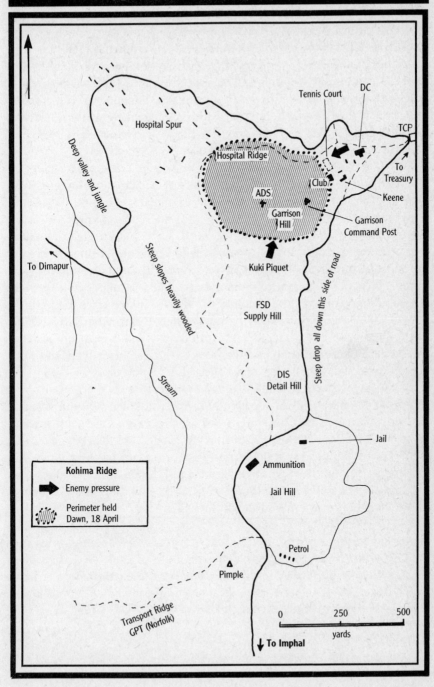

To Dimapur

Deep valley and jungle

Hospital Spur

Hospital Ridge

Steep slopes heavily wooded

Stream

ADS

Garrison Hill

Kuki Piquet

Tennis Court

DC

TCP

To Treasury

Club

Keene

Garrison Command Post

FSD Supply Hill

Steep drop all down this side of road

DIS Detail Hill

Jail

Ammunition

Jail Hill

Petrol

Pimple

Transport Ridge GPT (Norfolk)

Kohima Ridge

Enemy pressure

Perimeter held Dawn, 18 April

0   250   500

yards

To Imphal

As the sun rose on the morning of 18 April the gaunt survivors looked out on a scene of almost total devastation, with every tree and building blown to bits and the whole area littered with Indian, British and Japanese corpses – all infested with swarms of black flies. Over everything hung the stench of death and putrefaction. The enemy were within 100 yards of the command post and the dressing station where 600 badly wounded men lay helpless in a shallow slit trench. Most of the wounded had kept their personal weapon with one round in the breach, just in case. All suffered from the additional hazard posed by several hundred petrified non-combatants who were milling about completely out of control.

At about 0800 on 18 April the defenders noticed a change in the pattern of gunfire, and realized that 2nd Division's 25-pounders must have got within range. The ever accurate aim of Major Yeo, directed heavy bombardments on to all the Japanese positions, and RAF Hurribombers strafed the Japanese on GPT Ridge. Hardly able to believe it, the defenders watched as infantry, with tanks and artillery support, advanced towards them. Following close behind, came convoys of Bren carriers, 3-ton trucks and ambulances. By midday, the 1/1st Punjabis, who had themselves been surrounded in the Jotsoma Box, made the first contact with the Royal West Kents, and moved in to strengthen the positions of the battered, depleted and exhausted companies. The Japanese snipers did not give up, but took their toll of the Allied wounded as they moved down to the ambulances, and of the non-combatants as they rushed headlong down the hill.

After the initial advance of the Punjabis, the Royal Berkshires came in to relieve the Royal West Kents who were now at the end of their tether. Most had not washed, had not shaved, had not changed their clothes or their boots, and had hardly slept since 5 April. With bleary eyes sunk deep in their sockets, and drooping shoulders, they looked like scarecrows. They were too exhausted even to reply to the normal good-natured ribbing of the Royal Berkshires. In silence they slowly trudged down to the waiting transport. The padre, who had assumed heroic proportions in the eyes of his men, was still there, comforting and guiding. As the Royal West Kents moved out, their final view was one of utmost desolation. Jagged leafless tree stumps, churned-up earth, damaged weapons, blood-soaked clothes and boots, severed limbs scattered across the trenches, bloated corpses lying everywhere, and over all a mosaic of red, blue, green and white parachutes stretching down to Kuki Piquet.

Flung into an ill-prepared position, seething with indignation and frustration at the dithering incompetence of the base staff, removed from their brigade and divisional support, the Royal West Kents, helped by the

Assam Regiment and the Assam Rifles, for thirteen crucial days had held up the advance of the entire Japanese 31st Division. The Kohima siege was the turning-point of the Burma war and the Japanese never again made a major advance. Rarely has a single battalion of any regiment stamped its mark in the annals of military history as the Royal West Kents and the Assam Regiments did at Kohima.

THE BATTLE OF KOHIMA 2

As the Kohima siege was broken, another major battle for Kohima was only just beginning. The determination of the Kohima defenders had caused critical delay to Sato's 31st Division and prevented it taking part in the attack on Imphal. By 18 April, when the Kohima garrison was relived by the advance of 2nd Division, in the wider situation of Imphal the British and Indian forces, although surrounded by the Japanese, were in reasonably confident mood. 17th Division had reached its objective at Bishenpur by early April and, licking its wounds, was ready for the next round against its old adversary Yanagida and 33rd Division; 20th Division had completed its withdrawal to Shenam at approximately the same time, and was confidently holding the Shenam heights; on the north of the Imphal perimeter, the advancing Japanese 15th Division had already suffered a severe setback at the great battle of Nungshigum.

At Kohima, when the Japanese were attacking, they seemed prepared to sustain horrifying casualties, often showing little tactical imagination and throwing in one attack after another where previous attacks had already failed against strongly defended positions. After 18 April a significant change came about, and from that time onwards the Japanese were on the defensive, showing skill and enterprise, and defending every bunker with determination. Suddenly the balance had changed. The British and Indian forces, instead of conducting their defence against shrieking Japanese attacks, were now attacking an enemy who excelled at defensive warfare.

After its rapid advances of 1942, Sato's 31st Division had expected to sweep aside any resistance at Kohima. Their initial swift advance from the Chindwin reinforced these expectations, but it also masked some misgivings. One Japanese veteran, Mr Hirakubo, the Supply Officer of 3rd Battalion, 58th Regiment, who had joined the regiment on 10 March 1944, had been shocked when the division supply colonel addressed the new officers. He said that he and Sato objected to Mutaguchi's plans because they would not work, and throughout the campaign it would not be possible to get supplies forward to front-line units. He repeated that Division HQ would not send any supplies to the front, and that the responsibility for feeding the battalion depended entirely on the Supply

Officer. 58th Regiment, which had three battalions each of four infantry companies, reached Kohima on 5 April and by the 7th the 20 days' rations had been consumed. The question of supplies, which caused the ultimate clash between Sato and Mutaguchi, was a major cause of concern to the Japanese from the start of the Kohima battle. 31st Division had 15,000 soldiers, each carrying 50 kilograms. The division also had 10,000 oxen which were intended primarily to carry the heavier loads of ammunition, but they were not very good pack animals. Many fell down the steep slopes and, as the food ran out, many of them were eaten. Hirakubo's unit fared better than most, because had he discovered a British food store in a village they had just overrun and, working throughout the night with 50 men, he carried off enough rice to last the battalion for the rest of the campaign. The British bombarded the village the next morning. The Japanese were plagued by an acute shortage of ammunition and their heavier guns were rationed to a few shells a day, but until the very end of the battle it seemed to the British that every attack was met by a hail of gunfire and grenades.

31st Division had been surprised and taken aback by the strong defence of Sangshak and the determined resistance at Kohima. As the siege wore on, General Sato became increasingly alarmed at the heavy losses being sustained by his forward units, and although the Kohima garrison was at its last gasp Sato realized that with each passing day the build-up of Allied forces was increasing. His Intelligence reports showed that a new battalion of Indian or British troops was coming in every day, accompanied by a vast increase in artillery fire power and tanks. As the British supplies increased, his own dwindled ominously. Few supplies of food or ammunition reached him along the precarious road line from the Chindwin and his starving men began to kill their mules for food. The pressure to overrun Kohima became urgent.

The dispositions of Sato's forces at this time emphasize the remarkable achievement of the Royal West Kents and the Kohima garrison. Sato had 124th Regiment and a battalion of mountain artillery roughly in the area of GPT Ridge and Aradura Spur. 138th Regiment held Merema Ridge on the north side of the Dimapur road, while another battalion held the Naga village. This left 58th Regiment to maintain attacks on Garrison Hill and the areas around the DC's bungalow. These dispositions gave Sato a sound defensive position against any attack by 2nd Division, expected from the direction of Dimapur.

The new situation was to be illustrated on the very day the siege was raised. 58th Regiment attacked the DC's bungalow but was repulsed with heavy losses by the newly arrived Punjabis. Brigadier Warren thought that the Kohima perimeter was far too small and condensed for safety, and as his additional troops moved into the town he decided to recapture

Kuki Piquet immediately. An attack by the Punjabis was preceded by a bombardment from the whole of 2nd Division's artillery – 72 guns in all. An observer who watched this did not believe that anyone could possibly have survived it, but as the Punjabis put in their attack, the Japanese of 58th Regiment reappeared from the deeper recesses of their bunkers and, with withering fire, drove off the attackers – a situation which was to be repeated frequently during the coming weeks.

As the Japanese advance at Kohima suddenly changed to defence, General Mutaguchi, reviewing his different options, thought that a breakthrough might still be achieved if an additional regiment(brigade) could be hurled in on the northern Imphal front. He therefore ordered Sato to detach one regiment and send it immediately to Imphal. This order merely exacerbated their intense mutual antagonism. Sato, deeply concerned at his mounting casualties, decided to stall, and after some delay sent a signal asking Mutaguchi to send enough transport to move the regiment down to Imphal. Mutaguchi, realizing Sato's tactic, angrily replied that he was to use the transport he had captured at Kohima.

On the British side, disagreement was not so profound, but political pressures were building up. While Stopford and Grover had changed their tune when they saw the forbidding terrain of the Dimapur road at Zubza, the Chiefs of Staff in London and Washington still had a lot to learn. Pressure – notably from Washington, influenced by Chiang Kai-shek and Stilwell – came on to Mountbatten to return the aircraft he had commandeered at the start of the Imphal crisis. Under this pressure, he and Slim strongly encouraged Stopford to speed-up the drive forward to rescue Imphal. Chiefs of staff and war correspondents like to have big arrows on their maps and to move their pointers ever onwards, and the few miles of progress around Kohima compared unfavourably with, say, the advance in the Western Desert. They had little idea of the problems faced by 2nd Division, or that the terrain dictated attacks by a platoon or company, and rarely by an entire battalion let alone a division. Critics of 2nd Division were slow to learn the lesson that in the hills of Manipur one depleted battalion – The Royal West Kents – had been able to hold up an entire Japanese division.

On the British side, as the balance of the battle changed from defence to attack, 2nd Division moved forward to capture Kohima and open the road through to Imphal. Grover deployed three brigades made up as follows:

4 BRIGADE (Brigadier Goschen)	5 BRIGADE (Brigadier Hawkins)
Royal Scots	Worcesters
Royal Norfolks	Dorsets
Lancashire Fusiliers	Cameron Highlanders

6 BRIGADE (Brigadier Shapland)
Royal Welch Fusiliers
Royal Berkshires
Durham Light Infantry

NB. This simple order of battle can be misleading because, in the course of confused fighting, battalions were often switched from one brigade to another.

As 161 Brigade, with the remnant of the Royal West Kents, Punjabis and Rajputs were taken out of the line, 5 and 6 Brigades took over the forward areas. The Royal Berkshires occupied Garrison Hill, still over-looked by vigilant Japanese snipers, and soon encountered the ghastly conditions the defenders had suffered for so long, though initially the newcomers did not have to endure the constant Japanese attacks.

The demands from Slim and Stopford for a swift advance failed to appreciate that 2nd Division, attacking Kohima, were faced by nine battle-hardened battalions of a full Japanese division, effectively dug-in, in ideal defensive terrain, in well-prepared bunkers from which every man was prepared to fight to the death.

On 22 April 6 Brigade, supported by tanks and artillery, were ordered to make an immediate attack on the Japanese positions in the area of the DC's bungalow, and then to go on to occupy the Field Supply Depot. The attack went in but petered out in the face of heavy and sustained fire from the Japanese bunkers. At the same time, 5 Brigade set off from their base at Zubza, and approached Merema Ridge. They had a very difficult passage, in pitch darkness and heavy rain, clambering up precipitous cliffs, but they were fortunate in not meeting any Japanese, and the brigade eventually reached its forward unit, the Camerons, near Merema village.

While 5 and 6 Brigades were moving forward, Sato, still angered by the messages from Mutaguchi, decided to make a final attempt to capture Kohima. He sent two companies of 58th Regiment to advance from the DC's bungalow and attack the Royal Berkshires, and a full battalion of 138th Regiment to advance from Kuki Piquet to attack the Durham Light Infantry (DLI) which had just occupied Garrison Hill. The attack on the Durhams by wave after wave of men from 138th Regiment, whom Sato himself had ordered to capture the hill at all costs, was a fierce hand-to-hand encounter with heavy casualties on both sides. Machine-gun fire, grenades, phosphorous bombs and bayonets took their heavy toll in a screaming mélée, which lasted from just after midnight until dawn (23 April). The Durhams lost 76 out of 130 men, and eleven out of their fifteen officers.

The attack was less severe on the Berkshires who killed many men of 58th Regiment, with few casualties and without losing ground. Next morning Sato was told that of the seven companies taking part in the two attacks, four had been wiped out and no ground had been gained. The division clearly could not continue to sustain casualties at this level and Sato very soon had to decide whether to obey Mutaguchi and send a regiment to Imphal where 15th Division was delaying its attacks until reinforcements arrived from his division.

Grover planned to deploy his three brigades in a co-ordinated attack on Kohima, roughly as follows:

6 Brigade (Royal Berks, Royal Welch Fusiliers, Durham Light Infantry) supported by tanks, to advance on the Field Supply Depot and Jail Hill.

5 Brigade (Worcesters, Dorsets, Camerons) to advance around the north of Kohima and attack the Naga village which held Sato's advanced HQ.

4 Brigade (Royal Scots, Royal Norfolks – Lancashire Fusiliers now detached to 5 Brigade) to make a wide sweep to the south-west via Khonoma village and Mount Pulebadze, and to occupy Aradura Spur, thus blocking the road south from Kohima to Imphal.

Among several imponderable factors in this proposed plan for a divisional attack was the speed at which a unit could move through the precipitous jungle-covered hills west of Kohima. 4 Brigade discovered to its cost that, in spite of driving themselves to the point of exhaustion, on some days they advanced less than one mile. On the credit side they were to discover the amazing loyalty of the Naga people. Thanks largely to the inspiration of Charles Pawsey, more than 300 Nagas cheerfully gave their services to the British units as guides and bearers, and even during a battle would carry wounded men back to safety. Naga help was enlisted for the great march of the Norfolks and the Royal Scots to Mount Pulebadze, although the Nagas warned that the chosen route lay through impenetrable jungle, which even they had never traversed. They never asked for any reward, but Grover, through the local police, arranged for them to be paid for any work they undertook.

As the Norfolks hastily prepared to set off on their march, an incident took place which indicates some of the tension felt before a battle. The men were warned to take two days' rations, 100 rounds of .303 ammunition and two grenades. They had their steel helmets ready, but the CO – Bob Scott – thinking of their comfort during the march changed this order to bush hats. The MO then insisted that they wear steel helmets and he was backed up by Grover. So they had to unpack their kit again. Needless to say, the men's reaction was that they were being buggered about as usual.

During the first part of the march, at night, in heavy rain, and in very difficult country, even the Naga guides got lost – units were separated, and there was considerable chaos before they reached the village of Khonoma. The next day, trying to make up lost time, the men were driven to their physical limits, cutting their way through dense jungle, carrying heavy loads, climbing thousands of feet in rarified air which made their hearts pound and their limbs feel like cotton wool. In contrast the Naga porters made light of it all and ran laughing up the hills. The column bivouacked the second night because any movement was impossible, but it was wet and cold, fires were not permitted, and the men gained very little sustenance from crushed biscuit, tepid tea, or cold bully beef stew.

After several days of unremitting toil through thick jungle and up hillsides thousands of feet high, Brigadier Goschen, realizing that his men were completely exhausted, ordered a day's rest. This did little to help or improve morale, for they were in a deep, cold, mist enshrouded valley covered by slimy hostile vegetation. It was nicknamed Death Valley or Happy Valley – according to one's sense of humour. In this valley the column bumped an isolated Japanese patrol. This was a double blow, because secrecy was lost and, having had two of their men killed, the Naga porters left. One survivor of this march, Phil Dewey, who was the Norfolk's regimental signaller and carried the 48 wireless set, remembers that throughout this terrible march and battle he never fired his rifle and he was never hit – though some shrapnel hit the 48 set. He also remembers that, never having tasted alcohol, he was in a cold, flooded slit trench when he downed his rum ration and '. . . will never forget the wonderful warm glow which pervaded my whole body'. Another survivor, H May, was the company bugler, who during battles had to blow special calls for 2-inch mortar fire, smoke, 3-inch mortar fire, as well as advance!, retreat!, and other more normal calls. The daunting march continued until eventually, in a state of complete exhaustion, the Royal Scots and Royal Norfolks, having skirted the formidable sides of Mount Pulebadze, reached the fringe of Aradura Spur where they were attacked by the Japanese.

While 4 Brigade were making their trek towards Aradura Spur, 5 Brigade (Worcesters, Lancashire Fusiliers, Camerons) moved forward from Merema towards the Naga village. They had some worrying moments because of their lack of experience in jungle movement, but they reached their objective without alerting the enemy. In fact the Japanese were not expecting the British to be so far forward, and a small patrol of the Worcesters found a Japanese officer sitting outside his tent issuing pay to his platoon. The patrol attacked and killed the whole unit and took away the cash box and some valuable documents. The brigade lay low and continued throughout the day to intercept Japanese supply patrols coming forward to Merema. During the rest of the Kohima battle few victories were won so easily. By 26 April the Worcesters and the Lancashire Fusiliers had established themselves on a hill feature where they were able to receive their first air drop, as well as further supplies brought forward by the indefatigable Nagas.

While 4 and 5 Brigades were making their flank advances, 6 Brigade (Berkshires, Dorsets and Durhams) were already engaged in fierce clashes in Kohima itself, especially near the DC's bungalow. This feature where so many men, Japanese, Indian and British, were to die, was extremely steep with almost vertical drops of up to 40 feet between the four main terraces – the Club, the tennis court, the bungalow, and the road entrance. In a day and night of confused fighting, the antagonists often only twenty yards apart, both sides sustained heavy casualties. Simultaneously, the Japanese put in another heavy and determined attack on the positions held by the Durham Light Infantry on Garrison Hill.

These fierce battles, while not making any dramatic advances as required by the staff well to the rear in Delhi or beyond, did push back the Japanese from some of their more forward positions and, most important, opened up the road into Kohima, which enabled the first tanks to come forward. These were Lee Grant tanks from 149 Regiment RAC, and were to play an important part in the later stages of the battle. Sato, from his forward HQ, could actually see the build-up of tanks, artillery and trucks with supplies and reinforcements, while his own supplies dwindled to nothing and his reserves of ammunition dropped dangerously low. In this difficult situation, Sato finally decided that he could not send any troops to support the attack on Imphal. He therefore kept the badly reduced battalions of 124th Regiment, with Miyazaki, on Aradura Ridge, and 58th and 138th Regiments in Kohima and the Naga village. These were now mere shadows of the confident units that had forged westwards from the Chindwin just a few weeks before.

As 2nd Division's three brigades moved slowly forwards, fighting every inch of the way, pressure to move more swiftly came from Stopford (Corps), Slim (Fourteenth Army), Giffard (Delhi), Mountbatten (SEAC) and the Chiefs of Staff in Washington, who were demanding the return of the aircraft which Mountbatten had 'borrowed', and which were providing most of the supplies and air drops for both Kohima and Imphal. In this tense situation Mountbatten, giving total support to his fighting units, sent a signal to the Chiefs of Staff. He explained that he had two alternatives. First, he could hold on to the aircraft and keep up the supplies to Kohima and Imphal until the battle was won. Alternatively, if the aircraft were withdrawn, he would have to withdraw the Chindits and this would cause Stilwell to withdraw; he would have to fly IV Corps out of Imphal and hand over the whole area to the Japanese; he would then have to abandon the Ledo road and this would cut off all supplies going up to Stilwell. This alternative would enable the Japanese to achieve all their objectives. Mountbatten held on to the aircraft, but the incident shows how little the Chiefs of Staff really understood what was happening in Burma. His arguments show again the critical role played by the supply aircraft of the USAAF and the RAF in these battles. Mountbatten's cable did not completely remove the danger of the aircraft being sent elsewhere, and he was comforted shortly afterwards to receive a signal from Churchill saying: 'Let nothing go from the battle that you need for victory . . . I will back you to the full.'

The results of all this pressure fell upon Grover when Slim and Stopford came to see him outside Kohima on 3 May. Grover had planned for an assault on Kohima by all these brigades on 2 May, but this had had to be postponed because of the slow progress of 4 Brigade in its trek around Mount Pulebadze. Subsequently, Slim wrote that he did not wish to push Grover beyond what he thought was wise, but Grover felt that both Slim and Stopford were demanding immediate action and he therefore instructed Hawkins and 5 Brigade that they must attack the Naga village the next night.

In Kohima from 3 May, Grover had three brigades located as follows:

 4 Brigade on GPT (Norfolk) Ridge
 5 Brigade ready to attack the Naga village
 6 Brigade ready to attack central Kohima.

This was the start of the second main phase of the Kohima battle, which was to last from 3 May until 2 June, and in which every unit in the division would be involved in prolonged and bitter fighting against Sato's 31st Division. It was a period of considerable confusion because battalions were moved away from their brigades when urgent action demanded it, and several battalions lost so many men that they had to be amalgamated with other battalions.

The advance of 5 Brigade on 4 May towards the Naga village took them across the front of strongly held Japanese positions on Firs Hill, and Hawkins demanded that, to reduce noise, everyone should wear gym shoes. Somehow, after dramatic flaps among the 'Q' staff, enough gym shoes were provided, and the brigade moved off in fairly clear moonlight led by the Worcesters, who wheeled off to cover the Firs Hill flank, with the Camerons and Lancashire Fusiliers heading for the village. Active reconnaissance patrols had discovered that the Japanese slept between 0200 and 0400. The highly dangerous manoeuvre of moving an entire brigade, in almost single file, through very difficult country and across the front of a vigilant enemy, none the less succeeded perfectly. By daylight the Camerons had occupied Church Knoll and had a company forward on Hunter's Hill, while the Lancashire Fusiliers had set up a defensive position at the western end of the ridge. When the Japanese realized what had happened they opened up with heavy machine-gun and mortar fire, causing fairly heavy casualties to the units which had had little time to dig in. Church Knoll and Hunter's Hill were connected by a saddle which was highly vulnerable to Japanese fire. It soon became clear that Hunter's Hill was far too isolated to be held, and it was decided to withdraw the Camerons after dark on 5 May. This led to a disastrous incident when the withdrawal coincided with a heavy monsoon storm and a powerful and sustained Japanese attack. Extremely confused fighting continued throughout the night, and by daybreak the Japanese had successfully recaptured both Hunter's Hill and Church Knoll. The Camerons and Lancashire Fusiliers still held the western end of the ridge, but each battalion had sustained more than 40 casualties.

This attack of 5 Brigade on the Naga village was bloodily repulsed, and in Kohima the attack by 6 Brigade was equally unsuccessful. The brigade aimed to capture the series of hills which the Royal West Kents had defended in the first phase of the battle – Garrison Hill, Kuki Piquet, Field Supply Depot (FSD), Daily Issue Store (DIS) and Jail Hill. The Durham Light Infantry, Royal Berkshires and Royal Welch Fusiliers supported by tanks and artillery initially made some progress and got some platoons on to FSD and DIS, but all their positions were covered by penetrating Japanese fire, and they sustained severe casualties. At the end of a day of fierce and confused fighting, the Royal Welch Fusiliers still had a precarious hold on FSD.

As usual, the Japanese had sited their bunkers cleverly and had dug them deeply enough to withstand any amount of artillery or mortar fire. Inside the bunkers, every man expected to fight to the death. Brave and vigorous attacks by infantry following closely behind a heavy bombardment were invariably met by withering automatic fire and showers of grenades – as every unit in this grim, prolonged and bloody battle found to their cost. The arrival in Kohima of the first tanks, up the road from Dimapur, was the one factor which slowly swung the battle against the Japanese. While 5 and 6 Brigades were fighting their battles, the Dorsets, deployed around the DC's bungalow, now had the help of a tank (4 May). It soon became clear that only a tank firing directly into a bunker could dislodge the Japanese. The slope up to the bungalow was so steep that the tank had the greatest difficulty in climbing the hill, but, inching forward, it succeeded, and was able to blast the Japanese out of a main bunker; the supporting Dorsets, however, were driven back by fire from supporting bunkers. Both they and the tank had to withdraw, but they felt they had made progress and that the next attack would succeed.

After their long march around Mount Pulebadze, the Royal Norfolks and the Royal Scots had reached the fringe of Aradura Spur on 3 May and held their positions there prior to their proposed attack on GPT Ridge, which was to have been co-ordinated with the advance of 6 Brigade towards Jail Hill. On 4 May the Royal Norfolks, led by their bearded and cursing CO, Bob Scott, and supported by 99 Field Regiment, set off on the next stage of the operation and once again had to move through thick and difficult country. Throughout the march Scott had shown impressive leadership qualities, often moving with the forward sections. Now, carrying a large sack of grenades, he led his sadly depleted battalion in their assault on GPT Ridge. Fighting, cursing, shooting and hurling grenades, he created such momentum that the battalion overran one bunker after another and, despite suffering heavy casualties, captured GPT Ridge so swiftly that a pre-planned artillery barrage was never called down. GPT Ridge, where the Norfolks lost 120 killed or wounded, was renamed Norfolk Ridge.

The attacks on 4 May by three brigades, together with some help from 161 Brigade which had come back into the line, had made little progress, except for the Norfolks on GPT (Norfolk) Ridge. All battalions had sustained very heavy casualties. The Royal Welch Fusiliers lost 189 men and the Berkshires and Durhams lost so many that they had to be temporarily amalgamated. Grover urgently needed a short pause to reorganize and reinforce his depleted battalions, but he was ordered by Stopford to make another attack on 7 May.

To strengthen this attack Stopford, who was highly critical of Grover because of what he saw as the slow advance of 2nd Division, pushed forward another brigade, 33 Indian Brigade, under Brigadier Loftus Tottenham. This brigade comprised 1st Queen's Royal Regiment, 4/15th Punjabis and 4/1st Gurkhas who were already detached and operating with 161 Brigade. Slim had appreciated the serious situation at Kohima and therefore sent 7th Indian Division to operate alongside 2nd Division, as part of Stopford's XXXIII Corps. 7th Indian Division was to take under its command the recently arrived 33 Brigade, 268 Indian Brigade and 23 Long Range Penetration Brigade – a brigade of Chindits which was already operating around the north of Kohima and effectively disrupting Japanese lines of communication. Substantial reinforcements were welcome to Grover, but, except for 33 Brigade, they made little immediate impact on the Kohima situation. They had expected to come to Assam for a rest after heavy fighting in the Arakan, but immediately became involved in the battles in the centre of Kohima.

Stopford, aggressively overruling Grover, ordered him to renew the attack on Kohima on 7 May. Before that, on 6 May, the Royal Norfolks undertook to remove a particularly strong bunker on what became known as Bunker Hill. The attack was led by Captain Randle, a company commander. Although badly wounded by machine-gun fire from the bunker, he carried on and, to save his company from further casualties, threw himself across the opening to the bunker. For this selfless act he was awarded a posthumous VC, but even this gallantry did not succeed in driving out the Japanese, who still held on to their positions on the edge of Norfolk Ridge.

The attacks ordered by Stopford for 7 May ended in disaster. The 4/1st Gurkhas started with an attack on the remaining bunkers on Norfolk Ridge, but they came under very heavy fire and lost all their officers. The Queen's Royal Regiment assuming, wrongly, that the Gurkha attack had succeeded, advanced on to Pimple Hill and Jail Hill. Here Japanese fire from Norfolk Ridge and DIS – including a 75mm gun – began to cause them very heavy casualties, so heavy that before the end of the day Loftus Tottenham gave the order for them to retire. In spite of the gallantry of the Queen's, their attack was a bitter, bloody and costly failure. To add to the problems of this disastrous day, 4 Brigade, still stuck on Norfolk Ridge where they had not had a hot meal for ten days, were literally starving until a brave effort by the Gurkhas got water and rations forward to them.

The distinguished historian of Kohima, Arthur Swinson, gives a moving account of this critical phase of the Kohima battle: '7 May and the three days that followed were probably the bitterest time in the whole battle of Kohima. After thirty-four days and nights of close and bloody fighting, after hunger, thirst, discomfort, after appalling casualties, the enemy still held the main bastions of their position. No bombs, shells, mortars, flame-throwers, or grenades could seem to shift them. The 3.7 howitzers which could have reached many of their positions were silent through lack of ammunition; no amount of railing, correspondence, argument or anything else, could produce any. The Japs had lost thousands upon thousands of men, and reports kept saying they were weak and diseased and running short of ammunition. But all the British, Gurkhas and Indians knew was that as soon as they got near a bunker, the fire poured out of it as mercilessly as ever. The British battalions were now reduced to three or four hundred men; some had less. Few could muster four nominal rifle companies. All were desperately short of officers, and platoon commanders were almost non-existent. It would be untrue to say that the division faltered; but in these days, officers and men would sometimes look at the great ring of mountains encircling them, and wonder how on earth it could be taken, how flesh and blood could possibly stand much more . . . and how things would end.' (A. Swinson, *Kohima*, p. 183.)

After the costly failure of the attacks on 7 May Grover, having discussed the situation with the unit commanders, decided that the only way to capture Norfolk Ridge was to bring forward a 6-pounder anti-tank gun and reduce each bunker individually. To get this gun forward necessitated cutting a new track which could not be completed until 11 May. Stopford, after another fierce altercation, demanded a new attack within 24 hours. He and Slim insisted on speed because of the growing problems of keeping up the air supply to Imphal, but in the end agreed to Grover's plans for 11 May.

On 11 May the Queen's and the Punjabis led the attack on Jail Hill and DIS after an hour-long bombardment by mortars and artillery – including the 6-pounder – but enemy fire from bunkers on GPT and FSD still caused heavy casualties and prevented any major advance. The Queen's made some progress, often crawling to within a few yards of a bunker when there would be a hail of grenades in each direction. As the day wore on, the Queen's held about one-third of the hill, and by evening – literally digging for their lives – were safely dug-in, with the section posts linked up. While the Queen's were fighting hard, the Punjabis had occupied Pimple Hill virtually unopposed, and the Berkshires had established firm control on FSD.

After a night of heavy and driving rain and persistent Japanese firing, the Queen's started to advance supported by tanks which had been brought forward to deal with the bunkers that had wrought such havoc during the previous attacks. The tanks often fired at bunkers only ten yards from the nearest Queen's position. Then, to the amazement of the leading Queen's sections, first one, then two, then about twenty Japanese soldiers ran off down the side of the hill.

During the afternoon of 12 May, 4/15th Punjabis and the Berkshires, again supported by tanks, attacked DIS and FSD. Here resistance proved to be much tougher and both sides sustained casualties, but with the accurate fire of the tanks which were impervious to the small-arms fire and grenades of the defenders, the bunkers were slowly overcome. The Berkshires finally captured FSD and discovered a vast bunker with many stores, including 20 guns and piles of ammunition. The Queen's, Berkshires and Punjabis held on to the ground they had captured and stuck out another night of heavy rain. Then, at first light, they sent patrols probing forward and found the Japanese bunkers empty. At the top of Jail Hill they found a bunker which could hold 50 men, linked by tunnels to other bunkers, and so deep that no shells or mortars could touch it. At the same time, the Berkshires and Punjabis advanced over FSD and DIS, and the Royal Welch Fusiliers found that Kuki Piquet had been abandoned. Here they found gruesome evidence that a soldier of the Royal West Kents had been tied to a tree and used for bayonet practice.

By the morning of 13 May the main features of Kohima had been conquered, except for the DC's bungalow which was still holding out against the Dorsets and their supporting tanks. The Dorsets had been in the grounds of the bungalow for eighteen days of close and bloody combat, and had lost 75 men killed. The sappers had bulldozed a new route for a tank to get up the hill and level with the bungalow, and the mountain battery manhandled a 3.7in howitzer to accompany it. Then, on 14 May, Sergeant Waterhouse of 149 Regiment RAC, carefully manoeuvred his tank on to the tennis court. He started firing at point-blank range at the remaining bunkers, and the 3.7in poured 50 rounds in as well. The leading Dorset platoons stood ready, helped by pole charges prepared by the sappers. Suddenly, nearly 50 Japanese ran away, and the Dorsets rushed in. The tank and the howitzer continued firing at every bunker and then transferred their attention to the bungalow. Finally, the area was cleared, and more than 60 Japanese bodies were found. For the first time since 5 April there was no fighting on Kohima Ridge.

This hard-fought victory improved the morale of the British troops, but it did not immediately improve their conditions. All the forward troops were bearded, haggard and filthy because, with water rationed to a pint a day, washing, shaving or changing socks or clothes was impossible. One survivor recalled that he had not taken off his boots for 20 days, he had no change of underclothes, and his battledress was caked with blood, sweat and mud. Everybody stank because it was impossible to wash. The shallow latrine trenches were constantly hit by shellfire, and their contents scattered about, so that as the grim battle proceeded, dysentery spread rapidly. Water was available back at Zubza, where 44-gallon drums were cut in half and used as baths, but few of the forward units could get back as far as that.

Another irritant for the fighting units, also recorded by Arthur Swinson, was the deluge of official papers which followed them. One brigade, in the midst of the battle, received a bag of mail by mule transport. The documents demanded details of payments made to cleaners in 1943; the whereabouts of three tables issued in 1942; a set of divorce papers which should have been initialled; and a reprimand for a man who had not written to his wife – he had been killed three weeks earlier. Many units stacked such papers in the open, hoping they would be hit by shellfire, but they seemed to bear a charmed life.

The appalling conditions were made infinitely worse by the monsoon rain which had started in April and continued throughout May. Men lived in waterlogged trenches, their clothes and boots sodden, their food cold, and with only their inadequate ground sheets or gas capes to protect them from the rain. The only pleasant variation to this dreadful routine came when an air drop provided some extra rations, and the regimental cooks would work wonders with hot stew, tinned fruit and, best of all, hot tea.

All the forward units had sustained heavy casualties, and the plight of the wounded daily deteriorated. A man wounded in the area of the

Naga village had to be carried by Naga porters on a stretcher for a three-hour journey across precipitous hills down to the road. There followed a forty-mile journey back to Dimapur, and two further days in the train taking the wounded to hospital in Shillong. A medical officer said it was a miracle so many survived, but initially, for hundreds of wounded, their lives were saved by the patience, determination and cheerfulness of the Nagas who, at great risk to themselves, carried the wounded away from the battlefield. Mail, so often a morale booster, did not always bring joy. At one dressing station, a badly wounded man received a letter. A few minutes later the Sister in charge heard a noise, and when she looked round she saw that he had cut his throat. His letter told him that his wife had gone off with another man.

Brigadier Mike Calvert, one of the most successful of the Chindit leaders, showed his greatness as a commander by reminding his men that, however bad things were for them, things were probably much worse for the enemy. How true this was for Kohima! As more and more British reinforcements poured in, the Japanese fought on, with no reinforcements, no air support, no tanks, little ammunition, no rations, and, as Louis Allen wrote, 'The only relief they could expect was death.'

The bravery and devotion to duty of the Japanese soldier was unparalleled. He showed this by his fearless attacks even when his unit was being slaughtered, and equally by his stubborn and dogged defence. Throughout the Kohima battles, in the Japanese bunkers badly wounded men with malaria or dysentery or collapsing with starvation were propped up ready to fire or throw grenades at any attackers.

When Sato had first reached Kohima he attacked it with vigour and determination. Although 31st Division had sustained some heavy casualties, it was in good shape and full of confidence. His three regiments, 124th, 138th and 58th – which functioned particularly well under the able and aggressive Miyazaki – were highly trained and battle hardened. Things began to go wrong when, after 5 April, they failed to overrun the Kohima garrison led by the Royal West Kents. This was the date by which Sato calculated his division would have used up its initial supplies, and by which Mutaguchi estimated the division would be able to exist on supplies captured at Kohima. Thereafter, the question of supplies dominated the course of the battle, and dominated the worsening relationship between Sato and Mutaguchi. During the whole of the siege up to 18 April, Sato only received a couple of loads of ammuntion and a few cartons of cigarettes. Significantly, on the very day the siege was raised by the advance of 2nd Division, Mutaguchi ordered Sato to take Kohima by 29 April, and then to transfer one regiment and a mountain artillery battalion to Imphal. As 31st Division turned from attack to defence it became more deeply embroiled in the Kohima battle, and it became impossible for Sato to extricate any part of it. Sato had already disputed Mutaguchi's order to advance straight to Dimapur, and his objection had been upheld by HQ Burma Area, but now he was facing an even more difficult decision.

Slim wrote disparagingly of Sato, as the most unenterprising general he faced, but Louis Allen argues that Sato was neither stupid nor unenterprising. It is now known that Sato was ordered to attack Kohima, and was expressly told not to advance to Dimapur. He came very close to capturing Kohima, and he was determined that his men would not starve to death or lose their lives on what he saw as a madcap scheme of Mutaguchi's. Sato considered that Mutaguchi was prepared to sacrifice soldiers' lives for his own ambition and his insatiable craving for publicity. During the second half of April the situation became increasingly difficult for Sato because his division received no further supplies; partly because 23 Long Range Penetration Brigade, operating on the left flank of 2nd Division, had strangled all the Japanese supply routes coming up from the Chindwin, the Chindits had destroyed their supplies at Indaw, and also because the Nagas, encouraged by Charles Pawsey, were hostile to any Japanese patrols.

By the beginning of May the supply position for 31st Division had become critical, and Sato was totally at loggerheads with Mutaguchi. Sato then went over Mutaguchi's head and signalled both to the Commander-in-Chief for Burma, and Imperial Headquarters Tokyo, complaining of the complete failure to supply his division, and criticizing the handling of the battle. He gradually came to the conclusion that he had no hope of capturing Kohima, and because of his very heavy casualties which were not being replaced, there was no realistic prospect of his sending any units to Imphal. On 11 May he issued an order of the day for his division saying: 'You will fight to the death, and when you are killed you will fight on with your spirit.' His soldiers, realizing they had little prospect of survival, sent memorial letters home, often containing cuttings of their nails or their hair, and saying they would soon be going to a faraway place. A young officer replying to a letter from his son, wrote, 'You've done well even when Daddy is not there. Keep it up.'

During May, when his troops continued to fight in the area of the Naga village and on Aradura Spur, Sato's signals became increasingly critical of Mutaguchi. He said his troops were being slaughtered for nothing, that rations were exhausted, ammunition for artillery and infantry was used up, and 'the division would withdraw from Kohima by 1 June to a point where it can receive supplies'. Mutaguchi replied that he must hold his position for another ten days, by which time Imphal would have fallen and Sato would then be rewarded for his services. Mutaguchi was already sacking some of his other divisional commanders, and on

hearing of this Sato said publicly in front of his officers, 'This is shameful
. . . Mutaguchi should apologize for his own failure, to the dead soldiers
and to the Japanese people.' (Louis Allen, p. 288.)

Sato, with all his problems, and despite losing the centre of Kohima,
still held some powerful positions on Aradura Spur and around the Naga
village, which could hold up the British advance for a considerable time.
In the approach to the Naga village the British needed to recapture
Church Knoll and Hunter's Hill which had remained in Japanese hands
since the abortive attack of the Camerons (5 May). On 18 May, with an
air strike, a creeping barrage, and supporting fire from tanks, the
Worcesters moved forward. Naga village was heavily terraced and on
each terrace every bunker was supported by two others, so that even
when one bunker was captured with the help of tanks, anti-tank guns,
pole charges, and the newly arrived flame-throwers, the attackers still
met heavy fire and a shower of grenades from the supporting bunkers. In
spite of all this support, the Worcesters failed to capture Church Knoll,
and Grover had to agree to a withdrawal under cover of a further artillery
bombardment. The Worcesters lost 40 killed and wounded. As a result of
the attack some Japanese prisoners from 58th Regiment were taken and
one prisoner, talking quite voluntarily, said he had reached the limit of
endurance, that his company was reduced to 40 men, all the officers were
killed, the shelling was almost unendurable, and for ages they had only
had rice and salt to eat.

This setback at Church Knoll caused several days' delay while a
medium battery from corps artillery, and other reinforcements, were
brought forward. Stopford also chose this moment to tell Grover that 2nd
Division would probably be disbanded. A new attack was assembled and
led by 4/15th Punjabis, supported by Hurribombers, by 900 shells from
the medium guns, and by other artillery and mortar fire. Again, observers
thought that no one could possibly survive such a bombardment, but the
Punjabis, following a few yards behind the final barrage, were met by the
usual retaliation of machine-gun fire, 77mm gun fire and grenades. Like
the Camerons and the Worcesters before them, the Punjabis failed to
capture the feature and had to withdraw, thus causing further delay to
the two divisions.

A Japanese survivor confirmed the wonderful feeling of relief at
being in his bunker even though shells were falling, but added that many
comrades stayed in their bunkers because they were faint from starvation, beri beri or malaria, their clothes were soaked with sweat, blood or
filth, and all they could do was to go to the fire slit and pull the trigger or
throw grenades. Yet, men in such a state, could resist the attack of two
divisions supported by artillery. They also believed a rumour – totally

untrue – that they must hang on because another division was coming to their rescue.

Some regrouping of the British divisions then took place, so that 2nd Division would attack Aradura Spur, and 7th Indian Division would take on the Naga village. For the assault on Aradura Spur, Grover put 6 Brigade under Brigadier Shapland in the lead. The Durham Light Infantry, which had lost 75 men and eleven of its fifteen officers in a previous attack, was reduced to two companies, and the lead in the assault on Aradura Spur was taken by the Royal Berkshires and the Royal Welch Fusiliers (RWF). This attack illustrated several important military issues. Before the attack started there was a fierce dispute between Shapland – a gunner – and the COs of the two infantry battalions. Shapland insisted that they would advance by a leapfrogging tactic unknown to infantry training. Both colonels were horrified at Shapland's decision and appealed to the divisional commander. Because of these disagreements and days of prolonged heavy rain the attack was postponed.

The next day, 27 May, the Berkshires set off in driving rain, through thick bamboo which even an elephant could not penetrate, with huge trees, thorn bushes, creepers that ensnared men's feet, and up hills where men had to heave each other up on ropes. Single file was the only possible way to move, and it was impossible to use a compass because visibility was reduced to about ten yards, and frequent large trees or impenetrable clumps of bamboo necessitated lengthy detours. Because of the hills, wireless sets were almost useless, and the only communication was verbal. The Berkshires plodded on, getting more and more tired and hopelessly lost. To find out where he was, the CO managed to get a message to the gunners to put down smoke on to their objective, but this appeared to lie beyond range upon range of impenetrable jungle. Eventually the CO called a halt, and the battalion spent the night soaked to the skin, and wedged against trees to stop them sliding down the precipices. After a sleepless night in torrential rain, the Berkshires moved forward again, and then bumped a carefully sited position where they were met by accurate fire, and where their leading platoons sustained nearly 90 per cent casualties. The CO decided to withdraw, to prevent even more casualties among his fine battalion which had fought so bravely throughout the campaign.

The Royal Welch Fusiliers faced similar conditions and they too suffered heavy casualties from well-sited Japanese positions. To dig-in in thick and precipitous jungle was almost impossible because the continuous downpour would fill a trench with water, so the CO decided to stay where they were; in the morning the order to withdraw was given.

Several bitter lessons were to be learnt from this fiasco which cost so many lives. Commanders should take note of the views of the men on the ground. Attacks must not be demanded and chased forward by commanders in the rear who have not seen the ground. Personal reconnaissance is essential, for no officer can plan a successful attack unless he knows details of the ground he is attacking.

The attack on the Aradura Spur had been a disastrous failure, and a similar situation emerged on Church Knoll. Here an air strike and a heavy bombardment preceded yet another assault by 4/15th Punjabis. Yet this too failed and this proud regiment had to withdraw, leaving the hill littered with its dead.

Sato, the Japanese commander, was near to despair, but his troops, although sick, wounded, starving, with their units decimated, and though they were attacked by air strikes, artillery, mortars, machine-guns and flame-throwers, were still able to hold on and repel attack after attack by two experienced divisions.

At this depressing stage of the battle (28 May) Stopford conferred with Grover and Messervy (7th Indian Division). They faced a total lack of progress at Kohima, and realized that even when these defences had been overcome, they faced 80 miles of jungle containing superb defensive positions before they reached Imphal. Intelligence reports showed that in Imphal IV Corps was effectively resisting all Japanese attacks, but the sterling efforts of the air supply units could not keep pace with the demands for ammunition and supplies. There was no sense of impending victory at this meeting of the generals. The Japanese seemed as strongly entrenched as ever, and the way ahead almost hopeless.

Unbeknown to the top brass at that meeting, Loftus-Tottenham (33 Brigade) had decided to give the Gurkhas one final attempt to capture the Naga village. They had a new, young CO, Lieutenant-Colonel Horsford, aged 28. He refused to make another frontal assault, but proposed instead a night infiltration by the Gurkhas, after intensive patrolling to identify and pinpoint the Japanese positions, and to chart exact routes. For two nights, two-man patrols were sent off with explicit orders to patrol, observe, and identify the place, size and nature of all enemy defences. What a contrast to the bumbling direction of the unfortunate troops attacking Aradura Spur! Excellent and careful patrolling identified two features as undefended, and two strongly defended. Horsford made detailed plans to occupy the undefended positions on the night of 28/29 May, prior to a Company attack supported by tanks at first light on 29 May.

That night two Companies moved in to the undefended positions, wired up posts, and made a defensive fire plan. The main attack at dawn started with a barrage from 3.7-inch howitzers, 25-pounders and tanks, then close behind a moving barrage, the Gukha Company went in – the tanks changing their targets as the attack progressed. Such close co-operation enabled the Gurkhas to get right up to the bunkers and this time the defenders either fled or fell to the bayonets and kukris of the Gurkhas.

This first success still left some hard fighting ahead, but Horsford planned it carefully, and again refused a frontal assault because of the danger of heavy casualties. Renewed patrolling, the use of pole charges, and accurate attacks, gradually reduced the number of bunkers. Finally, at Horsford's request, there was a major barrage, followed by a company attack and the last Japanese position in the Naga village was captured. It was 2 June. While the Gurkhas captured the village, the Queen's cleared the ridge, and thus 33 Brigade, composed of the Gurkhas, Punjabis and Queen's Royal Regiment under Brigadier Loftus-Tottenham, had played a decisive and successful role in the Kohima battle.

Towards the end of May a series of increasingly angry signals passed between Sato and Mutaguchi. Sato said he was running out of ammunition, his men were starving, and he was going to withdraw to a position where he could obtain food and supplies. Mutaguchi ordered him to stay put and threatened to court-martial him if he withdrew. On 31 May Sato ordered the first units to withdraw; he wrote, 'We fought for two months with the utmost courage and have reached the limits of human fortitude . . . Shedding bitter tears I now leave Kohima.' (Quoted, Louis Allen, op. cit., p. 289.)

Sato had given the order to retire on 31 May, but he still left Miyazaki and a suicide rearguard on Aradura Spur. On 1 June 5 Brigade (Worcesters, Dorsets, Camerons) made a careful advance, but the Japanese, after holding their fire, unleashed a hail of bullets and grenades, and once again drove off the attackers. This caused further delay until, on 4 June, after artillery, tanks and medium machine-guns had been brought forward, the Camerons attacked and drove the Japanese off Big Tree Hill. At the same time, the Dorsets, in driving rain and mud, pushed forward on the other side of Aradura village, and discovered that the Japanese had withdrawn from Pfuchama.

Many units in the Kohima and Imphal battles, have recorded the moment when they heard the news of the Normandy landings. For the Dorsets and 5 Brigade, the news came just as they reached the top of Pfuchama, and they knew that at last after 64 days of fighting, the Japanese had been driven from Kohima. It was unfortunate that a major victory in Burma was pushed off the headlines at home by another action – the Normandy landings.

Miyazaki quietly withdrew his rearguard during the night and, under his iron discipline, troops of 58th and 124th Regiments continued to construct road-blocks and ambushes. Sometimes, as at Viswema, these led to battles lasting four or five days, fought in pouring rain and deep mud, and with casualties mounting both from wounds and from exhaustion. Miyazaki retreated past the great mountains mass of Mao Songsang, but except for his small group, the Japanese retreat was becoming a rout.

As 2nd Division advanced with tanks, armoured cars, sappers and infantry, they developed a sound technique, with the tanks taking on the Japanese, while the sappers made a reconnaissance of a bridge, and the infantry fanned out around a flank. This skilled arrangement was none the less severely criticized by Stopford for being far too slow.

The strategic and political squabbles continued. Mountbatten had to fight to obtain more aircraft, while IV Corps inside Imphal and XXXIII Corps fighting its way down towards them were both criticized by the rear staff for being too slow. Commentators from the safety of Delhi or even Washington, who had never seen a Japanese bunker, talked unrealistically of driving a convoy through to Imphal. One reasonable criticism must be made. Although Slim countenanced the Chindit operation, and massive air supplies were the key to the success of the Imphal and Kohima battles, he never used airborne troops in an attacking role. Quite a small airborne operation could have cut off Miyazaki's rearguard of 700 men and opened the road to Imphal considerably quicker.

Miyazaki's tactics were designed to one end – to delay the British advance while the battered remnant of 31st Division, with 1,500 stretcher cases, made their escape. The wounded had to be carried up precipitous slopes through teeming monsoon rain by men who were themselves starving to death. As the British advanced the pitiful plight of the Japanese became apparent. More naked and emaciated corpses lay among the litter of abandoned weapons and equipment. More of the corpses showed evidence that they had taken their own lives.

In the early days of June 1944, as Sato's HQ plodded in single file down a muddy rain-soaked track back towards the Chindwin, passing corpses by the dozen, Sato was approaching by Mutaguchi's Chief of Staff, and ordered to stop the retreat and advance towards Imphal. In a blazing row Sato refused, shouting that Kohima was a stupid battle, and he would ensure that the HQ in Singapore and GHQ in Tokyo discovered how foolish Mutaguchi had been.

On the Imphal road, the speed of the British advance increased, with the Worcesters and the Durham Light Infantry in the lead. Supported by tanks and armoured cars they swept aside the final resistance. On 22 June 1944 the Durhams, who had left so many of their comrades on Kuki Piquet, advanced to Milestone 108 and noticed some activity ahead. It proved to be the advanced units of 5th Indian Division. The road to

Imphal was open. After days of torrential rain, the sun shone and convoys rapidly drove through to the beleaguered units in Imphal.

Psychologically the Japanese commanders found it very difficult to adapt to the idea of defeat and withdrawal. General Kawabe, commanding the Burma Area Army in Rangoon, and Mutaguchi in Maymyo, still ordered new attacks. As late as 4 July Mutaguchi ordered 31st and 15th Divisions to attack Palel on the southern Imphal perimeter. Nothing happened; there was no attack, there were no troops to make an attack. Then, on 8 July, he faced the inevitable and ordered his broken divisions to withdraw towards the Chindwin whence they had set out in early March, intending to grab Kohima and Imphal quickly, before the monsoon arrived. A Japanese commentator later described the twin battles as the worst defeat of its kind ever chronicled in the annals of war. On 5 July Sato was removed from command of 31st Division. In a farewell speech he said that the operation had been mounted by the foolish desire of Mutaguchi, but that 31st Division had done its duty. 'Nothing can separate those of us who were tried in the fire at Kohima.'

In the Kohima battle, Indian, Gurkha and British casualties amounted to more than 4,000 killed and wounded. The Japanese lost 3,000 killed, 4,000 wounded and many more unaccounted for. 2nd Division, which bore the brunt of the heaviest fighting, had won a great victory and were to continue in the successful advance of Fourteenth Army. The moment of triumph for the division was quickly soured, for officers and men alike, when they heard with amazement that, on 4 July, almost in the hour of victory, Stopford had informed Grover that he was to be removed immediately from command of the division. Soon afterwards, Churchill's personal envoy had a meeting with groups of soldiers – with no officers present. They did not complain about their conditions, but gave him a very rough ride, demanding to know what had happened to 'their general'. The sacking of Grover at that point, still rankles with the veterans of Kohima; by a strange irony it was the day after Sato was sacked by Mutaguchi.

The moving motto on the 2nd Division memorial on Garrison Hill at Kohima, in a cemetery with more than 1,200 graves and many private memorials, has a special place in the hearts of all who have connections with Kohima:

> 'When you go home,
> Tell them of us and say,
> For your tomorrow,
> We gave our today.'

Another fitting epitaph was written on 14 April 1991 when, in the morning, with a congregation of 3,000 including fifteen Japanese veterans from 31st Division, and seventeen British veterans from 2nd Division, the new Roman Catholic cathedral of Kohima was dedicated. It stands on the lower slopes of Aradura Spur just above the Imphal road, overlooking the whole area where the battle took place.

In the afternoon, a formal act of reconciliation and a peace celebration was held in the new cathedral, with just as large a congregation, and with strong support from the Naga people of Kohima, now a prosperous town with a population of 83,000. In the peace celebration, prayers were read by Japanese, Indian, British and local Naga representatives. The climax of the act of reconciliation came when the Bishop said 'Let us offer each other the sign of peace.' At these words, and quite unrehearsed, one of the British delegation walked over, and in front of the whole congregation, held out his hand to shake hands with the leading Japanese delegate. Then both groups moved together to shake hands. Many who were present found this simple gesture to be unbearably moving. In his address the Bishop said 'From the cathedral we can see the War Memorial, but this is a peace memorial.' The service of reconciliation ended with the hymn 'Make me a channel of your peace'.

CHAPTER 7
THE CHINDIT ISSUE

N O STUDY of the Battles of Imphal and Kohima would be complete without a serious consideration of the issue of the Chindits and their eccentric leader, Orde Wingate. The question that lies at the centre of this highly controversial issue is how far the Chindits in Operation 'Thursday' affected the outcome of the two battles. Unfortunately this whole affair is still bedevilled by the intense bitterness which most veteran Chindits feel; first, at the way Wingate was treated and, more importantly, the disgraceful way the military establishment and the Official History of the Burma campaign deliberately set out to denigrate him and all he did – this despite the overwhelming evidence from Japanese sources that Operation 'Thursday' had a decisive effect on the supply and reinforcement of Mutaguchi's attacks on both Kohima and Imphal.

PERSONALITIES AND PLANS

The complex and dramatic story of Wingate and his creation of the Chindits involves high drama – when his wife was bundled off the Edinburgh to London night express in order to catch the Queen Mary sailing out of Glasgow with Churchill; elation, when, after a brilliant exposition, Wingate gained the support of Roosevelt, Churchill and the Joint Chiefs of Staff at the Quebec Conference; frustration, when he returned to GHQ India and met incompetence and deliberate obstruction; deep satisfaction when Operation 'Thursday' was launched on 5 March 1944, and he was able to fly in to one of the first Chindit Strongholds; finally, his tragic death nineteen days later.

General Wavell played a key role at several critical stages of Wingate's mercurial career. Their paths had crossed in the 1930s in Palestine, when Wingate organized Jewish night squads to counter Arab infiltrators. While most of the British forces sympathized with the Arabs, Wingate became a passionate Zionist supporter. He gained a DSO for his work, but what was considered his indiscreet enthusiasm for the Zionist movement caused his posting elsewhere. Later, when Wavell was fighting the Italians in Ethiopia in 1940–1, he remembered Wingate's outstanding work and appointed him to lead guerrilla forces behind the Italian lines. Two things emerged from this experience – his innovative and forceful ideas on guerrilla warfare, and his abrasive and difficult attitude to colleagues and superiors. In 1942, during the humiliating defeat of the British and Indian forces in Burma, Wavell again remembered Wingate's work in Palestine and Ethiopia, and called him to Delhi. Here, Wingate was briefed and given a fairly free hand to organize guerrilla forces behind the Japanese lines.

In February 1942 Wingate went into Burma and had his first meeting with Mike Calvert, who was running a commando school at Maymyo, north-east of Mandalay. Fortunately these two powerful characters hit it off and Calvert, through his outstanding bravery, became the most successful of all the Chindit leaders in the field. Eager to avail himself of Calvert's experience in commando-type actions, Wingate appointed him as his second in command. Calvert stayed with the general retreat – losing all his equipment and clothes, crossing the Chindwin, and eventually arrived at 17th Division Headquarters in Kalewa dressed as a woman – but Wingate, then a brigadier, had to go off to see Slim and Chiang Kai-shek.

Wingate and Calvert quickly organized the first Chindit expedition, which they led into central Burma in February 1943. Their expedition caused serious damage to Japanese road and rail communications, and the force marched more than 1,500 miles. When they came out, the majority of the survivors were suffering from malaria, dysentery and malnutrition, and of the 3,000 who had set out, 800 were casualties and were left behind.

This expedition, code-name 'Longcloth', almost immediately comes into the area of controversy which plagued it and all the subsequent Chindit activities. At a time when most of the news coming out of Burma was of pusillanimous retreat, 'Longcloth' was rightly hailed as an outstanding victory, but this was too much for his old opponents in Delhi to accept. The bedrock of the opposition to Wingate and all his schemes lay in the notorious sloth and inertia of the higher ranks of India Command centred at GHQ in Delhi where there were more than fifty brigadiers and 'Curry Colonels' by the dozen, who seemed petrified of any Japanese activity and were loath to contemplate getting out of their cushy headquarters jobs actually to fight the Japanese.

'Longcloth' was planned to coincide wih an advance by IV Corps from Imphal, but just before the expedition was due to set off, Wavell came to Wingate and advised that it should be called off because IV Corps Headquarters were adamant that they could not make an advance in case they suffered another defeat. Hardly a confident and aggressive attitude!

Having weighed up the likely effect of IV Corp's refusal, Wingate declined Wavell's advice, and continued with the operation. Under these circumstances it was perhaps natural that the Establishment would do their best to belittle the achievements of 'Longcloth'. Most of the official comment was that it had no strategic significance at all.

In fact, the effects of 'Longcloth' could hardly have been more significant. The effect on the morale of all the services in India by an expedition which could strike behind the Japanese lines and beat the enemy in straight fight was inestimable and, at a stroke, it broke the myth of Japanese invincibility. Although the Chindits paid a heavy cost with their high casualties, they learnt a number of lessons. They proved that, given air superiority, it was possible for units behind enemy lines or when actually engaged in battle, to be supplied by air. In practical terms the Chindits learnt lessons on the techniques of supply dropping, the significance of diet, the use of mules, the vital importance of wireless communication, and the problems of handling the sick and wounded. The worst aspect of 'Longcloth' had been the knowledge that the wounded or sick had to be abandoned, but this meant that for the next Chindit expedition – Operation 'Thursday' – the care and evacuation of the wounded became a high priority.

After the war, interrogation of Mutaguchi and other Japanese commanders made clear that Operation 'Longcloth' made a serious impact on them, and was a decisive factor in Mutaguchi's decision to launch his attack on Imphal and Kohima. The Japanese noted that after 'Longcloth' a tired Chindit column was able to march through the jungle from the Chindwin up to Kohima, and in March 1944 they used this route for the attack by 31st Division. Sadly, this lesson was not learnt by IV Corps HQ and this had serious consequences because Sato's divisional attack on Kohima took them completely by surprise. Acting on IV Corp's information, Slim assumed that an attack on Kohima would only be by a regiment at most.

All of these lessons were important, but far more significant were the wider implications of the Chindits' success, which was supported by an effective Public Relations exercise. It is here that the Chindit issue is drawn into the sphere of world strategy and Wingate, still a relatively junior brigadier, is suddenly lifted into the highest councils of the Allies. Churchill had long been critical of the inefficiency and defeatist attitude of the command in India and was delighted when at last there came news from Burma of at least one success, achieved through the drive and imagination of one outstanding officer, and against the scarcely veiled opposition of GHQ in Delhi. On 24 July 1943, after he had received news of 'Longcloth', Churchill wrote, 'In the welter of inefficiency and lassitude which have characterized the operations on the India front, this man of genius and audacity stands out, and no question of seniority must obstruct his advance.'

The following day he sent for Wingate who arrived in London on 4 August and reported that afternoon to General Sir Alan Brooke, the CIGS. That evening Churchill was dining alone and asked Wingate to join him. Churchill was immediately impressed and took an extraordinary decision. He was about to take the 10 p.m. train to Glasgow in order to travel on the Queen Mary to attend the Quebec Conference, and he decided to take Wingate with him. When Wingate said he would have liked to have seen his wife while he was in England Churchill, having ascertained that she was on the overnight train from Edinburgh to London, had the train stopped at the Borders, and she was taken off and brought to Glasgow to embark on the Queen Mary with her husband. So, from the Chindit columns in the Burmese jungle, Wingate was suddenly translated to the highest councils of war, to be interviewed by Churchill, by the British Chiefs of Staff, by Roosevelt and by the Joint Chiefs of Staff.

When the party arrived at Quebec for the Quadrant Conference, Wingate produced a short and excellent memorandum outlining his proposals for Long Range Penetration Groups. This paper illustrates Wingate's remarkable grasp of the wider strategic issues of the war in the Far East, and the role of the Chindits within it. He outlined plans for three groups of Chindit columns to operate: one to link up with the advance of Stilwell and his Chinese divisions; one to assist the advance of Chiang Kia-shek's Chinese divisions from Yunnan, and the third to concentrate on Indaw which was a road, rail and river centre for the Japanese armies facing both Stilwell in the north, and the IV Corps front at Imphal and Kohima. With considerable prescience Wingate predicted the Japanese assault with remarkable accuracy. The British Chiefs of Staff accepted Wingate's plan, and cabled the decision to Delhi that they supported Long Range Penetration on a larger scale, and that six brigades would be allotted to this scheme. After this, Wingate made another presentation to Churchill, Roosevelt and Mountbatten. When Churchill congratulated him on his exemplary lucidity, Wingate, somewhat lacking in modesty, replied that it was his normal practice. In these heady days, one of Wingate's most important achievements was to convince General Marshall and General Arnold, who thereafter backed him up, and also gave a new dimension to Wingate's ideas – namely that the Chindits should fly in on their next operation, and have air support throughout.

The enthusiastic American backing for Wingate's plan, related to their constant priority for the war in South East Asia, which was to drive back the Japanese so that a new supply route to Chiang Kai-shek in

Chungking could be established. This is why the road beyond Dimapur to Ledo and Fort Hertz was so important, and why Stilwell's operations with his Chinese divisions in the Hukawng valley leading down to Mogaung and Myitkying were to become so closely, and ultimately so disastrously, interwoven with the fate of the Chindits. The American hope was that, if an effective road could be opened to Chungking, 60 Chinese divisions could be trained and equipped ready to drive the 25 Japanese divisions out of southern China. This, in its turn, would make it possible to establish advanced airfields for American heavy bombers to bomb Tokyo and mainland Japan.

The American strategy also focused attention on one of the most colourful characters in the Far East War – Vinegar Joe Stilwell. He had shared the ignominy of the 1942 retreat with Slim. He had an acid tongue, a neurotic and pathological detestation of the English, and a generally misanthropic attitude to all races. Initially, this had made him a bit of a character, but when these qualities were displayed in a man holding high command, and in a position in which his unreasoning prejudice could and did cost the lives of thousands of British soldiers, his irresponsible offensiveness was disastrous. He publicly expressed the opinion that General Alexander was a coward and that the British were yellow and useless as soldiers. His conversation tended towards words like Chinks, Wops, Coons and Limeys – his ultimate term of abuse. This was bad enough, but his offensive and irresponsible attitudes rubbed off on his relations (his son and son-in-law were both in his headquarters) and other sycophantic staff with whom he surrounded himself. This was to have dire consequences for the later stages of the Chindit campaign.

Few Chindits will ever feel any sympathy for Stilwell whose intransigence caused the death of so many of their comrades, but he did have one of the most frustrating appointments of the war, as Chief of Staff to Chiang Kai-shek. Stilwell had to train those Chinese troops who completed the 1942 retreat by coming out to India where they were fed, equipped and trained at British expense. He was eager to lead them back and to drive the Japanese 18th Division under Tanaka out of northern Burma, but he had to operate in the corrupt quagmire of Chiang Kai-shek's court. Chiang received millions of dollars worth of aid, cash, and equipment – as the Americans thought – to forward the war against the Japanese, but, in fact, he had no intention of using these supplies to fight against Japan. He had realized that America and Britain were going to defeat Japan, and he used most of the American help to build up his own resources ready to take on Mao Tse-tung's Communists as soon as someone else had beaten Japan. Stilwell had long since seen through Chiang's schemes – hence their very sour relationship. To Stilwell fell the frustrating task of training and leading his Chinese divisions only to discover that his divisional commanders received secret orders from Chiang not to obey Stilwell's orders, and not to lose too many troops in attacks.

These were some of the imponderable factors with which Wingate had to grapple during the Quebec Conference. A further problem arose even before he left Quebec. General Auchinleck, who had replaced Wavell when he became Viceroy of India, cabled to the Chiefs of Staff posing the positive opposition of India Command to Wingate's proposal to raise six brigades for Long Range Penetration Forces (LRP). He produced some formidable arguments: there were not enough aircraft to support such a scheme; it would absorb troops needed elsewhere; there was no time to train these new units; the LRP forces would never inflict any real damage on the Japanese. Auchinleck kept his strongest argument to the last. The demand for six brigades would mean breaking up a tried and experienced British division – 70th Division under Major-General Symes – and this was totally unacceptable. As a gesture of compromise, Auchinleck offered a brigade from 81st West African Division or, as a last resort, the whole of 81st West African Division (then training in India) rather than lose 70th Division. Wingate vigorously rejected these arguments, and to his immense relief the Joint Planning Staff issued orders covering the following points:

(1) There would be a three-pronged attack in North Burma.
    Stilwell, with Chinese 22nd and 38th divisions to advance down the Hukawng valley.
    IV Corps to advance from Imphal, and XV Corps to advance in the Arakan.
    Chinese divisions to advance westwards from Yunnan and over the River Salween.

(2) More directly affecting Wingate and the Chindits, was the provision, positively supported by General Arnold, that the Chindits would have the support of Number One Air Commando, USAAF, under the leadership of two experienced pilots – Colonels Cochrane and Alison. The Air Commando was a very large force, including 100 gliders, approximately 100 light aircraft – the famous L1 and L5 – 30 Mustangs, 25 Mitchells, 20 Dakotas and twelve larger transport aircraft. There were even some helicopters – the first ever used in combat. This remarkable decision was accompanied by the proposal that instead of the Chindits infiltrating through the Japanese lines, they should fly in using Dakotas and gliders.

(3) Wingate was ordered to raise six brigades which would include a West African brigade, but involved breaking up 70th Division. He was to use these forces to land a brigade across the supply routes of

the Japanese forces facing the Chinese on the Salween, facing Stilwell in the north, and facing IV Corps at Imphal.

Churchill was determined to take action to overcome what he saw as the sloth, defeatism and inertia of India Command, by appointing a Supreme Commander to the newly established South East Asia Command. Both the British and American Chiefs of Staff rejected a number of very senior officers, so Churchill cunningly gained their agreement to the appointment of Mountbatten to the new post.

In the immediate aftermath of the Quadrant Conference at Quebec, Wingate went off to set up the Chindits on a much larger scale than he could ever have expected, and Mountbatten, who had been hankering after another command at sea, had to set up SEAC, having been promoted over the heads of all the commanders of the three services in the Far East, some of whom were consequently not too enthusiastic about the new arrangements. The appointment of Mountbatten and Wingate was to have a direct influence on the great battles of Imphal and Kohima.

Wingate returned to India from his exciting days at Quebec, buoyed up not only by the support of the Joint Chiefs of Staff and Roosevelt, but also by a personal letter from Churchill authorizing him to communicate with him direct if there were any obstruction or frustration of his plans for the Chindits. Wingate had always been a tempestuous and difficult colleague, a loner who often rubbed people up the wrong way. Louis Allen, a sympathetic commentator, described him as an inspired genius, but one whom some of his superiors found arrogant and insufferable. His image as an Old Testament prophet spouting Biblical texts did not always go down well with all his colleagues – even those who supported him fully. A few officers tended to laugh quietly at his stirring addresses, but many of the soldiers almost worshipped him. His impact varied – he excelled at the big occasion when speaking to a large audience, but was often ill at ease with smaller groups, and he did not always succeed. A Gurkha veteran recalls Wingate addressing a Column in his harsh metallic voice, 'I see a column, diseased and half-starved picking their way painfully through some of the worst jungle in Burma – by that I mean the worst jungle in the world. Some of you – the few who get back – will have known what it is to have suffered unendurable hardship. Good luck!' At which moment a young Cameronian said, "Then I'm nae bloody goin".'

When Wingate reached GHQ in Delhi in August 1943 as a newly appointed major-general, he faced a difficult situation. In his diary, Stilwell had previously described GHQ as a place where you tripped over generals in every corridor, most of them doing the work of captains or none at all. Wingate faced the added problem that because of his previous brushes with authority, and because many senior officers considered him a vulgar upstart who had gone behind the backs of his superiors, he was met by a wall of opposition, and an attitude of 'Who the hell does he think he is?'.

On his arrival he found that no accommodation had been provided for him; no office was available and his staff had to work in the corridor; no car was available and he had to apply to the pool to find out if one was free — usually it was not; there was no secretary or typist available, and again he had to apply to the typing pool; at Quebec he had been authorized to have his own aircraft, but his request for this was considered laughable. In case this appears exaggerated, it should be remembered that when Mountbatten arrived in Delhi from Quebec, he too received almost total opposition to all his proposals.

At the first conference about supplies for the Chindits, he met such resistance that he threatened to signal Churchill to inform him of the situation. Wingate faced blatant hostility from the moment he returned to Delhi, but there are two ways of viewing this. A fairly widely-held view was that he went out of his way to antagonize people who might have been quite ready to help him. In contrast, many who worked with him backed him completely, and considered that his assault on GHQ was necessary because the idleness, complacency, and inefficiency of India Command was so notorious that nothing short of direct assault would have achieved anything. Wingate's passion to get things done in a hurry did antagonize those who tended to drift along in bottom gear — most of GHQ — but Wingate was in overdrive all the time.

From Auchinleck downwards, there was great bitterness that 70th British Division had to be broken up to form brigades of Chindits, but, surprisingly, Major-General Symes, who commanded the division, and had to accept demotion to become Wingate's assistant, co-operated fully in the work of setting up and training the new Chindit units. Symes, who worked closely with Wingate for the next eight months, considered that while he could be charming, he was often fanatical, ruthless, arrogant and unorthodox, but he did know all the Chindits and had their complete confidence. Symes thought, 'He appeared deliberately to make enemies . . . and it was amazing that he got the help he did — a different approach would have got willing co-operation.' (Sykes, *Orde Wingate*, p. 56.) In contrast to this, there were many officers and men who dropped rank to join the Chindits. One was Brigadier Fergusson — whose career included Eton, Sandhurst, the Black Watch, and ADC to Wavell — who became a column commander; another, a lieutenant-colonel in the Gurkhas, who dropped to captain in order to join the Chindits.

From August 1943, in spite of the opposition, Wingate built up his Chindit organization. The Chindit striking force was based on the

Column, with each battalion forming two Columns. A Column, with about 250 men, consisted of a rifle company with four platoons; a heavy weapons platoon which handled the Vickers medium machine-gun and the 3-inch mortar; a commando platoon composed mostly of Royal Engineers – British and Indian – carried out most of the demolitions and booby-trapping; a Reconnaissance platoon, with usually at least one section of the Burma Rifles, was used to gain information and help from the local Karen and Kachin tribes.

In addition to rifles and Bren guns – the normal infantry weapons – and the Vickers and the 3-inch mortar, each Column had flame-throwers and the relatively new PIAT (an infantry anti-tank weapon). These heavier weapons necessitated mule transport, but at the start of Chindit training there were no mules available. The need for such weapons and their ammunition meant that even with mule transport each man had to carry a very heavy load, averaging 75 pounds. To some extent the weight the Chindits had to carry brought a change in their operational role; instead of being swift, lightly armed flexible groups behind the enemy lines, they tended to become slow plodding columns advancing in single file through the jungle.

With Wingate's passionate driving force and the enthusiastic support of his colleagues, the Chindit organization developed rapidly and the 20-week training scheme went ahead in the jungles of central India. Although Wingate would have used more colourful titles, his forces were referred to as the Third Indian Division or Special Force. The make-up of this force can best be illustrated from the brigades involved:

Third Indian Division (Special Force)

---

16 BRIGADE (Fergusson)
1st Battalion The Queen's Royal regiment – 2 Columns
2nd Battalion The Leicestershire Regiment – 2 Columns
Royal Artillery (acting as infantry) – 2 Columns
45th Reconnaissance Regiment – 2 Columns

---

77 BRIGADE (Calvert)
1st Battalion The King's Regiment – 2 Columns
1st Battalion The Lancashire Fusiliers – 2 Columns
1st Battalion The South Staffordshire Regiment – 2 Columns
3/6th Gurkhas – 2 Columns
3/9th Gurkhas – 2 Columns
4/9th Gurkhas – 2 Columns (originally in III Brigade)

III BRIGADE (Lentaigne)
1st Battalion The King's Own Royal Regiment – 2 Columns
1st Battalion The Cameronians – 2 Columns

3/4th Gurkhas – 1 Column

A section of 111 Brigade later became Morris Force (under Brigadier Morris), which was made up of 3/4th Gurkhas and 4/9th Gurkhas, and operated along the Bhamo–Myitkyina road.

In addition to the first three brigades to go in there were also:

---

14 BRIGADE (Brodie)

2nd Battalion The Black Watch – 2 Columns
1st Battalion The Beds and Herts Regiment – 2 Columns
2nd Battalion The York and Lancaster Regiment – 2 Columns
7th Battalion The Leicestershire Regiment – 2 Columns

---

23 BRIGADE (Perowne)

2nd Battalion The Duke of Wellington's Regiment
4th Battalion The Border Regiment
1st Battalion The Essex Regiment

This brigade, although it trained as a Chindit brigade, was removed by Slim from Special Force and used to cover the left flank of 2nd Division, and to prevent the Japanese reaching Dimapur. After the siege of Kohima, it harassed the retreating forces of Sato's 31st Division.

---

3 WEST AFRICA BRIGADE (Gillmore)

6th Battalion The Nigeria Regiment – 2 Columns
7th Battalion The Nigeria Regiment – 2 Columns
12th Battalion The Nigeria Regiment – 2 Columns

The final unit in the make-up of Special Force was an American unit with the uninspiring name of 5307 Composite Unit (Provisional). Named 'Galahad' by Wingate, it was later relieved of its miserable title by the American press, and given the name Merrill's Marauders. Initially trained with the Chindits, after a clash between Stilwell and Wingate it went under Stilwell's command.

Much of the training during the 20-week courses centred on the techniques of air supply in the jungle, and this was carried out both in training and in action by Number One Air Commando. Its commander, Colonel Cochrane, provided another insight into Wingate's character. Initially put off by Wingate's approach, Cochrane realized that Wingate controlled his Columns like an air command controlling aircraft on a mission, and he then added, 'I began to assimilate some of the flame of this guy Wingate.'

In October 1943 when the training was proceeding vigorously, Wingate became seriously ill. Treated initially for dysentery and malaria, it was eventually found that he had typhoid fever – caught, it was believed, when at an airport stop, disregarding all his own precepts, while waiting for a glass of water, he impatiently drank the water from a vase of flowers. He was near to death, but was nursed back to health by the redoubtable Matron McGeary, who had saved the lives of many Chindits after their first expedition. His illness lasted until November, but the training was loyally continued by Symes and Brigadier Tulloch – a lifelong friend and supporter of Wingate's. His serious illness brought some small advantage. Churchill sent a personal telegram wishing him well, and Wavell invited him to Viceregal Lodge for his convalescence. These indications of official approval helped to overcome some of the opposition he still met, but did not entirely remove it. He wrote ruefully to his wife that he felt like an ill-tempered dog when the world suddenly begins patting it.

Before the end of 1943 the Chindit Forces were well established and highly trained, but it was then that new strategic issues arose, of which Wingate was unaware or about which he was not informed. The climax of hopes for an effective large-scale Chindit operation had come at the Quadrant Conference (Quebec) when Wingate's personal performance had such positive results. Thereafter he had held firm to the clear plan made at Quadrant, but was unaware that very substantial changes were envisaged by subsequent high-level conferences. Churchill's support for the creation of Chindit Columns remained firm; his support for the planned offensive in north Burma did not.

A superficial reading of the Chindit story would give the impression that Wingate got support for his idea in August 1943, went back to India to create and train his Columns, and then successfully launched them in March 1944. Such a version is far from the truth. Some idea of the doubts and uncertainties surrounding the Chindit operation and the battles of Imphal and Kohima is given by the conference held in Cairo in November 1943, and attended by Roosevelt, Churchill, Chiang Kai-shek, Mountbatten and Stilwell. Named The Sextant Conference, it made the following military plans:

(1) Stilwell to advance down the Hukawng Valley.
(2) The Chinese to advance towards Bhamo (Yoke Force).
(3) British IV Corps to advance from Imphal.
(4) The Chindit Operation 'Thursday' to go ahead.

In addition, largely because of Churchill's enthusiasm for combined operations, it was agreed that an assault would be made on the Andaman Islands (code-name 'Buccaneer'). Almost as an afterthought it was proposed that 50 Indian Parachute Brigade would be flown in to capture Indaw.

From Cairo, Roosevelt and Churchill went on to Teheran to meet Stalin, who made strong and urgent demands for a second front in Europe. They accepted this demand, but, because of that decision, all available landing craft were immediately requisitioned for the European theatre – so 'Buccaneer' was cancelled. When that happened Chiang Kai-shek – who never really intended to attack – claimed that he had been betrayed and cancelled the proposed advance by Yoke Force towards Bhamo.

By December 1943, after the Cairo and Teheran Conferences, the 'Buccaneer' project, the Chinese advance to Bhamo, and the parachute attack on Indaw had all been cancelled. The only plans left were small advances from Imphal and in the Arakan. These decisions had serious consequences for the whole concept of Long Range Penetration, but some of these cancellations were kept secret or were not passed on to Wingate who, erroneously, continued to assume that the Quebec plans for Special Force remained unaltered.

While many of the Teheran decisions remained deliberately vague, some notion of the change in emphasis seeped down through India Command, and the obstruction of Chindit plans revived. As late as December a major exercise had to be cancelled because, ironically, all the available aircraft were required by 50 Parachute Brigade. Mountbatten continued to support Wingate without being able to give him the full facts.

Early in January 1944 Wingate was so frustrated that he wrote to Mountbatten complaining that 11 Army Group were opposed to any action in support of Long Range Penetration, and offered to resign because the plan agreed at Quebec had been abandoned. He also suggested that Galahad Force (Merrill's Marauders) should be put under Stilwell's command, and that Special Force should be broken up and returned to the normal infantry role.

The doubts and hesitations emerging from the Teheran decisions gave encouragement to Wingate's opponents in India Command, some of whom genuinely believed that the whole Chindit idea was a grave mistake, and others who, to preserve their complacency, thought that no aggressive action should be taken against Japan until Germany had been defeated. These feelings even spread to the Chindits themselves. When it became known that the Chinese were not going to advance towards Bhamo, Fergusson offered to resign because the whole purpose of the Chindit operation had been undermined. Stilwell, who was already advancing slowly down the Hukawng Valley, continued his sniping against the Limeys, saying he expected nothing from the feeble attitude of IV Corps or from 'Wingate's shadow boxing'.

While the High Command and political strategists were dithering and unable to decide whether to strike in Burma, in the Andaman Islands or in Sumatra, Wingate not only held to his main purpose but evolved a very clear military assessment. During January he assumed quite correctly that the Japanese would be making a large-scale attack on Imphal and

Kohima. He saw that this would create a situation in which the Chindits could play a proper role, and he then developed a new concept for their tactics, which showed him at his imaginative best. He called it 'Stronghold' – the word taken from the Old Testament 'Turn ye to the Stronghold, ye Prisoners of Hope'.

His plan was for a Stronghold to be established at a place sufficiently inaccessible from main roads or railways, to ensure that the enemy could not bring up tanks or heavy artillery to attack it. The essentials for a Stronghold were: to be located in wild and difficult country, but with a flat area large enough to create an airstrip for Dakotas, so that supplies could come in and the sick and wounded be flown out; a clearly marked supply dropping place within the perimeter, and a good supply of clean water. Essential for each Stronghold would be a garrison battalion, part of which would be used as a floater column lying in wait and ready to attack any enemy who approached the Stronghold. From the Stronghold other Columns would set off to harry and sabotage the enemy's communications, confident in the knowledge that there was a safe haven to which they could return, to replenish food, ammunition and water, and to bring back any wounded, who could then be flown out. All the Chindit leaders saw the brilliance of this new concept, and both the idea and the title caught the imagination of the entire force. Later there was a good example of the destructive and petty criticism from which all the Chindits suffered. General Kirby, the Official Historian of the Burma campaign, trying to belittle Wingate's achievements, ridiculed the word Stronghold, and suggested instead 'the pivot of manoeuvre' – a phrase which would really stir up the troops!

Having thought through the idea of 'Stronghold', Wingate sent another memorandum to Mountbatten. He suggested that in view of the likely Japanese attack over the Chindwin towards Imphal, the Chindits could operate most effectively by dropping well behind the attacking Japanese troops so as to disrupt their supplies and communications. The Chindits would fly in by aircraft and gliders, and within 36 hours would be able to establish a Stronghold of brigade strength, from which raiding parties could dominate the surrounding area. He then proposed in some detail the plan which, with very little change, became Operation 'Thursday'.

Mountbatten accepted Wingate's proposal and on 18 January 1944 Slim and Wingate met and agreed most of the necessary detail, including the provision of four battalions of infantry to act as garrisons in the Strongholds – though Slim did stipulate that he would control this provision. Things then moved rapidly. 77 Brigade under Calvert and 111 Brigade under Lentaigne completed their final training near Silchar. It had been planned that 16 Brigade would march into the Indaw area from

Ledo in the north, so Fergusson led his brigade up there ready for their long march. Wingate, buoyed up by the challenge of mounting an effective operation, visited all his units, and returned to Slim's headquarters on 25 January, only to find that Slim had changed his mind and had reneged on the agreement to provide four battalions for the Stronghold garrisons.

This appeared to Wingate as another example of the failure of Fourteenth Army to give him positive support, and he felt that to launch Operation 'Thursday' without the agreed garrison troops would put the whole operation in jeopardy. There are several descriptions of this incident, and nearly all differ substantially from Slim's account in *Defeat into Victory* (p. 128), in which he is condescending and dismissive of Wingate. Slim wrote, 'I found he had little appreciation of what a real Japanese attack would be like', and he followed this by hinting that he threatened Wingate with a court-martial unless he obeyed orders. 'I told him I had never had a subordinate officer refuse an order, but if one did I knew what to do.' (p. 220.) Slim does not explain why he agreed to the garrison battalions on 18 January but changed his mind one week later.

Slim then made a comment which comes close to the nub of the whole Chindit issue. In supporting his own argument, he stated, 'Wingate's men were neither trained nor equipped to fight pitched battles.' The Chindits would agree wholeheartedly with that, and would confirm that they were trained and equipped to undertake Long Range Penetration behind enemy lines for an absolute maximum of 90 days. Yet, after Wingate's death, Slim did not use the Chindits in their Long Range Penetration role, but instead handed them over to Stilwell – a virtual death sentence for many of them – to be used as normal infantry, attacking strongly held Japanese positions without any of the normal armour or artillery back-up. The Chindits were left at Mogaung long after they should have been withdrawn, and were slaughtered by the dozen because of Stilwell's paranoid dislike of 'The Limeys'. Slim did this at a time when – had he believed in the Chindit idea – he could have left them at Broadway, fulfilling their designated role, or he could have withdrawn them within the agreed time limit of 90 days and launched them on another Chindit operation.

Mountbatten did his best to smooth over this clash between Wingate and Slim, and the project went ahead. Slim issued his orders which reached the Chindit headquarters on 4 February. They equated very closely to the detail of Wingate's original memorandum for the operation, and because of the Establishment's opposition to a more colourful title, which Wingate would have preferred, it became known as Operation 'Thursday'.

The aim of the operation was couched in fairly general terms: to block supplies to Japanese 18th Division facing Stilwell's forces in the Hukawng valley; to create confusion, damage and loss to the Japanese in north Burma, and to help the Chinese operating near the River Salween. It was remarkable that this clause appeared, since Chiang Kai-shek had already made it clear that he was not going to launch an offensive over the Salween. The initial Chindit move centred on three brigades: 16 Brigade under Fergusson, 77 Brigade under Calvert and 111 Brigade under Lentaigne.

16 Brigade was ordered to march from Ledo to Indaw and to capture the two small airfields outside the town. Fergusson was given the added responsibility during his march of sending a column off to the east of his route to capture Lonkin, which was an outpost of the Japanese forces facing Stilwell. At the end of their long march they were to set up a Stronghold to be called Aberdeen.

77 Brigade was to fly in to Broadway and Piccadilly, establish a Stronghold, and from there attack road, rail and river traffic in the area, while 111 Brigade went into Piccadilly with the object of blocking both road and rail links south of Indaw to prevent Japanese reinforcements coming up from Mandalay. One element of 111 Brigade – which subsequently became known as Morris Force – was to be detached from the main brigade, to be landed at Chowringhee, and to block the road and rail link from Bhamo to Myitkyina.

The Chindits thought it was significant that, while they had orders to drop behind the Japanese lines, there was no mention of any advance by IV Corps even if Operation 'Thursday' proved successful. While the Chindits made their final preparations, there was yet another high-level conference, which illustrates the extremely uncertain support they received.

This conference – code-name 'Axiom' – took place at the end of February in both London and Washington. In London there was a clash between those who argued for a major offensive to recapture Malaya and Singapore, and those supporting the idea of a totally new operation based on Australia, aimed at linking up with the Americans sweeping forward over the Pacific islands towards Japan. Significantly, there was no mention of an aggressive drive in Burma. The Axiom mission went on to Washington, and the Americans were so alarmed at the pusillanimous attitude of the India High Command towards a Burma offensive, that Roosevelt cabled Churchill urging an all-out drive in Burma according to the pledges made at the Quebec Conference. The attitude of the British was reflected in a comment made by Brooke (CIGS) that the Long Range Penetration Groups were being launched for no definite purpose. While the complex, confusing and angry Axiom discussions were dragging on into March, with Anglo-American relations at their worst, once again

Wingate provided a solution. The initial success of Operation 'Thursday' – launched 5 March – enabled Mountbatten to cable Washington about the achievements of the Chindits and of Stilwell, and this resulted in the promise of 400 extra aircraft. The Joint Chiefs of Staff followed this on 21 March by pointing out that the success of the airborne operations of Special Force and of Stilwell's fighting in the Hukawng valley, showed that the difficulties of operating in Burma had been considerably overestimated, and they urged that an all-out effort should be made to capture Upper Burma in what was left of the dry season. To the Americans it again appeared that Wingate was the only leader on the British side in Burma who was prepared to take any offensive action, and these diplomatic and political repercussions must be weighed up when assessing the effect of the Chindit operations on the battles of Imphal and Kohima.

This wrangling, which went on even after Operation 'Thursday' had been launched, has been dealt with in some detail because it shows the extremely precarious nature of the support Wingate received even when he was actually in the jungle fighting the Japanese. In a subsequent comment on this unedifying episode Lord Ismay (Churchill's main link with the Chiefs of Staff) said, 'The waffling which has gone on over our Far East strategy will be one of the black spots in the British higher direction of the war.' (Ziegler, *Mountbatten*, p. 277.)

THE LAUNCH OF OPERATION 'THURSDAY' 5 MARCH 1944

The planners had decided that Sunday 5 March 1944 would be the ideal time to launch Operation 'Thursday' because all the factors, including the moon and the weather, were at their most favourable. The launch of this expedition, the first of its kind in history, was a night operation – hazardous enough in itself – but, far more hazardous was the fact that the landing grounds were not large flat open spaces, but confined clearings in deep jungle, surrounded by trees, which gave the glider pilots no second chance and no room for error. The courage and skill of the pilots and glider pilots of the USAAF Air commando were exemplary. Cochrane and Alison worked tirelessly to get the Dakotas and the gliders ready for the fly-in.

There were three possible landing grounds code-named 'Broadway', 'Piccadilly' and 'Chowringhee', and Calvert was to lead the fly-in with 77 Brigade to Piccadilly and Broadway. His brigade and their supporting aircraft and gliders were assembled at the Lalaghat airfield near Silchar. Previously there had been some reconnaissance of these places, but, so as not to alert the enemy, Wingate had ordered that there were to be no reconnaissance flights during the weeks immediately prior to the start.

On that fine Sunday afternoon, the climax of months of training for the Chindits, all was ready. The Dakotas, the gliders and their tow ropes were in place. Every detail of briefing to the pilots and to the Chindits had been completed and every man knew exactly what was expected of him and what he had to do when he landed. Every man understood the significance of the undertaking, and realized what a momentous and dangerous enterprise they were tackling. The presence of Slim and many other British and American commanders added to the tension.

Half an hour before they were due to embark, Major Russhon, USAAF whom Cochrane, against Wingate's orders, had sent to do a last-minute reconnaissance of the landing grounds, rushed up to Cochrane and the command group, with photographs showing that Piccadilly was blocked by large tree trunks which would make any landing quite impossible. Wingate's first reaction was to attack Cochrane for disobeying orders, but he quickly retracted and apologized – realizing that the reconnaissance had prevented a certain disaster.

This information changed the whole situation. Had Japanese Intelligence obtained details of the plans? Had they been betrayed by the Chinese? Were the enemy lying in wait for the Chindits? Had the plan been discovered, or was it, perhaps, pure chance? If Piccadilly could not be used, should the whole operation be called off? What alternative plan

Chindit Operations, March to July 1944

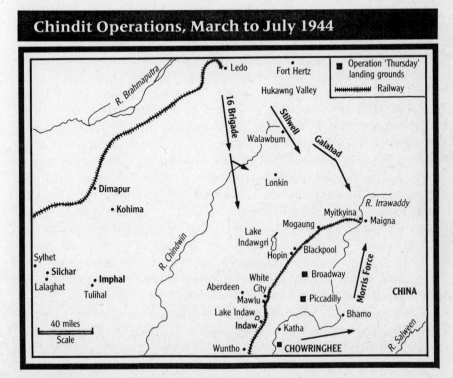

could be made at such short notice? Wingate, clearly upset at this last-minute hitch to his plans, consulted Calvert. Wingate, who was not flying in himself, was reluctant to ask his men to embark on what was now clearly a more hazardous enterprise. Calvert — who like Marshal Ney in a previous war, should be called the bravest of the brave — quickly summed up the situation and saw that, given the opposition and doubtful support of India Command, if the operation did not go ahead it would probably be cancelled altogether. He therefore said that he was prepared to take in his brigade, provided that they all went in to Broadway. His acceptance was relayed to Wingate, and to Slim who, clearly had to make the final decision.

It is one of the tragedies of the Chindit saga that these two fine soldiers, Slim and Wingate, were to be deeply and bitterly divided in their accounts of what happened during that fateful hour. Wingate wrote his at the time. Several others who were present — Calvert, Cochrane, Tulloch and Sir Robert Thompson — have written their versions, and have confirmed unanimously that Wingate's version was correct. In *Defeat into Victory*, written in 1955, Slim describes the moment when the photographs arrived, and gives the impression that Wingate got into 'an emotional state' and 'reiterated that the fly-in should be cancelled'. Slim added that after he took Wingate on one side, 'To prevent a scene in front of the Americans', Wingate 'became calmer and much more in control of himself', and then said to Slim, 'the responsibility is yours'. Unfortunately, this version, in which Slim even mistakes the name of the airfield, is at such variance with all the other eye-witness accounts, that it cannot stand.

Calvert, who was to command the leading brigade, has described how Wingate came to him and readily accepted the stipulation that he should take in his whole brigade, provided it stayed together and they all went into Broadway. The exact detail of what happened will never now be known, but there is no doubt that Slim's version, which was contradicted by all the others present, has caused deep and abiding resentment among the Chindits. In fact, a rapid decision was made and immediately acted upon. Pilots had to be re-briefed to go to Broadway instead of Piccadilly, but they rose to this challenge, Cochrane saying, 'Hey you guys, we've got a better place to fly to,' and the first aircraft and their gliders took off just over an hour behind their original schedule.

The entire operation had been mounted hurriedly and there had not been time adequately to rehearse all the towing techniques. Each aircraft towed two gliders, though some pilots had never practised this. Some of the gliders were overloaded and were unable to climb over the formidable mountain peaks beyond Imphal, so they had to turn back. Others surmounted that obstacle, but then their tow ropes parted and they crash-landed in different parts of Assam and Burma. Of just over 60 gliders, 37 landed at Broadway, but many of the others landed in friendly territory and the crews managed to return to base. These were serious losses, but they had the advantage of completely confusing the Japanese, who took a considerable time to identify the main base at Broadway.

Initially at Broadway things did not go well. There were two trees on the landing strip which had not shown up on the aerial photographs, and these caused several of the gliders to crash. Photographs also failed to show some fairly deep ditches which crossed the strip. These too caused some gliders to overturn, with the result that some of the later arrivals crashed into them. One glider had a small bulldozer on board, and crashed into the trees at the end of the strip. The crew were thrown out by the impact and the bulldozer shot through the front of the glider into the jungle. Watchers were amazed when shortly afterwards the bulldozer drove slowly on to the strip. For Calvert it was a nightmare because the crashed gliders, which could not be moved, caused more damage and casualties as more gliders arrived. He had arranged two code-words: 'Pork Sausage' if things were going well, and 'Soya Link' if things had gone wrong and further flights should be halted. In the early hours of the morning, fearing further casualties if more gliders came in, he signalled 'Soya Link'. This came as a depressing blow to Slim, Wingate and Tulloch waiting anxiously at Lalaghat. Tulloch advised Wingate to grab a couple of hours' sleep; he felt sure that they would get more encouraging information in the morning.

By morning Calvert, at Broadway, had assessed the situation and had been reassured by the American engineers that with the bulldozer and a lot of manual help they could clear the runway for Dakotas to land that evening. Hardly believing that this could be true, Calvert signalled 'Pork Sausage'. After the initial setback on the first night, when 77 Brigade had 30 killed and 20 wounded, the build-up at Broadway progressed rapidly. That night the chief air commanders, both American and British, flew in and watched as 64 Dakotas landed and took off. Air Marshal Baldwin described the scene: 'Nobody has seen a transport operation until he has stood on that jungle runway under the light of a Burma full moon, and watched Dakotas coming in and taking off in different directions on a single strip all night long at the rate of one landing and one take-off every three minutes.' On the second night Wingate flew in — to the delight of the Chindits who were building up the first ever Stronghold.

The success of the start of Operation 'Thursday' was greatly helped by a number of attacks by Cochrane's aircraft of the Air Commando and RAF Hurricanes on the nearest Japanese airfields. During the first two days 78 Japanese aircraft were destroyed and more damaged, and this accounted very substantially for the fact that there was hardly any interference from Japanese air forces during the entire operation. Another interesting comment about that dramatic Sunday night has come from the Japanese side. Thousands of their troops were waiting beside the Chindwin ready to start their attack. Hearing and seeing wave after wave of large Allied aircraft flying eastwards filled them with foreboding.

Lentaigne and 111 Brigade started their fly-in to Chowringhee on 6 March and by the 8th, before the Japanese had seriously reacted, 1,200 men, 2,000 mules and all the necessary equipment and ammunition had been flown in, as Wingate expressed it, 'into the guts of the enemy'. By then there were three Chindit brigades operating behind the Japanese lines: 77 Brigade (Calvert) building-up on Broadway; 111 Brigade (Lentaigne), which had flown into Chowringhee; and 16 Brigade (Fergusson), which was in the middle of its 600-mile march south from Ledo to Indaw, but because of the atrocious country it had to cross, was already nearly two weeks behind schedule – a delay which was to have grave consequences. In addition, Merrill's Marauders, which had trained as Chindits, were already in action under Stilwell's command in the Hukawng valley.

Broadway rapidly developed into a powerful Stronghold, with firmly constructed defences, carefully co-ordinated defensive fields of fire, an efficient and well-organized airstrip, a medical centre and a good supply of clean water. Most important, it was, according to Wingate's dictum, sufficiently far from major roads or railways to make it inaccessible to heavy guns or tanks. From the Stronghold Calvert sent out his different columns to attack and demolish the road and railway running north of Indaw towards Mogaung. The railway lay about twenty miles west of Broadway, so the columns had a lengthy march to their targets which were in the area of Mawlu and Hopin. The columns from the Lancashire Fusiliers, the South Staffordshires and the 3/6th Gurkhas probed aggressively in this sector of the front and by 12 March, one week after the launch, had totally blocked both the road and railway, thus denying supplies and reinforcements both to the Japanese 18th Division facing Stilwell, and to Sato's 31st Division at Kohima. Another column from 77 Brigade had marched south and had completely stopped all river traffic on the Irrawaddy.

Brigadier Calvert, ever one to lead from the front – unlike the fifty brigadiers from GHQ in Delhi – saw that Mawlu was the crucial point for road and rail traffic and determined to build up a defensive box there. The air supply was good and the Mawlu Box, because of the number of parachutes festooned in the trees, was nicknamed 'White City'. By this time the Japanese had begun to react in a big way, and at Pagoda Hill near Mawlu, there was a furious clash in which Calvert personally led a bayonet charge with the South Staffordshires — a fight in which Lieutenant Cairns won the VC. White City was a defended box rather than a Stronghold, but it was sufficiently well defended to have its own landing strip and dropping zone, pre-determined fields of fire for Bren guns and 2-inch and 3-inch mortars, large stocks of ammunition, telephone lines laid to platoon headquarters, a casualty clearing station, and the comforting knowledge that Mustangs were on call at two hours' notice. On 21 March the Japanese 114th Regiment, withdrawn from 18th Division facing Stilwell, made their first major attack on White City, but were repulsed with heavy casualties. This major fighting unit then moved back a short way from the White City defences, where they were attacked by waves of Mustangs and virtually destroyed.

Calvert was clearly the most successful and aggressive Chindit commander in the field, and under his positive leadership Broadway as a Stronghold and White City as a defended box were successes. Other Chindit operations were not so uniformly successful. 111 Brigade was flown out of Tulihal airstrip on 7 March to land at Chowringhee. Their flight went smoothly, there was no opposition, and the total silence after the landing has been described as a moment of enchantment. From Chowringhee the brigade had a long march to Katha on the Irrawaddy. An air drop of boats was made to assist with the river crossing, but this rapidly became a shambles. The mules refused to cross the water and as a consequence the brigade had to be split. Next an air drop went wrong and it took half a day (13 March) to collect — causing further delay. For five days the brigade seemed just to be milling about, becoming exhausted and achieving nothing. More significantly, it failed to reach its target, the railway south of Indaw, and this had disastrous consequences for Fergusson's brigade approaching from the north. During these trying and tiring days Lentaigne, who had only about half a brigade to manage — because the débâcle at the river had cut his numbers and he had lost 4/9th Gurkhas to Morris Force — began to suffer severely from strain and exhaustion. 'His exhaustion brought on a nervousness that was both obvious and acutely embarrassing.' (Rhodes-James, *Chindit*, p. 77.) Lacking effective leadership, the morale of the brigade dropped danger-ously, when it appeared that they had marched and countermarched for two weeks, and all they had achieved was to blow one bridge on a railway which did not appear to be used. An officer who trained with this brigade was not surprised at this failure because their training had been ineffective compared to that of 77 Brigade.

16 Brigade (Fergusson), made up of the Queen's Royal Regiment, the Leicesters and the Reconnaissance Regiment, had set out from Ledo on 10 February (when the Axiom Conference was still dithering over whether to support Wingate's operations), to cover nearly 600 miles of very

difficult country and to attack Indaw. They did not reach the Chindwin until 28 February, but were helped by the RAF which dropped inflatable boats for the river crossing. After this, at the behest of Stilwell, they had to detach a column to attack a small Japanese garrison at Lonkin. This diversion achieved little, but caused further delay to Fergusson's brigade. Fergusson had some serious problems on this seemingly interminable march, which did not appear to achieve very much, and occasionally he had to fall back on the eccentric punishments which Wingate had laid down for the discipline of Chindit columns behind the lines. This included curtailment of rations (77 Brigade was threatened with this for putting out incorrect landing marks), flogging, banishment to the jungle or execution. Fergusson's cases include being asleep on duty and stealing rations at an air drop.

The first columns of 16 Brigade arrived in the area where they were to set up their Stronghold, Aberdeen, on 20 March, two weeks behind schedule, while two columns of the Reconnaissance Regiment were still ten days behind after having had to wait at Lonkin. Wingate's original plan had been for 16 Brigade to wait in the area of the Aberdeen Stronghold before attacking Indaw. He now changed this plan. Although Fergusson asked for some days delay for his sick and exhausted men, Wingate insisted that they attack Indaw at once, before the Japanese had time to defend it.

This meeting, on 20 March at Aberdeen, was the cause of bitter criticism by Fergusson, and indirectly involves the future role of the Chindits and the wider strategy for the battle of Imphal. By 20 March the Japanese attack on Imphal and Kohima was looking extremely menacing, and the question arose as to how far the Chindits, by operating in the Indaw and Wuntho areas, could give more direct help to the defenders at Kohima and Imphal. Wingate, after another clash with Slim, had obtained permission for 14 Brigade (Brodie) to fly-in to Aberdeen as soon as its airstrip was ready. The leading unit of the brigade landed at Aberdeen on 23 March. The crucial question was whether 14 Brigade should go immediately to help Fergusson at Indaw, or whether it should march south-westwards from Aberdeen to attack the supply routes of the Japanese 15th and 31st Divisions attacking Imphal and Kohima. After his meeting with Wingate at Aberdeen, Fergusson was convinced that 14 Brigade was coming in to help him at Indaw as soon as possible, but Wingate's orders to Brodie for 14 Brigade contain no mention of helping Fergusson at Indaw.

Just as Mountbatten could not always pass on to Wingate all the vagaries of strategic planning with which he had to cope, so perhaps Wingate, in a rapidly changing situation, did not pass on all his information to Fergusson. Certainly Fergusson felt that he had been let

Right: The jungle-covered hills surrounding Kohima, through which the Royal Norfolks and the Royal Scots fought their way.

Right: The hills around Kohima showing the very difficult terrain over which most of the fighting took place.

Right: Shells falling on a Japanese position near Shenam.

Left: Sometimes the generals in the rear wondered why progress was slow. The Tiddim road.

Left: Jeep ambulances, seen here approaching Kohima, saved hundreds of lives.

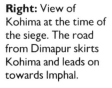

Right: View of Kohima at the time of the siege. The road from Dimapur skirts Kohima and leads on towards Imphal.

Right: The new Roman Catholic Cathedral, dedicated in 1991, was built on the first rise towards Aradura Spur. The dedication also included a service of reconciliation between British and Japanese veterans.

Left: The track leading to 161 Brigade Box outside Kohima. Note the chains on the wheels.

Right: Kohima after the siege, showing convoys of 3-ton trucks.

Left: Kohima with references to the main features in the battles.
1 The Deputy Commissioner's Bungalow 2 Garrison Hill 3 Kuki Piquet 4 FSD 5 DIS 6 Jail Hill 7 The road to Imphal 8 Pimple 9 Congress Hill 10 GPT Ridge 11 Norfolk Ridge 12 Rifle range 13 Two Tree Hill 14 Jatsoma Track 15 & 16 Mount Pulebadze

Right: Garrison Hill after the siege – the scene which reminded observers of the Somme battlefields of 1916.

Left: Kohima. The tennis court which was the scene of prolonged hand-to-hand fighting and is now a cemetery with a Cross of Sacrifice.

Right: The devastated Naga village after the battle.

Above: View from Naga village across Kohima towards Aradura Spur and the mountains behind it on the way to Imphal. After the battle of Kohima these daunting obstacles faced 2nd Division as it tried to open the road to Imphal.

Below: Unloading stores in Kohima after the monsoon started in May.

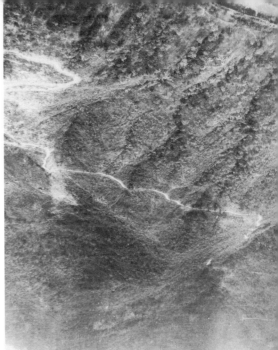

Above: Wingate, Cochrane and Alison.

Above right: The Tiddim road where 17th Division suffered heavy casualties as it retreated towards Imphal.

Below: The Tiddim road where the Gurkhas and Jats fought many delaying actions against the Japanese 33rd Division.

Right: The Tamu road where 20th Division withdrew in good order up to the heights of Shenam.

Left: The north end of the Imphal plain showing the airstrip and the hills near Nungshigum, where the Japanese were finally stopped.

Left: The scene of the Battle of Naram when 2nd Division advanced down the road to Imphal. The mountains in the background gave the Japanese ideal defensive positions.

Left: The flat southern part of the Imphal plain showing bomb and shell craters.

Right: Many of the battles around Imphal were fought during the monsoon in conditions like this. Gas capes and groundsheets gave little protection and keeping weapons in working order was a constant problem.

Right: Miserable monsoon conditions in Bishenpur just after the battle.

Right: The misty heights of Shenam where 20th and 23rd Divisions held the Japanese advance through weeks of bitter hand-to-hand fighting.

Left: Men of the Devonshire Regiment in the fighting at Shenam.

Left: Shenam – the Devons prepare to attack.

Left: Sappers laying anti-tank mines during the battles at Shenam.

Right: The Gurkhas during the prolonged battle for Scraggy — another reminder of the Somme.

Right: The West Yorks advance near Molvom.

Right: A Sikh patrol moves through flooded paddy fields on the Imphal plain.

Above left: General Wingate in a Dakota, with the rifle he always carried, setting off to fly to Broadway. He is wearing his medal ribbons including the DSO and two bars.

Left: 'Piccadilly is blocked'. This dramatic photograph shows Wingate, Cochrane, Calvert, Alison and Tulloch just after they received the photographs showing that the proposed landing ground at Piccadilly was blocked by teak logs.

Left: Mules were vital to the Chindit columns but did not always take kindly to flying in a Dakota.

Above: A Dakota tows a glider over the mountains to the landing ground at Broadway.

Above right: The Sentinel L5 flying out wounded Chindits. This invaluable aircraft, which could land on very short strips, saved the lives of many wounded men.

Below: A Chindit in an isolated valley watches as a Dakota drops supplies.

Right: The difficulties of pinpointing the drop-zone were greatly increased when operating in this sort of country.

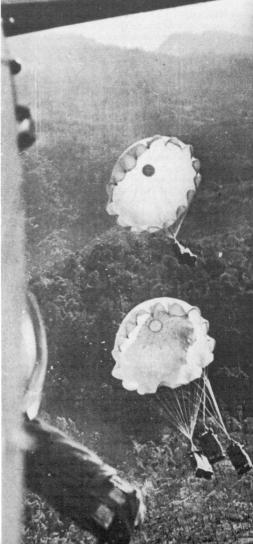

THE GENERALS

Above: General Slim posing in front of the Fourteenth Army sign which he helped to design.

Right: General Scoones who commanded IV Corps during the Imphal siege. He won the MC in the First World War.

Below: General 'Punch' Cowan who commanded 17th Indian Division during the whole of the retreat and through to final victory.

Opposite page, top: Mountbatten, Supreme Commander South East Asia Command, did much to improve morale by his cheerful, informal addresses to groups of servicemen.

Opposite page, bottom left: The inscription at the base of the Cross of Sacrifice, with a wreath laid by a Japanese group at the time of the dedication of the new Kohima cathedral.

HERE AROUND THE
TENNIS COURT
OF THE DEPUTY
COMMISSIONER
LIE MEN WHO FOUGHT
IN THE BATTLE OF
KOHIMA
IN WHICH THEY
AND THEIR COMRADES
FINALLY HALTED
THE INVASION
OF INDIA
BY THE FORCES
OF JAPAN
IN APRIL 1944

Below: The 2nd
Division Memorial in
Kohima Cemetery
with the inscription:
'When you go home
tell them of us and
say for your tomorrow
we gave our today'.
Wreaths from the
2nd Division
Pilgrimage, 1991.

WHEN YOU GO HOME
TELL THEM OF US AND SAY
FOR YOUR TOMORROW
WE GAVE OUR TODAY

Above: The Cross of Sacrifice with the Aradura Spur and Mount Pulebadze in the background.

Below: As 2nd Division advanced from Kohima they had many fierce battles with the Japanese rearguards. This is the scene of the battle at Kigweima.

down at a critical moment for him and for 16 Brigade, though Tulloch, in discussing this matter, writes that to imagine 14 Brigade could actually give any support to Fergusson's attack on Indaw, '. . . does not make any sense at all'. (Tulloch, *Wingate in Peace and War,* p. 262.)

By the time the first units of 14 Brigade had arrived at Aberdeen Fergusson had already left for his attack on Indaw. This was not a success. Because Wingate had hustled him forward he had not had time to make a proper reconnaissance and this, as ever, proved disastrous. His columns – the Queen's and the Leicesters – were to suffer severely because there was no water on the route they followed. Fergusson faced another serious problem because, during the advance to Indaw, Wingate was in the process of moving his headquarters from Imphal to Sylhet, and for those vital days Fergusson could not contact him.

Fergusson planned to rendezvous at the village of Auktaw, and from there to send two Queen's columns off to the west of Indaw, and the Leicesters and the Reconnaissance Regiment to the east. Even this plan had to be changed, and the Reconnaissance Regiment column was ordered to veer off to Thetkegyin, on the northern edge of Lake Indaw, to get water for their men and, more importantly, for their mules. In both these places – Auktaw and Thetkegyin – the advancing columns, because of inadequate reconnaissance, bumped unexpectedly into Japanese defensive positions. The Chindits drove the Japanese out of Auktaw – but all surprise was then lost – and they found that Thetkegyin was strongly defended. The engagement here lasted for two days (26–27 March) during which Japanese mortar fire hit the mules carrying the flame-throwers, and this resulted in an inferno of smoke and flames, with grenades, mortar bombs and ammunition exploding, and, over all, the sickly stench of roasting mule. After inflicting more than 80 casualties on the enemy, the column withdrew – having themselves lost heavily.

The two columns of the Queen's, which were sent on two different routes to the west of Lake Indaw, were not markedly successful. They did ambush some Japanese truck convoys, but in another skirmish Japanese grenades caused the Chindits' mules to stampede with the result that the heavy weapons, the reserve ammunition and the unit's wireless set were lost.

Of the columns in 16 Brigade, the Leicesters were the most successful. A proud county regiment, they did not really respond to Wingate's style. Their comment about one of his messages was 'Some message about guts and God'. They were an excellent infantry battalion with effective leadership. They reached Indaw east airfield, and having checked on an adequate water supply, dug-in as quickly as possible. The Japanese attacked them over a period of three days, but they held out with the help of accurate supporting strikes from the Air Commando.

They killed 90 of their attackers and suffered few losses themselves. Had any of the other columns managed to reach the Leicesters, Indaw could have been taken and held, but this did not happen, and after the third day of fighting, Fergusson ordered a general retreat to the Stronghold at Aberdeen. Although 16 Brigade failed at Indaw, it had one major achievement to its credit. Near Indaw it came across a huge supply dump which turned out to be the main supply base for all the Japanese divisions in northern Burma. Fergusson contacted the Air Commando and had great satisfaction in knowing that the dump was completely destroyed by Mitchells and Mustangs.

The Attack on Indaw, March 1944

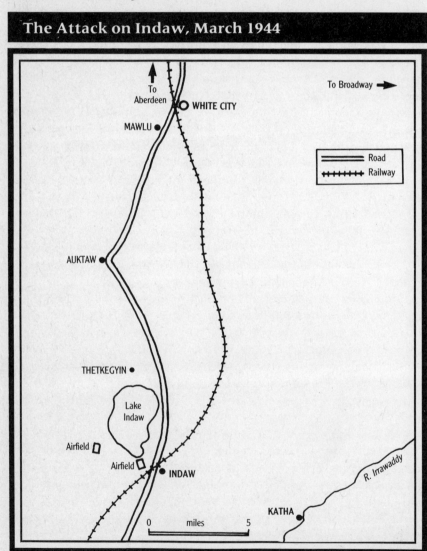

It had been Wingate's plan to occupy Indaw well before the Japanese had reacted to the Chindit fly-in. This did not happen for two reasons. First, the delay of two weeks on 16 Brigade's long march, and secondly the activities of 111 Brigade, which had flown into Chowringhee. They failed to destroy the road and rail link south of Indaw which Wingate had ordered them to do, and thereby allowed Japanese reinforcements to reach Indaw. In addition, while they were marching about, to confuse the Japanese they told local villagers that they were making for Indaw. In view of this it was not surprising that 16 Brigade had such a violent reception when they arrived.

As assessment of the role and impact of the Long Range Penetration Groups must include the activities of the American brigade which trained with the Chindits and became known as Merrill's Marauders, or Galahad Force. As 5307 Composite Unit (Provisional), they had trained in India on the same lines as the Chindits, though they were not subject to British military discipline. They appeared to the Chindits as a wild and undisciplined bunch, and they caused serious problems when, for example, from their troop train they shot at cows and Indian peasants. In January 1944 Stilwell gave command to his son-in-law, Brigadier Frank Merrill, who had little infantry experience, but the unit was welded into an efficient fighting force by Colonel Hunter, an experienced regular soldier. Hunter relied on regulations rather heavily, but he was determined enough to stand up to Stilwell and to Wingate – for example he refused Wingate's order to cut the vocal cords of his mules. He was also strong enough to tell Stilwell that he had gravely mishandled the whole of the Galahad operation. In contrast Merrill was a mere yes-man to Stilwell.

During February and March, while Stilwell was driving and cajoling his Chinese divisions slowly down the Hukawng valley, he sent Merrill's Marauders on a wide detour to the east of the valley, intending to cut off the main forces of Tanaka's 18th Division. This strategy led to the Battle of Walawbum, which started on 8 March, just after the Chindit fly-in. Galahad Force did well and, at a cost of 45 casualties, inflicted 800 casualties on the enemy. This action did not bring the reward it deserved, partly because the two Chinese divisions – 38th and 22nd – obeyed Chiang Kai-shek's instructions instead of Stilwell's, and partly because his orders were vague and his staff work was appalling. Tanaka, a tough and experienced general, had worked out his tactics in advance, and although he sustained heavy casualties he was able to slip away from Walawbum on a pre-prepared route.

At the height of this fighting (10 March) Merrill had a heart attack and was flown out to safety, while the rest of the campaign of Galahad Force, including a violent battle lasting two weeks, was directed by

Hunter. Stilwell's treatment of the Chindits was scandalous, but he treated the Marauders little better. One Marauder is reputed to have said 'To think that I had that bastard in my sights and did not pull the trigger.'

While these battles were under way the diplomatic wrangling again influenced events in north Burma. Sato's 31st Division was posing a serious threat to Kohima, and because of that Stilwell slowed up his advance in case the Japanese captured Dimapur and cut him off from all his supplies coming up the road and railway to Ledo. He continued with his normal vituperation of Mountbatten and the British. He wrote in his diary, 'Off to see Louis who, to put it mildly, has his hind leg over his neck ... What a mess the Limeys can produce in short order.' These irresponsible comments, coming from the man holding the high office of Deputy Supreme Commander SEAC were bad enough, but unfortunately Stilwell surrounded himself with sycophantic followers, and his attitude to the British was to rub off on to his staff and cause dire problems for the Chindits in their later campaigns. Following Stilwell's lead, Chiang Kai-shek, at the height of the Kohima battle, took the opportunity to order his divisions not to advance further – all of this just at the time when Operation 'Thursday' was launched, ostensibly to help Stilwell and the Chinese. So much for Allied solidarity!

Wingate was to have one final fling on the political and strategic stage. When the initial press release gave details of Operation 'Thursday', it spoke of moves by Fourteenth Army. Wingate was furious – sensing the mean hands of GHQ – and telegraphed Mountbatten to protest. In reply Mountbatten pointed out that the whole programme for publicity was carefully designed to build up to a climax giving the maximum publicity to Wingate himself and to the Chindits. He then added an interesting comment, 'Your telegram made me realize how you have achieved your amazing success in getting yourself disliked by people who are only too ready to be on your side.'

Slim's comment is also, in a different way, significant. (*Defeat into Victory*, p. 266.) He said he agreed to the publicity because 'The Japanese were much more likely, if Wingate's name were given, to take this expedition as merely a repetition of his minor and ineffective raid of 1943.'

This fracas had hardly subsided when Wingate received a telegram from Churchill congratulating him and the Chindits on the outstanding success of Operation 'Thursday'. Wingate replied to Churchill's message by asking for four additional squadrons of Dakotas and arguing that if their success were exploited there was an opportunity to destroy four Japanese divisions (15th, 31st, 33rd and 18th). He concluded, 'Slim gives me his full backing.' This statement caused another bitter dispute between Slim and Wingate. Slim later denied giving his backing to this request from Wingate, but Tulloch, who was Wingate's Chief of Staff, wrote that it was absolutely true, and that he had checked it personally with Slim's Chief of Staff. Finally, on 24 March, Mountbatten sent a signal to Special Force Headquarters passing on the thanks and congratulations of the Prime Minister and adding that the Prime Minister gave Special Force his full backing, and would support the demand for four Dakota squadrons. Tragically, Wingate was killed before this message could be delivered.

THE DEATH OF WINGATE AND THE FINAL CHINDIT CAMPAIGN

On 24 March 1944 Wingate flew into the Broadway Stronghold in a B-25 Mitchell bomber from Air Commando. He spent a busy day, visiting White City where he conferred with Calvert, then went to Aberdeen, which Fergusson had already left, and finally after returning to Broadway he flew on to Imphal. Here he had another discussion with Air Marshal Baldwin about the problems of communication with the new headquarters at Sylhet. Baldwin flew a Lockheed aircraft and Wingate took the Mitchell he had used that morning. At about 1700 hours, Wingate, who was flying to Lalaghat, offered a lift to some war correspondents and took-off, with Baldwin following in his aircraft shortly afterwards. An hour later Wingate's aircraft crashed in the hills around Bishenpur and everyone on board was killed.

There is conflicting evidence about the flight. Baldwin was adamant that although there were isolated storms about, the weather between Imphal and Silchar was clear and fine, and he had had no problems flying an almost identical route. In contrast, a pilot from 194 Squadron who flew out of Imphal at the same time, recorded that the weather was particularly bad, with poor visibility. He recalls also seeing a Mitchell which seemed to be far too low, near the Bishenpur hills. Yet another witness maintains – in total contradiction of Baldwin's evidence – that Wingate took off 'in pissing rain'. Many years later Tulloch received information that while the Mitchell was at Broadway the young pilots had told Colonel Rome (Officer Commanding Broadway) that one engine of the Mitchell was not developing full power, and they thought that they should wait for a replacement, but they were in awe of Wingate and did not like to delay him. Rome passed this information to Wingate who discussed it with the pilots, but it is not known whether he overruled them.

A crashed aircraft was identified the next day (25 March) and on the 27th a patrol brought definite confirmation. Tulloch issued an order of the day for the Chindits, telling them of Wingate's death, and adding that the most fitting memorial to him would be the early achievement of his purpose.

Wingate's death created an immediate problem for Slim who had to appoint a successor, and at a time when the Japanese assault on Imphal and Kohima was at its height. Slim telephoned Tulloch and asked his advice on this sensitive issue. There was an urgent need to find a leader who believed in Wingate's philosophy, who had the experience to lead Operation 'Thursday' to a successful conclusion, and to defend it against the inevitable opposition of the old guard Indian Army critics. Almost inexplicably, Tulloch suggested Brigadier Lentaigne who was leading 111 Brigade in the vicinity of Indaw. Tulloch ruled himself out because, although devoted to Wingate, he had not commanded a column in the field. Perhaps for the same reason Tulloch did not mention or suggest General Symes as a candidate. Tulloch recommended Lentaigne as the man most in tune with Wingate even though he knew that the two men had been totally at odds. There was a long-standing and deep antipathy between them, and Lentaigne was among those who regarded Wingate as an upstart, whose ideas were unsound and completely unproven. Wingate, for his part, had had Lentaigne imposed upon him, and never established a good rapport with him.

Tulloch's suggestion of Lentaigne seems all the more remarkable given that he already knew that Lentaigne's leadership of 111 Brigade after it had landed at Chowringhee had been seriously inadequate. He was too old, he suffered from fatigue after a few days, and he had caused serious concern to the officers of his column. Did Tulloch perhaps think that since Lentaigne was a Gurkha officer, this would be more acceptable to Slim who always liked to have ex-Ghurkas in command of his units? Lentaigne would certainly be more amenable and would not threaten to bring Churchill down on the heads of the generals. Lentaigne at this time was a worried man and inspired no one with confidence. He had had the unnerving experience of being in a battle and knowing that his officers had lost confidence in him. He had, unwittingly, contributed to the defeat of Fergusson at Indaw, by failing to block the railway south of Indaw, and by alerting the Japanese to a possible attack. He was not in tune with the other Chindits and, quite wrongly, thought that Broadway and White City would be overrun almost at once. Thompson says categorically that the appointment of Lentaigne was a mistake (Sir Robert Thompson, *Make for the Hills*, p. 54) because in particular he was too weak to stand up to Stilwell.

Interestingly, although Calvert was outstandingly the most successful Chindit leader, it does not appear that he was thought of as a possible successor to Wingate. It seems that he was considered exclusively as a tough fighting man in the field, and yet he had a fine and original mind, was a brilliant engineer (second class honours at Cambridge) and would have had the enthusiastic loyalty of every single Chindit.

In accepting the advice of Tulloch, Slim made a serious blunder, by completely overlooking the claims of General Symes, who had commanded 70th Division before it was broken up into Chindit columns. With remarkable loyalty and self-control, he had knuckled down to being Wingate's Number Two, and had shown fine leadership qualities when Wingate was seriously ill with typhoid in the autumn of 1943. Symes was furious when he heard from Tulloch that he had been passed over, and Lentaigne appointed. He went at once to Slim and asked where he stood. Symes' diary (Louis Allen, p. 350) gives details of a thoroughly unsatisfactory interview with Slim, who initially said he did not know Symes was at Chindit headquarters, then that he did not know what Symes' status was. Next, he added that the suggestion of Lentaigne had come from Tulloch – but later hedged about that – and finally agreed that he had made the decision in a hurry and had not had time to think it out. Symes and Tulloch had never got on well and it seems fairly clear that Tulloch deliberately refrained from suggesting Symes' name to Slim. Symes, dissatisfied with Slim's interview, appealed to Giffard and then to the CIGS to be relieved of his post.

Wingate's death was a serious blow to the Chindits, but Operation 'Thursday' had to go on, and his death did not interrupt the battles which were taking place at Broadway, White City and on the Bhamo road. The concentration of Chindit forces at Broadway and White City under the aggressive leadership of Calvert had at first been underestimated by the Japanese High Command. Then, because Calvert's block had done such serious damage to the supply and reinforcements for Mutaguchi's divisions and for the divisions facing Stilwell, on 6 April the Japanese launched a strong attack on White City. They started with heavy shelling of Mawlu and the White City Dakota airstrip, and followed this on 7 April by a substantial air attack carried out by 27 bombers – twelve of which were destroyed. Infantry assaults followed the air attacks, but they were repulsed with heavy losses. On 10 April Lentaigne flew in to see Calvert and it was agreed that Calvert would take command of a counter-attacking force. For another six days a confused battle raged between the White City defenders, the attacking Japanese, and the counter-attacking Chindits. At the end of the battle the Japanese Independent Mixed Brigade had sustained more than 50 per cent casualties, was destroyed as an effective fighting unit and fled southwards towards Indaw. The Chindits too had sustained casualties, in particular from a new Japanese weapon – the 6-inch mortar.

THE FINAL CHINDIT CAMPAIGN

Two weeks after the battle of White City, Lentaigne – under orders from Slim – ordered that 16 Brigade (Fergusson) would be flown out from Aberdeen; Broadway, White City and Aberdeen would all be abandoned, and a new block would be established at Blackpool, about 60 miles north of Indaw on the road and rail route to Mogaung and Myitkyina. This was really the end of the Chindits – after this they never again operated in what was their correct role. After their success at Broadway and White City they should have been taken out, reformed and used again in another Chindit operation for which they had been trained and equipped. This decision clearly illustrates that Slim never genuinely supported the Chindit concept, and it highlights the tragedy of Wingate's death; with Churchill's strong support he would never have accepted such a decision which was virtually the death-knell for the Chindits as a force.

In response to Slim's orders, 77 Brigade, 14 Brigade and 3 West African Brigade abandoned their Strongholds and, against opposition, moved north towards the proposed site of Blackpool. Their move had one fortunate consequence; by that time the Japanese had realized the danger from the Stronghold at Broadway and the block at White City, and the whole of 53rd Division put in an attack on White City. After the recent defeat of the Mixed Brigade the Japanese division approached the block with caution, only to find that it had been evacuated the previous day. While the three Chindit brigades were moving towards Blackpool, 111 Brigade by a different route had reached Blackpool on 7 May. The brigade was commanded by Major John Masters, because Morris, nominally in charge, was leading his part of the brigade up on the Bhamo road. Blackpool fulfilled few of the requirements of a Stronghold, and before 111 Brigade had time to build adequate defences the Japanese attacked it in strength.

Slim's decision to abandon Broadway, White City and Aberdeen was soon followed – on 17 May – by his decision to hand over command of Special Force to Stilwell. Slim justifies this decision as an issue of tidying-up the command of units approaching Mogaung and Myitkyina which were Stilwell's main objectives. In doing this Slim showed a total misunderstanding of the role of the Chindits, and condemned them to virtual slaughter at the hands of Stilwell whose venomous and vitupera-tive attitude to the hated Limeys now had full scope. Lentaigne who had only been in his post for a few weeks had come under the influence of Slim, and thereafter was to be no match in argument with Stilwell. Calvert and Fergusson had argued forcefully in favour of retaining the Broadway complex for a short time, after which Special Force should have been evacuated, rebuilt and re-launched.

An even stronger argument in favour of Broadway, was that the Stronghold was the perfect example of Chindit strategy, whereas by moving the brigades up to Blackpool, and then on to attack the heavily defended Japanese positions at Mogaung, Slim completely changed their role. He himself had said that they were not trained or equipped to be normal infantry, yet, by handing them over to Stilwell he condemned them to be used as normal infantry, but without armour or artillery support, against prepared Japanese positions.

An even more remarkable aspect of Slim's decision is that it infuriated Stilwell, who saw it as the yellow Limeys giving up Broadway and allowing reinforcements and supplies to reach Japanese 18th Division which he was fighting. This is exactly what happened. 'Bloody Limeys letting him down again!' This certainly was an odd decision of Slim's and for the Chindits it proved disastrous, a tragic error which led directly to their very high casualties during the rest of the campaign. Before Wingate's death, when they were being used in their proper role, they had inflicted 12,000 casualties on the enemy with negligible casualties themselves. From Blackpool onwards it was to be a very different matter.

The move from Broadway to Blackpool proved to be difficult and hazardous. 77 Brigade reached there on 17 May – the black day when Slim handed over the Chindits to Stilwell. By this time the whole of Japanese 53rd Division was in the area of Blackpool and Mogaung. Although Stilwell knew that strong Japanese forces were already attacking Blackpool, he demanded that the Chindits attack Mogaung at once. He also knew that the Japanese had more than 4,000 men and had strongly fortified the town.

While most of the Chindits were being forced into a role for which they were not armed or equipped, one group, Morris Force, was fulfilling the true Chindit role. Originally a part of 111 Brigade, they had landed at Chowringhee at the start of Operation 'Thursday'. From here they marched east and north to sabotage the road from Bhamo to Myitkyina. They operated effectively in different columns from early March to the end of May and during that period they virtually blocked the road, and very few Japanese vehicles got through. With Morris Force blocking the Bhamo road, and the Broadway complex blocking the road to Mogaung and threatening the roads going west from Indaw to Mutaguchi's divisions, the decision to abandon Broadway seems even more inexplicable.

By the end of May the three Chindit brigades – 77, 111 and 3 West African – together with Morris Force, which had advanced up the road from Bhamo to Myitkyina, were brought into the orbit of Stilwell's forces in the area of Mogaung and Myitkyina. In a daring swoop Merrill's

Marauders had captured Myitkyina airfield (17 May), but despite a very substantial build-up of forces by air supply, Stilwell had failed to capture the town. He became so violently frustrated that many people even on his own staff thought that his failure to capture Myitkyina town had temporarily unhinged him. His antipathy to everything British got even worse. Boatner, Stilwell's Chief of Staff – who was renowned for playing craps at every opportunity, and only fed Stilwell information he wanted to hear – was told to capture the town at all costs. He in turn ordered Morris Force to capture the village of Maigna at all costs. The American staff informed the Gurkhas that the village was not occupied, but in fact the Japanese were there in force. Then Stilwell's staff – following his lead – criticized the Gurkhas, saying that they lacked courage. Thus a very dangerous antipathy grew up.

In the first part of June Merrill's Marauders and 20,000 Chinese were besieging Myitkyina and to the fury of Stilwell were making no progress. Stilwell then once again ordered the Gurkhas to capture the village of Maigna at all costs. The Gurkhas were by then reduced to less than 500 men and their attack failed. Stilwell then announced that it was the fault of the Gurkhas that Myitkyina had not been captured – even though he had 25,000 troops surrounding it. His obsession with Myitkyina, probably stemmed from the pressure he was under from the American High Command to re-establish land communication and an oil pipeline to China, so as to reduce the huge cost of maintaining supplies over The Hump.

Stilwell kept fuelling antagonism towards the British, and on 3 June he complained to Mountbatten that 77 Brigade had refused orders to attack Mogaung, and that Morris Force had also refused orders. Mountbatten sent Slim – the only British general with whom Stilwell would ever co-operate – to see if he could calm things down. He did manage to get Stilwell to realize that he was getting extremely biased reports from his own staff – notably from the egregious Boatner.

By early June 111 Brigade, 14 Brigade and the West African Brigade were concentrated near Lake Indawgi which was used by flying-boats to evacuate the sick and wounded because so many airstrips were unusable in the monsoon rain. These brigades were reorganizing after suffering heavy casualties in the fighting around Blackpool and Mogaung. John Masters, commanding 111 Brigade, wrote in *The Road Past Mandalay* (p. 279), that morale became a serious problem 'as the men became convinced that Stilwell meant to murder us'.

Slim succeeded briefly in pacifying Stilwell, but immediately after the visit Stilwell ordered 77 Brigade 'to capture Mogaung at all costs'. The phrase 'at all costs' became a grim standing joke for the Chindits. Calvert worked out a very careful plan of attack, which started on 6 June, when the brigade still numbered 2,000 men, but they were exhausted by their prolonged jungle campaign, by the constant monsoon downpour, and by the high incidence of malaria, dysentery and typhus. By the second day of the battle the Chindits had suffered more than 300 casualties, and as the battle progressed, commanding officers informed Calvert that each battalion had been reduced to the strength of a Company. The battle continued and by 13 June their numbers stood at 550, and there was a major crisis over evacuating the sick and wounded. Regular shelling by Japanese artillery on a fairly confined position caused more casualties each day, and on 14 June Calvert sent his Second in Command to Stilwell to alert him to the situation. He was not received with any sympathy. Despite his losses Calvert continued his attack on 16 June with an air strike, accurately brought down by Thomson, followed by a mortar barrage of 400 bombs and an infantry assault. This brought some progress and killed 150 of the enemy. Calvert then heard that the Chinese were coming to support the assault on Mogaung. The promise of help was slightly encouraging and on 24 June Calvert, who realized that the Chinese were generally reluctant to put in frontal assaults, planned a final effort with his emaciated and depleted units. During the night there was another substantial air strike on the Japanese positions, followed by a barrage of 1,000 mortar bombs, and then the Gurkhas, the South Staffords and the Lancashire Fusiliers went in using automatic weapons, grenades and flame-throwers. The Chinese were to attack on one flank, but twice they failed to achieve their object, and caused additional casualties to the British. They then withdrew. The Chindits continued with fierce fighting against the Japanese for several more days – during which two more VCs were won – and then, on 27 June, after a final bloody onslaught in which the Chinese again refused to attack, the Japanese were driven out. 77 Brigade was reduced to 800 men, having suffered more than 50 per cent casualties in the battle for Mogaung.

They had suffered enough, but the next day they had to endure another typically underhand blow from Stilwell. The world radio announced that the Chinese–American forces had captured Mogaung. Showing admirable restraint, Calvert signalled Stilwell, 'Understand Chinese have taken Mogaung. Please record we have taken umbrage.' The Chindits enjoyed a moment of grim satisfaction when they heard that Stilwell's son, who was his Intelligence officer, announced that umbrage must be a very small village because he could not find it on the map.

In the aftermath of this prolonged battle, 77 Brigade lost hundreds more men, from total exhaustion, from wounds and from the ravages of sickness to which they no longer had any resistance. Their resistance was so low that if a man cut his finger it would go septic and in a few days he would be dead. Mountbatten, alerted to the crucial situation, flew to see

Stilwell to discuss the withdrawal of Special Force. Stilwell virtually said that the Chindit commanders were lying, but grudgingly agreed to a medical inspection of all the men by an Anglo-American team of doctors. Their report was decisive. It found the men were physically and mentally worn out, many had suffered several attacks of malaria but had kept fighting; most were suffering from prickly heat, footrot and septic jungle sores, and there was a rising number of deaths from typhus and cerebral malaria. When Mountbatten received the report he ordered Stilwell to evacuate the sick and wounded at once. Stilwell prevaricated disgracefully – saying that he had never kept unfit men in battle. In this final miserable wrangling, Mountbatten sent senior officers – including Merrill – to supervise the arrangements. This was a wise move for Merrill knew that Stilwell had treated the Marauders almost as badly as he had treated the Chindits. The Marauders had been driven over the limit of endurance and on several occasions had broken down and had refused to fight.

It was agreed that 77 Brigade and 111 Brigade should be taken out, but 14 Brigade and the West Africans did not get out until August, by which time Myitkyina had fallen. Calvert commented, 'It left a bitter taste when the Chindit Brigades were treated like malingerers by the Supreme Command.'

This tragic anti-climax, when the sick and emaciated remnant of a once fine fighting force was flown out to hospital in India, was caused largely by the treatment they had received at the hands of Stilwell – his judgement blighted by his almost insane antipathy to everything British. It must be said too that their troubles really stemmed from the decision of Slim not to use them in their role of Long Range Penetration Groups, but to deliver them as normal infantry into Stilwell's hands. The Chindits almost to a man believe that this would not have happened if Wingate had lived.

The Chindits had some months of recuperation in India, and then the decision was made that they should be disbanded. Mountbatten wrote, 'It was the hardest duty in my life to agree to give the order to break up the Chindits. But now that the whole Army is Chindit-minded, there is no need for Chindits. We are all Chindits now.' These were comforting words to the battered survivors of Wingate's Special Force, but whether they were true is open to serious doubt.

CHAPTER 8

THE BATTLE FOR IMPHAL

S LIMS'S STRATEGIC PLANNING for his showdown with Japanese 15th Army under Mutaguchi centred on drawing the enemy forward and fighting the decisive battles in the area of the Imphal plain. The Japanese, whose aims were more straightforward, expected to advance swiftly from the Chindwin, seize Imphal and Kohima before the monsoon broke in May and, in the mind of Mutaguchi at least, use that victory for a triumphant march into India. When that happened he expected the Indian masses to rise and welcome the Indian National Army commanded by the fiery Subhas Chandra Bose, and to throw off the hated British imperial yoke. The Japanese, given their defeats and withdrawals in the Pacific theatre, were under considerable pressure to achieve some striking success in Burma, and Mutaguchi, with his passion for glory and self-advancement, was convinced that he was the leader to achieve just that.

THE SCENE IS SET

Prior to February 1944, IV Corps under Scoones was preparing for an advance into Burma with three divisions, and had built up a huge network of roads and supply bases on the Imphal plain. Most of these lay in the relatively flat area between the town of Imphal and the village of Palel. The bases had been built up ready for a major advance southeastwards and were in no way prepared for a defensive role. The difficulty of communications had weighed heavily with Slim when he considered the great strategic issue of whether to attack eastwards over the Chindwin; try to hold the line of the Chindwin against Japanese attack; or withdraw 17th and 20th Divisions from Tiddim and Tamu to the Imphal plain where his supply route would be at its shortest, and where his superiority in guns, tanks and aircraft could be used to the greatest advantage. He had also reckoned that when the monsoon came it would produce a major hazard for the Japanese, whose supply routes would become more and more difficult. He then made the decision to withdraw to the Imphal plain, knowing that this might cause some resentment in 17th and 20th Divisions who had fought hard, had captured valuable territory at some considerable cost and had established a local superiority over their Japanese opponents. As a result of Slim's decision, in February 1944 the Imphal plain became a hive of industry as all units hastily dug trenches and erected wire defences, and large numbers of civilian workers and other non-combatants, called 'useless mouths', were moved out.

The Battle of Imphal was unusual in that Corps Headquarters, normally located some way behind the lines, was actually under siege. The Imphal Headquarters had been built up during 1943, when 8,000 labourers were engaged in laying out an extensive camp with bamboo

Imphal

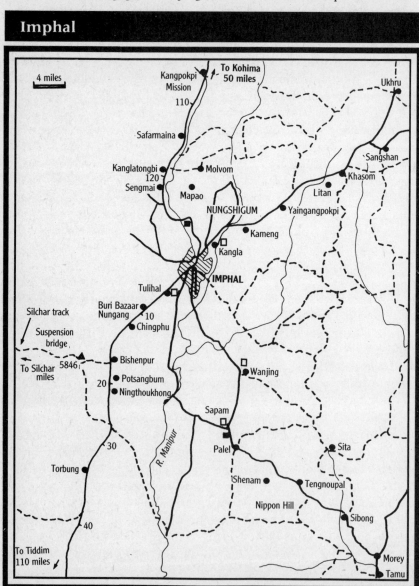

bashas and tents. This permanent layout to some extent produced a peacetime mentality, when for example senior officers disputed whose office should be next to the Corps Commander's, and officers' messes were kept strictly divided according to rank. As the Japanese approached and 'useless mouths' were sent out, to the amusement of the fighting units Corps HQ was not reduced at all.

By the beginning of April when the Japanese were less than six miles away, life at Corps HQ was continuing much as before. A young doctor, (Dr Maurice) recorded details of the excellent medical services available in 41 Indian General Hospital and 14 British General Hospital. The hospitals found that 90 per cent of the wounded recovered, but most deaths were caused by scrub typhus, malaria or dysentery. Mobile surgical units and field ambulance units, close to the front line, were well staffed and provided with good, up-to-date equipment and modern drugs such as penicillen.

As late as 9 April, when the siege was well under way, there were regular open air film shows, with the officers sitting at the front, of course. The war had been brought home to the HQ on 17 March when a bomb attack killed twenty men in a unit near the HQ buildings, but a good idea of the confidence felt by the staff is given by Dr Maurice's remark in a letter home, 'I am having a grand time which I would not miss for anything.' On 10 April he was furious at being posted away, and saw General Scoones before he left. The General kept him for half an hour, explaining the various aspects of the Corps involvement in the battles. This is in surprising contrast to a common criticism of Scoones that he failed to pass on information to his officers. Just before he left the doctor had had to give the general a medical examination. After one test Scoones asked what the test was for, and received the answer 'Syphilis, Sir.'

This fairly comfortable and relaxed situation did not prevent Corps HQ from receiving very angry criticism from the fighting units for failing to provide supplies and transport when needed and, above all, failing in their most important function of passing on Intelligence information. 20th Division was extremely critical of Corps HQ for the inadequate orders and confusion over the supply base at Moreh before they withdrew to Shenam, and 17th Division, notably General Cowan, clashed seriously with Scoones over the timing of the order to withdraw up the Tiddim road. Similarly, Scoones' tardiness in sending 37 Brigade to the help of 17th Division caused deep resentment. These are serious criticisms, but the most damaging allegations of incompetence at Corps HQ, arise from their handling of the Battle of Sangshak. The leading units of Sato's 31st Division attacked the forward Company of 50 Indian Parachute Brigade on 19 March. Up to that moment Brigadier Hope

Thomson had received no orders and no information about a Japanese advance, although Intelligence reports of a swiftly moving Japanese regiment approaching the Ukhrul area reached Corps HQ on 16 March; which means that Corps HQ failed, over a period of three days, to pass on this crucial information to 50 Brigade. In addition, Corps HQ failed to provide transport to bring the Gurkha parachute battalion to Sangshak, and failed to provide any barbed wire for its defences. These criticisms, and the fairly widespread criticism of Scoones' failure to pass information even to his senior commanders, do suggest that during the siege, IV Corps headquarters fell down on its job in several ways. The Japanese attack came earlier and more swiftly than Slim had expected, and came close to destroying 17th Division as it withdrew from Tiddim to Imphal (Chapter 2). The Japanese fared less well against 20th Division which withdrew in good order from Tamu up to the heights of Shenam, but the greatest threat to Slim's overall plan came from the rapid advance of 31st Division under Sato towards Kohima. Slim, who was always prepared to shield his subordinate commanders, openly admitted that he had made a mistake in not ordering 17th Division to withdraw earlier, and that he made a second mistake in underestimating both the speed and the size of the Japanese force heading for Kohima. He added, generously, that he was saved from the consequences of his mistakes by the stubborn valour of his troops.

By the first week in April 1944 the main framework for the Battle of Imphal had been laid. 17th Division had reached Bishenpur on the southern edge of the Imphal perimeter, and 20th Division was established in strength on the Shenam heights. The Japanese 31st Division had made rapid progress towards Kohima, but had had a bloody fight with 50 Indian Parachute Brigade at Sangshak (19–26 March). In spite of the delay caused by the battle at Sangshak, some Japanese units had plunged forward and had cut the Impahl–Kohima road so that IV Corps was completely cut off from Kohima and from its supply base at Dimapur (29 March). During the first week of April Slim's main worry was the Japanese threat to Kohima and, as he saw it, to Dimapur – though it is now known that Sato did not intend to attack Dimapur.

Decisions made in the middle of March by Slim, Mountbatten and Baldwin, notably about air supply, began to come to fruition in this critical first week of April. By 27 March 5th Indian Division had been flown in from the Arakan, 9 and 123 Brigades had gone to Imphal, while 161 Brigade had gone to Kohima and was destined to play a key role in the siege (Kohima siege 5–18 April, subsequent battle 18 April–6 June). Thanks to excellent work by Indian Command, 2nd British Division had begun to arrive at Dimapur by 1 April.

So, to face Mutaguchi's three divisions – 31st (Sato), 15th (Yam-auchi), 33rd (Yanagida) – Slim had 17th (Cowan), 20th (Gracey), 23rd (Roberts), 5th (Briggs) – all at Imphal, together with 2nd (Grover) and 7th (Messervy) at Kohima. In addition, he had 3 Special Service Brigade made up of one army and one Royal Marine commando which he positioned at the western end of the Silchar track in case the Japanese broke through there; also 23 Long Range Penetration Brigade, which had been trained as a Chindit unit in India and was initially used to defend the road and rail routes from Dimapur to Ledo, and later to sweep round to the north of 2nd Division and cut the Japanese supply lines from the Chindwin; finally, and in some ways most significantly, 254 Tank Brigade, which so often swayed the balance in hard-fought battles. In addition to all these forces, it must be remembered that as Mutaguchi's forces crossed the Chindwin, Wingate's Chindits, the equivalent of six highly trained brigades, or two additional divisions, had been launched on Operation 'Thursday', to drop in the area of Indaw to threaten and destroy Japanese lines of communication and supply routes. During the first few days of April Slim had a worrying time, fearful that 31st Division might make a dash for the virtually undefended Dimapur, but it can be clearly seen that when that threat did not materialize, he had a huge superiority in infantry divisions, a substantial superiority in tanks and an overwhelming superiority in the air, both in terms of supplies and of offensive action.

SHENAM

From the end of March, when IV Corps was cut off in Imphal, the most straightforward section of Scoones' front was Shenam, where 20th Division under Gracey was well dug-in after its model withdrawal up the steep hills from Tamu and Moreh.

From Gracey downwards, the division had resented handing over the vast stores at Moreh to the Japanese, but in the final days before it was lost it had been a scrounger's paradise. Many units had grabbed additional equipment and extra rations which stood them in good stead during the long weeks of the siege. One field regiment acquired a compressor which was adapted on a trailer to become a mobile charging plant. In monsoon conditions, keeping batteries charged was a constant headache for the gunners and this unofficial charger was a godsend. Other units constructed water trailers and other equipment – always showing their ingenuity to supplement the official provision. Even in Moreh there were some shortages, and one gunner unit which had been trying for months to obtain bush hats for its men, failed in its quest and they had to fight their way through the Shenam battles wearing side caps.

The Shenam saddle was nearly 5,000 feet above sea level, and the scrounging at Moreh enabled most units to face the bitter night-time cold with extra blankets and great-coats.

The Shenam saddle consisted of a long uneven ridge, running roughly east-west, with hills of varying height rising from the ridge. These hills, named only by the soldiers who fought there, hold the graves of thousands of Japanese, Gurkha, Indian and British soldiers who took part in the most prolonged battle of the entire Imphal campaign. The ridge, barely 50 yards wide in parts, swept down steep jungle-covered cliffs to a precarious road, and at the eastern end of the ridge to a jeep track. 20th Division knew that they had to hold this position to the last man and the last round, while the Japanese of Yamamoto's force knew that the south-eastern approach to Imphal over the Shenam Pass was the quickest and easiest route for the whole Japanese advance. It had a metalled road all the way, and the chances of the Japanese ever taking Imphal really depended on their breaking through at this point. They knew that if they could advance the few miles along the ridge they would be able to dominate the all-weather airstrip at Palel, capture the supplies in the large dumps scattered around Palel, and have an ideal spring-board for a successful attack on the Imphal plain.

By the beginning of April both sides had had time to construct

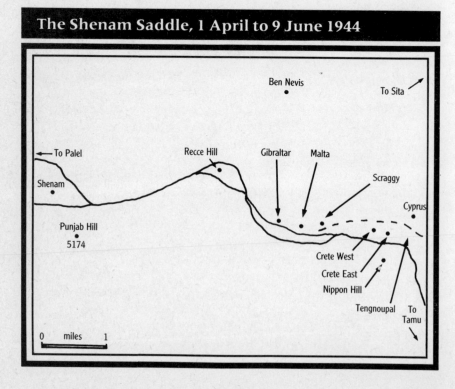

The Shenam Saddle, 1 April to 9 June 1944

defences with deep bunkers and well-sited supporting trenches. The soldiers of 20th Division had experience of the Japanese in attack, but they were amazed at their sheer determination to defend their bunkers and die rather than surrender. In hopeless positions, totally cut off from all assistance, pounded by artillery, attacked by overwhelming numbers, and offered honourable surrender by loudspeaker messages in Japanese, they still fought on to certain death. Even airstrikes by Hurribombers with 500-pound bombs failed to overcome their resolve. Platoons attacking a Japanese position nearly always found that even if they captured it, they came under effective fire from another well-concealed bunker on the reverse slope.

British troops quickly came to rely on and appreciate the RAF and USAAF, both in close support work and in bringing supplies. A young officer wrote, 'They brought rations, petrol, shells, stores and mail. Everything from a tin of bully beef or a soya link sausage, to a medium shell or a new jeep engine – from a ton of barbed wire to a spare wireless valve. No praise is too high for this wonderful organization and the splendid young men from the Empire and the United States who flew the machines. Without them Imphal could not have been held.' (Written soon after leaving Imphal in 1944 by Colonel J. Henton Wright, who was then a young officer in 9 Field Regiment.)

The artillery played an important part in the fighting, and gunner units were frequently and rapidly transferred to where they were most needed. In one action around Bishenpur, an infantry attack had the support of two batteries of 25-pounders, a battery of mountain guns, some 6-pounders and Bofors guns, a battery of 5.5in howitzers, together with a sound-ranging and flash-spotting troop from a survey regiment. The gunners relied on accurate information to range on their targets, and because of their better-quality wireless and telephone equipment often acted as the communications centre between brigade headquarters and the forward infantry units.

The first major clash with the Japanese on the Shenam heights took place on what became known as Nippon Hill. On 1 April, 2nd Borders had taken part of the hill, but the Japanese put in a powerful counter-attack and drove them off. The hill overlooked the road from Tamu to the Shenam heights, and it was decided that 4/10th Gurkhas from 100 Brigade should make an immediate Company attack. Nippon Hill had some scattered trees and vegetation on the lower slopes, but the top was bare of cover. The Gurkhas advanced to within a few yards of the top, but as they charged with fixed bayonets they were met by a storm of automatic fire and grenades and were driven back. Two more attacks were similarly repulsed. The fight for Nippon Hill continued for ten days, while 20th Division consolidated its other positions. At this stage, 80

Brigade (1st Devons, 9/12th Frontier Force Regiment and 3/1st Gurkhas) took over the defence of Shenam from 100 brigade, while 32 Brigade was detached to assist 17th Division in its struggle at Bishenpur.

At the eastern end of the Shenam ridge, 9/12th Frontier Force Regiment held carefully defended positions near Crete and Scraggy. 3/1st Gurkhas held Gibraltar, and the Devons lay slightly to the north on Patiala Ridge. The Japanese on Nippon Hill overlooked most of the positions and inflicted casualties by accurate sniping and shelling. Brigadier Greaves, commanding 80 Brigade, decided to make a major assault on Nippon Hill on 11 April, with two Companies of Devons leading the attack supported by Hurribombers and much of 20th Division's artillery. The Japanese had spent ten days preparing elaborate and effective defences, with skilfully sited underground bunkers. The Devons followed closely behind a heavy and prolonged bombardment, but the Japanese, who held their fire until the last moment, met their attackers with machine-gun fire and grenades. The Devons lost eight officers and 80 men. Despite their heavy losses the Devons kept going and drove the Japanese off the hill, which they then occupied in Company strength. The Company quickly dug-in, put up wire defences and brought in stocks of ammunition ready for the expected counter-attack. This was a wise precaution because the Japanese mounted three attacks during the night, but the Devons, helped by accurate defensive fire from the artillery, drove them off. The Japanese losses were so heavy that for several days wounded survivors who had been buried under piles of corpses would emerge and try to throw a grenade before they were shot down. On the day after the battle the Devons, proud of their capture of this famous landmark, handed over their positions to the Frontier Force Regiment and moved over to Patiala Ridge.

The Frontier Force battalion defended the hill for another week, but the Japanese, desperate to break through to Imphal, put in one attack after another. Yamamoto, who kept well forward with his attacking battalions, was bitterly frustrated by the stubborn defence of the Shenam features. Even though he had some reinforcements, withdrawn from the operation against the Chindits, and tank support, his force still made little progress. Here, as elsewhere in the three Japanese divisions, when things started to go wrong the relationship between commanders rapidly deteriorated. After the failure of a tank attack, Yamamoto openly accused the commander of cowardice, and his relationship with the CO of 213th Regiment − his main infantry force − was little better. Eventually, with tank and artillery support, Yamamoto Force drove the Frontier Force Regiment off the hill and immediately established a very strong and carefully defended position. Gracey, to whom the road up from Tamu was now less important, decided not to risk sustaining further heavy casualties in trying to recapture such a heavily defended feature and left the Japanese in occupation until July.

While this struggle had been raging, the forward units of Yamamoto Force had been probing a hilly area at Sita, a few miles north of Nippon Hill. This very isolated post, connected to Tengnoupal only by a mule track, had just been taken over by 3/1st Gurkhas on 14 April, when Japanese 213th Regiment put in a strong attack, supported by 75mm guns, medium machine-guns and mortars. The Gurkhas had prepared their defences very carefully, with a lot of barbed wire and well-sited anti-personnel mines. The Gurkhas were warned of an impending attack at 0300 hours when the mines started exploding. The attack was beaten off, but the Japanese advanced with a Bangalore torpedo – a metal pipe full of explosives which was pushed forward to blow a gap in barbed wire defences. The brave Gurkha platoon commander saw what was happening, rushed forward, threw grenades at the Bangalore torpedo party, and then attacked another group who were assembling ready to break through the gap. At the cost of his life he had repulsed a dangerous attack. In the assault on Sita the Japanese lost 500 killed and wounded against Gurkha causalties of less than 50.

After the battles at Sita and Nippon Hill, Yamamoto's forces continued their attacks. Believing that the Indian and Gurkha soldiers could be suborned from their loyalty, a battalion of the Indian National Army was sent off on a separate mission to infiltrate the defences near Palel. They were ambushed by a small Gurkha unit and fled in all directions, leaving weapons, ammunition and stores behind them. In considering Yamamoto's constant attacks on positions on the Shenam Saddle, carried out at such a high cost in casualties to 213th Regiment, it must be remembered that the Japanese considered this to be the most likely route for a successful advance on Imphal. On the British side, it was clearly understood that if Shenam and Palel fell to Yamamoto the whole of the Imphal defences would be put at risk. These factors account for the unending battles and the almost total devastation of this relatively small area which was the scene of fierce and close hand-to-hand fighting from early April until July. The monsoon, which broke in May, added another dimension to the horrors of this place. It is small wonder that the survivors compared it to the battlefields of the Somme.

The 1st Devons, who had established well-defended positions on Crete, Cyprus and Scraggy near the village of Tengnoupal, bore the brunt of the next wave of Japanese attacks, and were engaged in close-quarters fighting. During one clash a Devons NCO, Sergeant Leech, tried to capture a wounded Japanese officer, who in the struggle sank his teeth into the sergeant's hand. He only let go when the sergeant killed him with his own sword. The persistent Japanese attacks, which cost them

appalling casualties, gradually pushed back the British line and enabled
the leading companies of 213th Regiment to occupy Cyprus and Crete
East, which overlooked Tengnoupal. On 23 April after a bombardment
lasting two days, the Japanese attacked Crete West which was defended
by 3/1st Gurkhas. The attackers advanced and captured four of the well-
prepared bunkers, but a Gurkha platoon commander led a counter-
attack, and when the Gurkhas charged, waving their bloodstained kukris,
the Japanese fled. Despite this setback the Japanese continued to attack
Crete West, and bloody close-quarters fighting went on through April and
into May.

On 1 May the Devons replaced the Gurkhas on the Crete positions, to
take on once again the brunt of the Japanese attacks. Daily raids and
nightly jitter raids continued until 7 May when the Japanese mounted
another major assault. Then, in the course of a long and bitterly fought
encounter the Devons and Gurkhas were pushed off Crete, having
sustained 200 casualties in that brief phase of the fighting. After losing
Crete, 80 Brigade pulled back to Scraggy, where the line was once again
held by 3/1st Gurkhas.

The Devons, like many other units during this struggle, found that
whenever they recaptured a position the Japanese had always turned it
into a fortress. Japanese veterans do not remember that their digging of
bunkers was anything very special, but their ability to create deep
bunkers with heavy timbers overhead still amazes the British veterans
who recall trying to attack them. In particular the British were puzzled
that the Japanese could fell so many trees for overhead cover, and
remove so much soil from their trenches, and yet have them so
completely camouflaged that neither direct observation nor aerial
reconnaissance could detect them. A veteran of a Devons platoon on
Crete remembers a Japanese attack on their slit trench (which did not
have overhead cover). 'There were eight men there in a bunker – real
good mates of mine – when they got a direct hit. Seven of them were
killed and one buried alive. I gave the one that was buried some water
and the old favourite of ours, bully beef.' The narrator, Mr L. T. Collins of
Plymouth, was then wounded in the head and paralyzed down his left
side. He lay overnight in a bunker and was then taken to the Regiment
Aid Post, and then down to Imphal from where he was flown out to
hospital.

The Japanese were still under urgent pressure to make a clear break
through at Shenam, and at midnight on 10 May made yet another assault
on the forward Gurkha positions on Scraggy. These posts were effectively
wired and well defended, but the Japanese sent in wave after wave of
attackers, and so many were killed on the Gurkha's defensive wire, and
so many bodies were piled up that some of the later waves were able to

run straight up over the barbed wire. They overran the first Gurkha trenches and kept up their momentum. The pressure was so severe that the Gurkha CO warned his men to crouch well down in their trenches and then called down an artillery barrage on his own positions. This gave some respite and caused casualties to the attacking Japanese troops. As daylight broke a Company of 2nd Borders came up to relieve the Gurkhas, and found more than 800 Japanese dead around the barbed wire.

Scraggy was the most bitterly contested hill on the whole Shenam Saddle, and in places the Japanese trenches were less than ten yards from the British. It was impossible to erect wire in such a situation, and because the ground was shale, even the Japanese found it hard to dig deep enough to afford effective cover. Decomposing corpses and their attendant flies littered the area, and the nauseating stench of death and putrefaction was everywhere. Such was the strain of being in these trenches that men were often relieved after half an hour, and were allowed to smoke to offset the stench. They looked out from their trenches to a landscape in which every living thing had been destroyed – shell-holes surmounted only by charred tree stumps, smashed equipment and putrefying corpses.

Slim and Scoones realised that 20th Division, which was operating with only two brigades (32 Brigade was detached to assist 17th Division), had had a long period of gruelling fighting since before they left Moreh and until their recent battles on Crete and Scraggy. The order was therefore given that 23rd Division would replace them and on 13 May the changeover started. 20th Division then moved to the area of Yangang-popki north-east of Imphal.

Slim's strategic plan had been to lure the Japanese divisions forward to the Imphal plain and there to engage and destroy them. This he did, but there was no single dramatic battle such as at Alamein, for example, but rather a series of fierce, separate, hard-fought battles at Sangshak, Bishenpur, Kohima, Shenam, Nungshigum and Molvom. These were the killing fields, the battles where IV Corps with the RAF and USAAF achieved Slim's goal of destroying Japanese 15th Army under Mutaguchi. The Japanese were maintaining relentless pressure on the Shenam positions so the divisional changeover had to take place one battalion at a time. 37 Brigade went forward and occupied the advanced positions on Gibraltar, Malta and Scraggy, but was supported by two additional battalions – the Seaforths from 1 Brigade and the Rajputs from 49 Brigade. Also in support were tanks, medium machine-gun units and 159 Field Regiment. This was a powerful force, but the Japanese from Nippon Hill and Crete could overlook most of these places and had pinpointed many for shell or mortar fire. It has been suggested that by this time the

Japanese were running short of ammunition – not an impression shared by the Gurkhas when 250 shells fell on Malta in the course of a single day, or when Gibraltar received more than a hundred shells in the space of an hour. Daily shelling and mortar fire, jitter raids, sniping, and full-scale attacks meant that units in the forward trenches had virtually no rest or sleep, so they were changed frequently – sometimes twice a week.

37 Brigade was able to occupy its new positions over a period of days when there was the usual harassing fire but no all-out assault. This did not come until 20 May when the Japanese, after a substantial bombardment, attacked the Rajputs occupying Gibraltar. The Rajputs had prepared their defences very carefully and had accurately co-ordinated defensive fire plans with 158 Field Regiment. Their thorough work paid off, and although wave after wave of attacks were thrown against their defences, the attackers were repulsed leaving nearly 100 dead behind them. This was the type of action in which Mutaguchi's 15th Army lost its momentum and finally ground to a halt. With all his bravery and his readiness to die, there was a limit to what even a Japanese soldier could stand. When, day after day, he put in fearless attacks but hardly gained a yard, and when he saw his comrades slaughtered by his side, he must have begun to realize that there was not going to be a triumphal entry into Imphal, and there was not going to be a victorious march on Delhi.

No description of the battles on the Shenam Saddle would be complete without the mention of the work of the American Field Ambulance Service, details of which are movingly described in Evans and Brett-James's masterly book *Imphal*. The Ambulance played its most dramatic role in the battles between 37 Brigade and the Japanese in the hills and valleys around Scraggy, Malta and Gibraltar. The hero of this

Units Involved in Shenam 2

23rd Indian Division (Major-General Ouvry Roberts)
1 Indian Infantry Brigade (Brigadier King)
1st Seaforth Highlanders
1/16th Punjabis
1st Patialas

---

37 Indian Infantry Brigade (Brigadier Marindin)
3/3rd Gurkhas
3/5th Gurkhas
3/10th Gurkhas

---

49 Indian Infantry Brigade (Brigadier Esse)
4/5th Mahrattas
6/5th Mahrattas
5/6th Rajputanas

---

ambulance unit was a young man, Neil Gillian, who had been rejected for military service on medical grounds. Instead, he joined the Field Ambulance Service and after experience in the Western Desert eventually arrived at Shenam. The Field Ambulance Service used big Chevrolet ambulances which could not reach sufficiently far forward on the difficult terrain of Shenam. With the help of the gunners and REME craftsmen, Gillian managed to get some jeeps modified with a structure that could take two stretchers. He organized his team so that when a battalion was engaged it would have the support of the jeep ambulances and their crews from the other battalions. In one of the most violent battles around Gibraltar, he got his jeeps almost into the front line. After the company commander and the medical officer had been killed, he stayed on and organized a first aid post for the very large number of wounded. When the Japanese attacked again, Gillian personally saw to it that the wounded were got out and taken to the jeeps, which were loaded up with more than a dozen wounded men and driven off to safety. His heroic work continued day after day among the fiercest fighting, and the Gurkhas reckoned that he personally saved hundreds of lives. In one battle when the Gurkhas had to evacuate a part of Scraggy, Gillian was still there rescuing wounded men from almost under the noses of the Japanese. After the battle he was recommended for the VC, but as an American he was not eligible for this, but to the great satisfaction of all the units he had served so well, he received the George Medal.

The attack on the Gurkhas and Rajputs of 37 Brigade, which started on 20 May, continued for days, and by 24 May the Japanese had taken a precarious hold on Gibraltar and had cut off the British positions on Malta. This created a very grave situation so the Gurkhas and Rajputs put in a swift counter-attack along the ridge. This led to hand-to-hand fighting with kukri and bayonet, but gradually the Japanese were driven back. Eventually they broke and fled down the steep side of Gibraltar, leaving 150 dead and many more unaccounted for. In this action 37 Brigade lost eleven killed and more than 100 wounded, but it inflicted such damage on the Japanese that there was no major attack for another two weeks. This battle on Gibraltar is of great significance, for it finally showed Yamamoto that he had little chance of breaking through to the Imphal plain via the Shenam Saddle.

While the strengthened 37 Brigade were fighting around Scraggy, Malta and Gibraltar, 1 Brigade had been sent on a broad sweep to the north of the Shenam Saddle to prevent any Japanese advance on that flank, and to remove them from one position they were known to have occupied. As ever, the nameless, gaunt and formidable hills which rose jungle covered out of the monsoon downpour, were quickly given nicknames by the troops, and on this occasion the hill occupied by the

Japanese became 'Ben Nevis'. The Patialas and Punjabis cleared the defenders from several minor positions, but Ben Nevis presented a major obstacle, with the Japanese very well dug-in around a difficult hill feature. It was necessary to bring forward 25-pounders and other heavy weapons to support the attack on Ben Nevis, and this presented serious problems because the basic jeep track became a sea of mud and totally impassable. Gunners and sappers sweated away using all their ingenuity, and, helped by a bulldozer and teams of men, managed to bring four 25-pounders and their ammunition sufficiently close to help with the attack. All was ready on 24 May when there occurred one of those tragic mistakes which occasionally happen during confused fighting in close and difficult country. As the Punjabis were forming up for their attack, they were strafed by a Hurricane and sustained casualties, but this did not deter them. After a susbstantial bombardment they advanced and by midday had captured one of the twin peaks of Ben Nevis. The attack on the other peak proved more difficult, but after an initial setback a second attack went in during the late afternoon and the Japanese were driven off.

The defeat of the Japanese on Ben Nevis confirmed the impression gained in the battles around Scraggy and Gibraltar that they no longer had the reinforcements and supplies to keep up their constant attacks or to mount their usual rapid counter-attacks. After being pushed off Ben Nevis they lay low for four days, and then after an artillery bombardment they attacked again but were driven off.

In the central sector around Scraggy there was an even longer lull in the fighting until, on 9 June, when the whole area was deluged with monsoon rain, the enemy again attacked the Gurkhas on the side of Scraggy. The Gurkhas sustained heavy casualties and the Japanese occupied a part of the hill. The Gurkhas then withdrew to a strong position where they had a good field of fire and some protection from direct enemy observation. It was then decided to abandon that part of Scraggy rather than risk heavy casualties in attempting its recapture.

The final struggle for Scraggy had cost the Gurkhas dear – 23 killed and 113 wounded – but the Japanese had suffered even more heavily. After 9 June they did not make another major attack on 37 Brigade, and the lines remained fairly static for several weeks. 23rd Division had been told to hold the Shenam Saddle to the last man and the last round. That had not proved necessary, but they did sustain heavy losses before the Japanese impetus was finally halted on the devastated ridges of Scraggy. 20th Indian Division deserve the honour for blunting the initial progress of Yamamoto's advance, when he appeared to be carrying all before him, but both divisions are equally deserving of praise for their brave and stubborn defence of this vital sector. From 1 April, when the Borders had been driven off Nippon Hill, every day that passed had reduced the chances of the Japanese achieving the breakthrough they so urgently needed.

THE BATTLE FOR IMPHAL

At the beginning of April, while Slim was extremely worried about the danger of 31st Division advancing past Kohima towards Dimapur, within the Imphal perimeter, the Corps Commander, Scoones, was facing a more stable situation despite the losses suffered by 17th Division during its withdrawal from Tiddim to Bishenpur. The majority of 5th Indian Division had arrived from the Arakan and had been swiftly and successfully deployed to counter the Japanese attack on the north-west of Imphal near Nungshigum, and 20th Division was holding Yamamoto's approach to the Shenam Saddle. This left the south-west approach where 17th Division, reinforced by 32 Brigade from 20th Division, faced its old rivals, Japanese 33rd Division under Yanagida.

One of the first actions in this sector occurred on the Silchar Track. This track led west from Bishenpur through the mountains to Silchar and

Units Involved at Bishenpur

BRITISH FORCES

17th Indian Infantry Division (Major-General Cowan)

---

48 Indian Infantry Brigade (Brigadier Cameron)
9th Borders
2/5th Gurkhas
1/7th Gurkhas
1st West Yorks

---

63 Indian Infantry Brigade (Brigadier Burton)
1/3rd Gurkhas
1/4th Gurkhas
1/10th Gurkhas

---

32 Indian Infantry Brigade (Brigadier Mackenzie)
(Detached from 20th Division)
1st Northamptons
9/14th Punjabis
3/8th Gurkhas

JAPANESE FORCES

33rd Division (General Yanagida/General Tanaka)
214th Infantry Regiment
215th Infantry Regiment

---

the airfields and supply dumps of upper Assam, and it was an obvious target for the Japanese in their attempt to cut off Imphal completely. On 14 April a unit of 20 volunteers from Japanese 215th Regiment, after two weeks of marching through the jungle west of Bishenpur, attacked and destroyed the suspension bridge which took the track over a very deep gorge. Slim, in his book, inaccurately gives the impression that all the men involved perished in the attack, but in fact they sustained few losses and received a hero's welcome when they returned to their unit. This incident signalled the start of the long-drawn-out series of battles in the Bishenpur area between Yanagida's 33rd Division and Cowan's 17th Division supported by 32 Brigade and other units which joined in during the prolonged struggle.

32 Brigade, when it moved down from Shenam, centred on the village of Bishenpur itself, and faced elements of Yanagida's 214th and 215th Regiments. As the front slowly stabilized, 32 Brigade sent a Company of 9/14th Punjabis down the road to Ningthoukhong. During the next few weeks this village, thickly wooded with dense bamboo, and with a stream running through it, witnessed as much heavy shelling and fighting as any village in Burma. The surrounding countryside of marsh and paddy fields skirting Logtak Lake forced a complete change of tactics on the battling forces. The initial clashes of two Punjabi Companies with the Japanese in the village on 7 May were costly and unsuccessful. Tanks took part in the first skirmish, but discovered that the Japanese had brought up a 47mm anti-tank gun, a far more effective weapon than any they had produced before. After the Punjabis had been forced to withdraw, 1/4th Gurkhas mounted a battalion attack, with support from Lee Grant tanks of the 3rd Carabiniers. Very soon two of their leading tanks had been knocked out and two more damaged by the unexpected anti-tank gun. Realizing that Imphal was cut off and no replacement tanks could be expected until the siege was raised, Mackenzie decided to withdraw from Ningthoukhong rather than risk losing any more tanks.

Whenever the leading Japanese units came up against determined resistance and failed to carry all before them, it tended to cause bitter clashes between Japanese commanders at different levels. In the middle of April the CO of 214th Regiment, Colonel Sakuma, was severely criticized for failing to advance, but he maintained that he was facing a wall of steel. Japanese commanders, even the aggressive Mutaguchi, were often a long way behind their forward units and had little idea of the situation on the ground. Sakuma had set out in March with more than 4,000 men in his regiment, but now, before the end of April, he could muster less than 1,000 fighting troops. On 22 April Mutaguchi appeared near the front at Yanagida's 33rd Division Headquarters and demanded to know what was happening. He was highly critical of Yanagida and the performance of 33rd Division and announced that he would take over the direction of the division himself. So confident of victory had he been, that he had brought twenty geisha girls from his HQ in Kalewa, intending to install them in Imphal as soon as it was taken. Ignoring the reality of the situation, he ordered an immediate attack, even though one Company of 214th Regiment was reduced to 80 men and another to only twenty. When Mutaguchi addressed the officers of the division, Yanagida sat in his tent and refused to attend. Later he tried to argue with Mutaguchi, but his senior officers did not support his objections. Secretly, Mutaguchi told 33rd Division's Chief of Staff, Murata, that if necessary he was to overrule Yanagida, who, in any event was going to be replaced as soon as possible.

Although Yanagida was in serious dispute with Mutaguchi, his division still operated quite effectively. It put strong pressure on 32 Brigade, but found that 17th Division could muster strong artillery support for its forward brigades. At this stage of the battle – early May – 32 Brigade had more than twenty guns, including 25-pounders, 3.7in howitzers and six-pounders, and this artillery support was being used, particularly in the area of the Silchar Track and Point 5846 – about halfway between Bishenpur and the ill-fated suspension bridge.

The gunners had a difficult and complex task in this type of fighting, where it was hard to identify a particular target and where positions often changed hands rapidly. In one incident at this time, an Indian unit on a hill known as 'Bastion', came under intense Japanese pressure and gave way. Their men went rushing back, but the gunner unit held firm. As the hill had been lost, the gunners requested permission to fire on it before the Japanese could dig-in, but permission was refused for fear that some of the Indian troops might still be there. It was a tense situation. In the dark and the noise and the rain, it was difficult to know how far the Japanese had penetrated and, for security, the forward units burnt their secret codes and documents. The gunner officers, who did not know Urdu, were unable to cope with the Indian unit that had given way, but a brigade officer who could speak Urdu managed to rally the men and stop the retreat. At daybreak the unit that had given way put in a counter-attack supported by tanks. This failed, but another attack by an Indian Parachute battalion, supported by Stuart tanks, regained the hill and drove off the Japanese. During this engagement, which is scarcely mentioned in official histories, the Japanese lost more than 300 killed.

The 1st Northamptons and 3/8th Gurkhas from 32 Brigade fought a series of close encounters with the Japanese in and around Point 5846. This was an area of such thick jungle and impenetrable bamboo that it did not even receive a nickname. On one occasion the Northamptons were clearing their way through a bamboo thicket and heard movement a few yards away; they found it was a Japanese patrol equally lost in the dense jungle. The Northamptons and Gurkhas established a very strong 'Box' at Point 5846, and repulsed many attacks, but they sustained more than 100 casualties. The Japanese suffered even more. 215th Regiment, under Colonel Sasahara, had had heavy losses in the battles on the Tiddim road, and was now reduced from more than 4,800 to about 400 men fit enough to fight.

The Japanese could not dislodge the defenders of Point 5846, but they did manage to cut the Silchar Track and cut all routes to the defensive Box. For the Northamptons, water became the most important issue, and they had to send armed working parties with their mules down a slippery track to fetch water back up – a climb of more than 1,000 feet. These parties gained considerable protection from Sergeant Kelly, who later became the battalion RSM. He was a sniper, and watched the track day after day – even after he had been wounded – and he claimed 23 victims. As they defended their Box, and struggled to get water, the Northamptons took part in days and days of close and confused fighting, while other units fought to break the Japanese hold on the track and rescue the beleaguered battalion.

In this close and steep country, the British often had the edge in the fighting because of the tanks of 254 Tank Brigade, under Brigadier Scoones, the brother of the Corps Commander. Before the main Imphal battle had started, Scoones had spent a great deal of time with experiments to determine whether tanks could operate in this type of country. Fortunately for IV Corps, arguments as to the feasibility of the concept overcame very strong opposition from the tank experts, and he was given command of 254 Brigade to enable him to prove his point, which he did most effectively.

On 30 April the road was opened and a convoy was able to bring supplies forward to the Northamptons, and to take out some of their wounded – another exercise in which The American Field Service Ambulance distinguished itself. Even this success did not put an end to the dour struggle around the Northamptons' perimeter. Japanese patrols from 214th and 215th Regiments continued to attack convoys on the Silchar Track, and to harass the work parties climbing the 1,000 feet down to the water point and back.

At the end of April, when the Northamptons were still holding on to their positions around Point 5846, Mutaguchi's plan to seize Imphal and Kohima by a quick dash up from the Chindwin had obviously run into serious difficulties, but his forces were still making some progress. This was the time when the Devons and Gurkhas were pushed off Crete by Yamamoto and withdrew to Scraggy, and when the Royal Scots and Royal Norfolks were still plodding through their march to Mount Pulebadze prior to Grover's planned assault on Aradura Spur and

Kohima. In Kohima, since 2nd Division had broken the siege and were being strongly reinforced by 7th Indian Division, Sato's 31st Division were clearly on the defensive. It is little wonder, therefore, that Mutaguchi, who had already had serious clashes with Sato, had left Maymyo and had gone forward to urge more aggressive action by Yamamoto on the Shenam Saddle and Yanagida on the Silchar Track. It had been a grave psychological shock to Mutaguchi when he began to realize that he was not going to capture Imphal and Kohima, and that his personal ambition of leading a victorious march on Delhi was dashed.

Slim kept in close and frequent contact with IV Corps in Imphal, and his assessment of the overall situation in early May was more cheerful than Mutaguchi's. Slim, after his worries in early April, now reckoned that his worst anxieties were over. The Japanese had failed to take Kohima, had not moved towards Dimapur, and were clearly on the defensive as 2nd Division began to advance up the Imphal road. Slim considered that Yamamuchi's 15th Division had been 'well hammered and was losing cohesion' (*Defeat into Victory*, p. 332). To the south of Imphal, Yanagida's 33rd Division was slowly being reinforced by units from the Arakan, but Slim considered that, even with reinforcements, 33rd Division was not strong enough to pose a serious threat to Imphal as a whole. In addition to the British military build-up, British and American control of the air was not effectively challenged and he considered that, as the monsoon came on, although air supply would face additional problems, the difficulties facing the Japanese – especially the supply problem – would increase dramatically.

While the Northamptons continued to defend their Box at Point 5846, the rest of 32 Brigade, based on Bishenpur, were coming to grips with the Japanese in a small village a couple of miles south of Bishenpur, Potsangbam – which inevitably became 'Pots and Pans'. A Company of 9/14th Punjabis, patrolling carefully into the village, found to their surprise two 47mm anti-tank guns, with their crews sitting in the sun brewing tea. The Punjabis, led by their Jemadar (warrant officer), who won the MC, attacked and killed the crews and captured the guns. Soon more Japanese arrived, then more Punjabis, and this initial skirmish developed into a fierce battle involving additional troops from 32 Brigade as well as tanks and artillery. The Japanese were driven off and the Punjabis returned to Bishenpur with some prisoners and four guns. These included a 70mm mountain gun and the 47mm anti-tank guns which were towed back behind the unit's Bren carriers – valuable captures because neither the 47mm nor the 70mm had been taken before.

This fierce short prelude led to a long-drawn-out struggle for Potsangbam itself, where the Japanese were strongly entrenched. Although tanks were to be a valuable support for the Indian and British infantry attacks, at Potsangbam they did not have an easy time. Paddy fields, with deep water-filled ditches surrounded the village; these proved to be dangerous obstacles for tanks and restricted their movement to the main roads. The Japanese defenders had realized this, and had sited their 47mm anti-tank guns at strategic spots, and covered other roads with anti-tank mines. The first attack in support of the Punjabis lost several tanks to enemy fire; one overturned in a ditch, two pulled out with damaged tracks, and another with a faulty starter motor. As the action proceeded, others sank in the mud or got bogged down in ditches. Despite these set-backs the tanks were not badly damaged, and continued to use their guns and machine-guns to support the advancing infantry. The Punjabi battalion sustained heavy casualties – 40 killed and 100 wounded – and were dangerously reduced in numbers. After this clash, because 32 Brigade had been so heavily involved at Potsangbam and on the Silchar Track, 63 Brigade (Burton), with three Gurkha battalions, took over the responsibility for Potsangbam, and 9/14th Punjabis withdrew.

17th Division's Support Battalion, 1st West Yorks, were sent to occupy positions forward of Potsangbam and down the road towards Ningthoukhong. They held this unpleasant waterlogged spot for several weeks during May while both British and Japanese wheeled all round them, engaging in fierce encounters which cost both sides heavy casualties. The West Yorks could not dig in properly because of the waterlogged, low-lying soil, and their positions were exposed to artillery and sniper fire. From their exposed positions and under the monsoon downpour, they began to lose men from footrot – another link to the Battle of the Somme.

While the position stabilized around Potsangbam, Cowan decided to counter-attack by sending a brigade-strong unit southwards, parallel to the Tiddim road, to cut off the forward Japanese units and strangle their supply lines. He intended that when this force was in place, he would send 63 Brigade to advance south through Potsangbam and crush the Japanese between his two brigades. 2/5th Gurkhas and 1/7th Gurkhas from 48 Brigade set off in early May (the actual date is disputed) and took a wide sweep eastwards past Logtak Lake. They had to traverse high steep hills through very dense jungle under heavy monsoon rain, but reached their objective, Torbung, on 16 May. Here they were able to take an air drop on a hill overlooking the road. The Gurkhas set up an ambush, destroyed some tanks, and then destroyed several convoys of trucks which were bringing up food, weapons, ammunition and reinforcements for the forward units. The leading driver of one convoy asked a Gurkha sentry if the road was clear, and was waved on – into the bag! The Gurkha positions on high ground east of the road enabled them to observe all traffic and destroy large quantities of supplies. The Japanese quickly realized what a serious threat this posed to them and mounted swift counter-attacks, but these were beaten off. 33rd Division was determined to break this hold on their life-line and put the Gurkhas under considerable pressure.

At the same time, when Cowan sent 63 Brigade to advance southwards from Potsangbam, it quickly ran into trouble. The brigade moved off into the hills south-west of Bishenpur, but met very stiff opposition which, without tanks and artillery support, could not be overcome. When 63 Brigade failed to advance, it created a difficult situation for Cameron and the Gurkha battalions of 48 Brigade, still holding out at Torbung. They were now dangerously isolated and were having to form a defensive Box as they fought their way north. This was not an easy operation, and at the village of Ningthoukhong, where the Japanese were powerfully entrenched, they had to make a wide detour before they could join up with 63 Brigade. Cowan's plan had not succeeded and the Japanese had not been crushed between his pincer movements, but the Gurkhas, at a fairly heavy cost to themselves, had inflicted another 1,000 casualties on the Japanese.

In all the actions in the area of Bishenpur, the Silchar Track and Potsangbam, the infantry had remarkable support from the artillery. Each Indian Division included one field regiment – three batteries with two troops of four 25-pounders; one jungle field regiment with 25-pounders, 3.7in howitzers and 4.2-inch mortars; and one mountain regiment, a combined anti-tank and anti-aircraft unit with Bofors guns. In addition, each Corps HQ controlled one medium regiment with 5.5in gun/ howitzers. At the end of April when the battles around Bishenpur were starting, the artillery was concentrated as a brigade group, located in the Gunner Box about a mile north of the place where the Silchar Track joins the Tiddim–Imphal road. A large concentration of guns had obvious advantages, but despite dummy decoys it could not be concealed, and the Japanese not only engaged in counter battery fire, but also put in infantry and air assaults on the Gunner Box during May. In one infantry attack on 8 May, one gun was destroyed, but the battery inflicted thirteen casualties on the enemy, and on 10 May twelve aircraft attacked the Box and four were destroyed.

In the type of battle which took place around Bishenpur, where visibility was so poor, there had to be very close liaison between the gunners and the infantry units. Usually forward observation officers, or occasionally the battery or troop commander, would patrol with the infantry. Nearly all the actions mentioned had the direct support of field or medium artillery, as did the units fighting at Shenam where the gunners sustained heavy losses around Scraggy and Gibraltar. As the initiative in Imphal was slowly wrested from the Japanese, 8 Medium

Regiment deployed one of its troops with each of the four divisions, thus providing heavier support for the divisional guns.

By the middle of May, although Yanagida knew he was to be replaced by Tanaka as commander of 33rd Division, he was still attempting to carry out Mutaguchi's orders to capture Bishenpur and Imphal, and decided on a fairly straightforward plan. He ordered 214th Regiment (Sakuma) to advance northwards over the Silchar Track to Nungang, a point just to the west of Buri Bazaar, and from there to put in an attack on Imphal with two battalions. Simultaneously, he ordered 215th Regiment (Sasahara) to capture Bishenpur and advance up the road to Imphal to link up with 214th Regiment. Sakuma criticized this plan, pointing out, reasonably enough, that if 215th Regiment failed to take Bishenpur as ordered – and they had already failed several times – 214th Regiment would be hopelessly isolated and in a very dangerous situation.

Being a well-disciplined officer, Sakuma, despite his objections, set off on 16 May with 214th Regiment on a forced march to Nungang, the point from which he was to attack Imphal. For four days, in torrential monsoon rain which turned streams into dangerous torrents that swept his men away, and through floods which covered his heavily laden men up to their waists, Sakuma's men grimly kept going, but not without open grumbling and criticism of the senselessness of the whole expedition.

Sakuma had been wise to doubt the ability of 215th Regiment to take Bishenpur, but in fact they achieved a considerable degree of success. Sasahara's men, supported by part of 213th Regiment, which had slipped up past Potsangbam, made a surprise attack on 32 Brigade HQ and the Gunner box in the early hours of 20 May. The main attack fell on 9/14th Punjabis and 3rd Carabiniers. In a wild mélée in pitch darkness and driving rain – the same storm that had dogged the march of 214th Regiment – both sides lost many men. By daybreak more than 100 Japanese were dug-in with machine-gun and mortars on the north-east of Bishenpur village – a very dangerous threat to Mackenzie's 32 Brigade.

There then followed one of the extremely unpleasant accidents of war, caused in this case by units having to be hurriedly moved from one part of the front to another. When 63 Brigade had set off from Bishenpur on its march to Torbung, it left behind its administrative tail, including nearly 300 mules. There was a mix-up in the arrangements for the mules, and the unfortunate animals were caught up in a chaotic battle in which Brigade HQ, 9/14th Punjabis, 3rd Carabiniers, 9/12th Frontier Force Regiment (hurriedly brought in from 20th Division), and various batteries of gunners all took part. The Japanese intruders became hopelessly enmeshed in the area where the mules were tethered, and began to use them as cover from enemy fire. The British, trying to contain the Japanese, hurriedly erected wire so that in the end the Japanese were herded in with the mules and subjected to artillery, rifle, automatic and mortar fire. Tanks were brought in, but in the driving rain and flooded conditions several got bogged down – only adding to the chaos. Close-quarter fighting, firing and mortaring went on for several days, during which the stench from the disintegrating bodies of both men and mules was so overpowering that the troops had to be issued with field dressings soaked in eucalyptus to stop them vomiting. Finally, the Japanese intruders were overcome, and when the position was taken, more than 120 of their casualties were found, together with the carcasses of 300 mules. Such was the stench that bulldozers were brought in to dig a huge pit, and the bodies were covered with tons of lime. Two small groups of Japanese managed to get away from the main body and on 25 May, with no thought of returning safely to base, they attacked the Gunner Box, but were cornered and killed.

While this gruesome battle was taking place, Sakuma's 214th Regiment came close to achieving a remarkable *coup*. Having set out on 16 May, after three days of torrential rain they reached Nungang and prepared to cut the Bishenpur–Imphal road, and establish a strong point at the tiny village of Chingphu. Unbeknown to Sakuma, General Cowan had moved the HQ of 17th Division to this very spot. When a Company of 214th Regiment attacked this lightly defended position, it created an extremely dangerous situation and caused considerable alarm in 17th Division.

To contain this new threat, units were hurriedly brought in from 17th Division, 20th Division and the Corps reserve – 3/1st Gurkhas, 6/5th Mahrattas, 9/12th Frontier Force Regiment and tanks from 3rd Cara-biniers. The battle started with the usual confusion while the platoons in the immediate vicinity engaged in hand-to-hand fighting with bayonets, kukris and grenades, and tried to establish how large an incursion had been made. 214th Regiment, even after their long march, and with their men exhausted and sick, had managed as they always did to set up an effective strongpoint which they defended with great skill and deter-mination, and from which they vigorously repulsed every attack. After two days Cowan decided to bring up 50 Indian Parachute Brigade, which had been reformed after the battle of Sangshak. Both sides sustained heavy casualties, and neither side made much headway. Hurriedly assembled units quickly ran out of ammunition, and Bren carriers bringing up more ammunition got bogged down in paddy fields, and themselves had to be rescued. In one incident a British wireless operator was in touch with a Gurkha unit, but all the officers had been killed, and there was no one in the unit who could speak English. Eventually some Gurkhali phrases were passed on and this led to a successful attack. On 30

May the Japanese withdrew from a small hill they had held from the start of the battle, leaving behind more than 100 bodies and some prisoners in the last stages of shock, exhaustion and starvation. One prisoner confirmed that except for him his entire Company had been wiped out. 214th Regiment was so completely isolated that even the sick and wounded were forced to fight on. This usually meant standing in a slit trench up the waist in water, under an incessant monsoon downpour, shivering from beri-beri, malaria or dysentery, and waiting for another attack by Indian, Gurkha or British troops who appeared well fed and fully supplied with ammunition.

Sakuma had sent another group – about 400 men – to make a second block on the Bishenpur road. They too dug in carefully, but they had no anti-tank weapons, and when the 3rd Carabiniers advanced with tanks the whole unit was destroyed. Of the 900 men of 214th Regiment who had set out on their forced march with Sakuma, only 60 survived to march away.

The two famous Japanese Regiments, 214th and 215th, had been virtually wiped out in their attack on Bishenpur – as effective fighting units they were finished. Some battalions were reduced to less than 40 men and many of those were sick or wounded. Some Companies numbered as little as three men with not an officer among them. In 33rd Division as a whole, only two battalion commanders had not been killed or wounded.

On 30 May Sakuma, with the pathetic remnant of his once fine regiment, faced almost total disaster, but then learned that another battalion was coming to support him. This proved to be not a fresh well-trained infantry battalion, but a motley collection of about 250 sick and wounded men, about 100 of whom were caught and killed by an artillery barrage before they reached Sakuma's HQ. At the same time Tanaka, who had now replaced Yanagida, issued a resounding order of the day. It is not difficult to imagine the effect of this order on the broken and emaciated troops who had lost hundreds of their comrades, who were being harried both on the ground and from the air, and were at the end of their tether. Tanaka said, 'Our death-defying infantry expects certain victory when it penetrates the fortress of the enemy . . . this will decide the success of the Great Asia War . . . regard death as lighter than a feather . . . expect that the Division will be almost annihilated . . . the infantry group is in high spirits and afire with valour. All officers and men fight courageously.' (Evans and Brett-James, *Imphal*, p. 305.)

Tanaka's aggressive orders had rather more effect on the units lying to the south of Bishenpur, in the area of Potsangbam and Ningthou-khong. On 7 June, using reinforcements from 154th Regiment which had just arrived from the Arakan, the Japanese mounted a strong attack on the fringe of the village of Ningthoukhong which was still held by 1st West Yorks. The attack fell on the leading platoon of the West Yorks — itself reduced to twenty men. The platoon was stretched to the limit to hold their carefully prepared positions, but the platoon sergeant, Sergeant Turner, rushed at the Japanese attackers hurling grenades. Five times he went back for more grenades, and five times charged the enemy until they withdrew. In the final clash he was killed. He was awarded a posthumous VC. The Japanese lost 60 out of 80 men, but the West Yorks had 50 casualties, and were shortly afterwards replaced.

Despite their setback at the hands of the West Yorks, the Japanese advance continued against 1/7th and 2/5th Gurkhas of 48 Brigade, holding another part of Ningthoukhong. The Gurkhas were well prepared, but they had heard tank engines coming closer during the night. The Japanese had a slight advantage at this time because their lighter tanks could move over the paddy fields where the heavier British tanks got bogged down. However, the Gurkhas were not too apprehensive about the approaching tanks because they had been issued with the new PIAT (Projector Infantry Anti-Tank). This was a cheap, light, mass-produced weapon which was remarkably effective against tanks, as the Japanese were about to discover. The Gurkhas were being hard pressed to hold their positions against attacks by both tanks and infantry, when a young Gurkha rifleman, Ganju Lama, though he had been wounded three times, crawled forward with his PIAT and destroyed the two leading tanks. He had won the MM a few weeks before, but for this exemplary bravery he received the VC.

Tanaka's hollow words had done little to encourage Sakuma and the remnant of 214th Regiment, and at the end of May they withdrew to approximately the line of the Silchar Track where Japanese and British units still faced each other, but with gravely reduced numbers. The Northamptons, Gurkhas and Punjabis of 32 Brigade had continued to hold out during weeks of close fighting in the area of Mortar Bluff and Water Piquet, close to Point 5846. Somehow, despite all their losses and suffering, the Japanese managed to put in a strong attack on Mortar Bluff. Attack and counter-attack continued in pouring rain, and the Northamptons were reduced to fewer than two Companies. In hand-to-hand combat the Japanese were brought to a standstill. One action illustrates the type of fighting which continued for so long. A platoon of Gurkhas, led by their platoon commander, Netrabahadur, set out to retake Mortar Bluff. They occupied the small hill in pouring rain and pitch darkness, but were immediately surrounded and subjected to powerful Japanese attacks. The Subadar kept in wireless contact with his CO at Battalion HQ during the hours of blackness and chaos as more and more attacks fell on the unit. At about 0400 hours contact ceased and Battalion realized that the Gurkha platoon had been overrun. The Subadar, Netrabahadur, had displayed indomitable leadership of his platoon, and when the position was recaptured his body was found, still clutching his kukri with which he had decapitated his attacker. He was awarded a posthumous VC. Further desperately fought battles continued in this whole area, and in these another VC and many other bravery awards were won. Fighting along the Silchar Track and around Point 5846, which the Northamptons and the Gurkhas had held for so long and at such a high cost, continued throughout June and into July.

Both sides continued to suffer heavy casualties, but while 32 Brigade could be reinforced by units and men drawn from 48 Brigade or 63 Brigade, and could when necessary receive supplies, food and ammunition by air, the Japanese received very few supplies or reinforcements, and they knew they could not save their wounded. In early July Sakuma and 214th Regiment were at last ordered to withdraw from the Silchar Track – the scene of such prolonged fighting – and to move to a point about four miles further south. There are harrowing descriptions of the sufferings of the badly wounded Japanese during this move. A group of 50 wounded men, with an escort, set out ahead of the main body. Many had lost a leg or an arm, or were seriously ill with dysentery or malaria. Some could only move 100 yards before having to stop to rest. They passed hundreds of corpses, and a few wounded men, many of whom begged for a grenade so that they could put an end to their suffering. Many of the group took their own grenades and went off the track and into the jungle to kill themselves. Of the 50 who set out, only eight survived the four-mile journey.

After a campaign that had seen his regiment decimated and the few survivors too ill or badly wounded to fight, Sakuma had no relief from trouble. Tanaka came to a forward post to meet him. Sakuma argued that his regiment was in such poor shape that it should be pulled out so that it could be reinforced and reformed as a fighting unit. He added that Mutaguchi had completely misjudged the strength and determination of the British defences around Imphal, and that it was time that the senseless slaughter stopped. Tanaka was able to see the pitiful state of 214th Regiment, but any sympathy he might have felt was overruled when he and Sakuma received orders that the regiment was to move at once to attack Palel. One of Sakuma's officers protested at this further futile sacrifice, and when rebuked left the tent and killed himself with a grenade. Sakuma was forced to set out towards Palel with a tiny band of men fit enough to march, after the sick and wounded had been left behind. After another day, having made scarcely any progress, on 8 July his orders were changed again and he was told to make for Tiddim – a hundred miles to the south. He was to see Bishenpur no more.

THE NORTHERN SECTOR

The struggle on the northern sector really started on 26 March when the advanced units of the Japanese 15th Division under Yamauchi, which had skirted south of the great battle at Sangshak, reached the village of Litan, about seven miles south-west of Sangshak and sixteen miles north-west of Imphal. This position was lightly held by 2/1st Punjabis from 123 Indian Infantry Brigade which, as part of 5th Indian Division, had just flown in from the Arakan. The Punjabis had been hurriedly sent forward

Imphal: The Northern Sector, 12 April to 22 June 1944

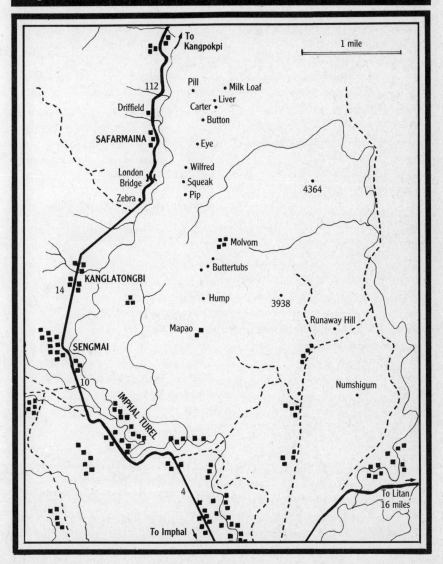

to Litan, and it was soon realized that they were in a dangerously isolated position. They were therefore withdrawn to Kameng, where a firm and well-defended position was established across a wide valley. The main road from Imphal to Ukhrul ran down this valley which, in contrast to most of the Imphal battle area, featured not dense jungle but fairly open scrubland with just a few trees.

Yamauchi felt reasonably pleased at his progress as far as this. In stark contrast to the coarse and brutal Mutaguchi with his coterie of comfort girls, Yamauchi, a sensitive and intelligent man who was already seriously ill with tuberculosis, was deeply worried about the huge

Units Involved at the Battle for Imphal

BRITISH FORCES

THE NORTHERN SECTOR
5th Indian Infantry Division (Briggs)

9 Indian Infantry Brigade (Salomons)
2nd West Yorks
3/9th Jats
3/14th Punjabis

123 Indian Infantry Brigade (Evans)
2nd Suffolks
2/1st Punjabis
1/17th Dogras

(161 Brigade at Kohima)

89 Brigade (Crowther) Attached later from 7th Indian Division
2nd King's Own Scottish Borderers
7/2nd Punjabis
4/8th Gurkhas

23rd Indian Infantry Division (Roberts)

1 Indian Infantry Brigade (McCoy)
1st Seaforth Highlanders
1/16th Punjabis
1st Patialas

37 Indian Infantry Brigade (Marindin)
3/3rd Gurkhas

3/5th Gurkhas
3/10th Gurkhas

49 Indian Infantry Brigade (At Imphal)

20th Indian Infantry Division (Gracey)
This division came down from Shenam and replaced 23rd Division

80 Indian Infantry Brigade (Greeves)
1st Devons
9/12th Frontier Force Regiment
3/1st Gurkhas

100 Indian Infantry Brigade (James)
2nd Borders
14/13th Frontier Force Rifles
4/10th Gurkhas

ARMOUR
254 Tank Brigade (Scoones)
3rd Carabiniers
7th Cavalry
150 Regiment RAC

JAPANESE FORCES
15th Infantry Division (Yamauchi)

51st Regiment (Omoto)
60th Regiment (Matsumura)

military potential of America now geared up against Japan. He had served as a military attaché in Washington and had a good understanding of the global situation, but in spite of his worries, his latest and perhaps his last command had gone well. He had had to divert some of his infantry battalions to go to Indaw to face the attack by Wingate's Chindits, but even with this drawback, the leading reconnaissance units of 15th Division had driven forward, and on 28 March had cut the Imphal–Kohima road at Kangpopki Mission. Both 51st Regiment (Omoto) and 60th Regiment (Matsumura) quickly established strong defences near Mission at Kanglatongbi, and at Mapao. These were important strategic positions giving them control over a range of hills which looked down over the Imphal plain and dominated the road to Kohima.

To cut this road had been a great achievement, and created a major crisis for Slim and Scoones, but the front Japanese Companies had serious communication problems. They were separated from 15th Divisional HQ at Kasom by high jungle-covered peaks and deep precipitous valleys, and their supply route was precarious. Before they actually cut the Kohima road they had noted, enviously, that 120 trucks an hour were going into Imphal. After this they were even more envious, as, cut off from nearly all supplies, they watched a constant stream of aircraft bringing food, ammunition and reinforcements into the airstrips at Imphal and Kangla.

On this section of the front, too, the Japanese attackers were soon to discover, as their comrades at Shenam and Bishenpur had, that the British forces could no longer be lightly brushed aside. On 1 April at Kameng, a Japanese platoon was hurled into the attack – against the wishes of the platoon commander who wanted to carry out a reconnaissance. Eighty men started the attack, and a few hours later eight broken men limped back and reported that the British had both tanks and flame-throwers in their defences.

When Intelligence reports had brought in sufficient detail of the attacking Japanese forces, Scoones made a fairly straightforward plan. Using 5th Indian Division – less 161 Brigade which had been detached to defend Kohima – he placed 123 Brigade (Evans) to defend the road going north-west through Kameng to Yangangpokpi; and 9 Brigade (Salomons) to face the threat from the north on the main road from Imphal to Kohima going past Sengmai and Kanglatongbi.

After the Punjabis had been withdrawn from Litan, the Japanese did not follow up very quickly and 123 Brigade had sufficient time to create a powerful defensive position just behind Kameng. The 2nd Suffolks and 1/17th Dogras held the forward posts at Kameng, while the Brigade perimeter included 2/1st Punjabis, a squadron of 3rd Carabiniers, a squadron of 7th Cavalry together with 28 Field Regiment, a sapper field company and a field ambulance. On 4 and 5 April the first serious attacks were made on the Dogras' positions, but with the aid of carefully hidden barbed wire and carefully sited light and medium machine-guns and mortars the attack was driven off fairly easily. More than 100 men took part in the attack, and 98 corpses were found on and around the barbed wire defences in front of the Dogras' positions.

This setback to the Japanese advance took place while the units from 60th Regiment were probing southwards, from where they had cut the Kohima road, towards the large British stores dump at Kanglatongbi. Some of the stores were rescued by 9 Brigade, but the Japanese took the dump and then, sensibly, sent a small patrol to destroy the water-pumping station which supplied Imphal. The patrol went in and wrecked the valves, thinking they had effectively cut off all water supplies to Imphal. The night watchman, who fortunately for him had slipped away before the Japanese arrived, and, fearful that he would be ticked-off for leaving his post, merely switched over to the reserve system which continued to function throughout the siege.

The incident of the pumping-station and the setback to 51st Regiment in its attack on the Dogras, were the prelude to one of the biggest and most significant battles on this front – the battle for the great hill feature of Nungshigum. This was an uneven ridge, more than three miles long and rising from the level of the Imphal plain to peaks of more than 3,700 feet. Yamauchi realized that from Nungshigum – only six miles from IV Corps Headquarters – his forces could dominate the roads going north from Imphal, and could directly theaten the Kangla airstrip beside the road to Litan.

On the British side the defence of Nungshigum was switched to 9 Brigade. Salomons had few men to spare so he sent only two platoons of the 3/9th Jat Regiment to hold Nungshigum. On 6 April they sweated up the steep hills and reached the summit. By this time the Japanese had grasped the significance of Nungshigum, and before the Jats had had time to dig-in or put up wire, a powerful forces from 51st Regiment mounted a major assault. The two Jat platoons sustained heavy casualties and had to be withdrawn, but the next day the Jat Battalion counter-attacked and drove the Japanese off the hill again. Yamauchi calculated that if he captured and held Nungshigum it would pose a serious and permanent threat to IV Corps and the whole of the Imphal defensive system. He therefore sent forward heavier guns, including a troop of 75mm guns, and on 11 April after frequent and determined attacks by 51st Regiment, the Jats were again driven off Nungshigum.

On 12 April at 5th Division HQ, a major conference took place, which included Briggs, the commanders of 9 and 123 Brigades, Brigadier Scoones, commanding 254 Tank Brigade, and Wing Commander Archer from 221 Group RAF. It was decided that 1/17th Dogra Battalion from

123 Brigade would attack the hill on 13 April, supported by two squadrons of Vengeance dive-bombers, a squadron of Hurricanes, all the 5th divisional artillery and 'B' Squadron, 3rd Carabiniers.

The steepness of the sides and the narrowness of the top ridge on Nungshigum to some extent dictated the type of attack that could be launched. The plan was for the attack to start with bombing and strafing by the Vengeances and Hurribombers, then a bombardment from more than 80 guns from 5th Divisional artillery, followed by another machine-gun attack from the Hurricanes, before two Companies of the Dogras and a troop of tanks made the actual assault.

At first light on 13 April, the tanks and infantry got into position, and at 1030 hours the assault started with the air attack. At 1050 the artillery took over and 9 Brigade created a diversion on the west side of Nungshigum to distract the defenders. Following the pounding by the aircraft and guns, the tanks and infantry moved up. One remarkable thing about this battle was that, because of the configuration of the ground, the troops of Japanese 51st Regiment from their defences could see the whole of the attack forming up. Similarly, while the battle raged the British commander and troops of 5th Indian Division could see everything that was happening. One Japanese soldier recalled that he had had to dig a trench for the adjutant, and another for the sergeant-major, and then he was too tired to dig his own properly. He woke early in the morning to a brilliantly fine day, and looked down to see all the activity below him – guns, men and, most ominously, tanks. Japanese soldiers had been told that the British had no tanks in Burma, but as they looked down from Nungshigum most were not too worried, because they were convinced that no tank could possibly climb such steep inclines.

By 1130 the two Companies of Dogras and six tanks had arrived very close to the summit, and at the end of the very narrow ridge which would restrict tank movement to single file. As soon as the supporting artillery ceased fire, the tanks moved slowly forward, a few yards ahead of the infantry. The ground was so steep that the guns from the tanks could not be depressed sufficiently to engage the enemy bunkers, and so the commander of each tank had to stand up and look out of his turret in order to direct the fire. The tanks advanced on the front Japanese bunkers and some Japanese ran forward to fix magnet mines to the tanks. The tank commanders, with pistols and grenades, drove these attackers away, but having to stand up in full view of the enemy made them extremely vulnerable to small-arms and sniper fire.

Within a few minutes of reaching the crest of the hill, and with close hand-to-hand fighting continuing all round them, the tanks inched slowly forward, only to suffer disastrous casualties as, first one tank commander, then another, then five of the six commanders were killed or seriously wounded. In the midst of this mêlée, a tank slithered on the edge of a hill, and to the horror of the spectators, including the top brass down on the plain, it fell over a cliff and dropped 100 feet. Everyone assumed it would be a total write-off, but the crew were not seriously hurt and only one of the tracks was damaged. The tank was recovered the next day.

The infantry and tanks were not in radio contact, and this caused further casualties when officers of the Dogras had to climb on to the tanks to explain their needs to each tank commander. The situation became critical. All the officers in the tanks had been killed, and all the Dogras' officers, including the two Company commanders, had been killed or seriously wounded, and at this stage the whole attack could have failed. That it succeeded, was due to the remarkable bravery of Sergeant-Major Craddock of 3rd Carabiniers, and the senior Viceroy Commissioned Officer of the Dogras, Subadar Rambir Singh. The Japanese defences centred on three bunkers, deeply dug and with heavy timber providing good head cover which had already withstood the air and artillery bombardment. Craddock and Rambir Singh decided to get the tanks close enough to fire at point-blank range into the bunkers, while the accompanying infantry went in with the bayonet. The Dogras rushed forward to within a few yards of the bunkers but even then were driven back. Craddock and Rambir Singh quickly conferred again, and then managed to get another tank to go up the hill so that it could come down on top of a bunker. The sight of this was too much even for the stoical defenders inside the bunkers and they broke away and fled down the hill.

The commander of 51st Regiment, Colonel Omoto, had also been observing the progress of the battle. At first he refused to believe that tanks could be fighting on the crest of the hill and when, through binoculars, he saw the final tank assault, he cried, 'We're done for! That's it!' (Louis Allen, p. 257.) Soon afterwards, an officer in the final stages of exhaustion staggered into Omoto's HQ and told him that the battalion on Nungshigum had been overrun by tanks and annihilated. Omoto discovered that all the Japanese officers involved in the fight had been killed or wounded, and so, after an ineffective counter-attack which was easily repelled, 51st Regiment withdrew from the peak of Nungshigum, having lost 250 men and a large quantity of arms and equipment.

The victory at Nungshigum, brought about by the remarkably close co-operation between the infantry and tanks, the Dogras and the Carabiniers, had been won at a heavy cost – including the loss of all the officers of 'B' Squadron. Sergeant-Major Craddock's bravery and deter-mination is still commemorated annually when on the anniversary of Nungshigum, 'B' Squadron 3rd Carabiniers (Now the Royal Scots Dragoon Guards) parades under command of the Squadron Sergeant-

Major. For the bravery shown in this action, Sergeant-Major Craddock won the DCM. One DSO, three MCs, two MMs and one Indian Order of Merit were also awarded.

Both sides quickly appreciated the significance of the victory at Nungshigum. IV Corps HQ, hoping to exploit the victory, sent off 1 Brigade (McCoy) from 23rd Division to try to outflank the Japanese, and to attempt to capture Yamauchi's divisional headquarters in the area of Khasom. 1 Brigade (Seaforths, 1/16th Punjabis, 1st Patialas) with 16 Mountain Battery set off as rapidly as possible on a long march east and north to Khasom. At the end of their march, assisted by an accurate RAF attack on Khasom, the Seaforths rushed in and drove out the Japanese garrison. The Punjabis and Patialas attacked other positions in the area, and all three battalions quickly dug-in and wired up their positions against the inevitable counter-attack. Soon after these successful actions, 37 Brigade (3/3rd, 3/5th and 3/10th Gurkha) drove northwards from Kameng, past Yangangpokpi, and cleared the road as far as 1 Brigade in Khasom. 23rd Division had a relatively easy task during this phase of the fighting, when 15th Division were making fairly rapid withdrawals, but in early May they were withdrawn from this sector and sent to replace 20th Division on the forbidding heights of Shenam.

The British victory at Nungshigum made an immediate impact on Yamauchi's 15th Divsion, especially those units lying to the north-west and holding the Kohima road near Sengmai. If Omoto withdrew from the Nungshigum area, he would put 60th Regiment (Matsumura), holding Sengmai, in serious trouble. Such a decision would have to be made by Yamauchi himself. Already a sick man, he had been devastated by the losses his troops had suffered at Nungshigum, and by the realization that he had absolutely no answer to the British tanks. This weighed heavily with him, but knowing that Omoto's fine 51st Regiment had been reduced to a miserable remnant with little will to fight, Yamauchi made the decision to withdraw. Later, Japanese historians attributed their overall defeat in Burma to the disastrously mistaken assumption – made before Mutaguchi's three divisions crossed the Chindwin in March – that they would not encounter British tanks.

Yamauchi ordered the withdrawal of 51st Regiment from Nung-shigum, but he still had scattered units around Kanglatongbi on the Kohima road, and in strong defensive positions in the mountainous country around Mapao. Even from here the Japanese could see Imphal and the airstrips in constant use, with aircraft bringing in supplies and taking out the wounded. These Japanese units now had to face the advance of 5th Indian Division. Compared to their great victory at Nungshigum, the next phase of their fighting was more routine. 9 Brigade slowly pressed the Japanese towards Mapao Ridge, and in one action

Jemadar Hafiz of the 3rd Jats won the VC for his inspiring leadership in an attack on an enemy position at Mapao; under his fierce onslaught the defenders broke and ran away, and the hill became known as Runaway Hill.

The Indian and British soldiers of 5th Indian Division faced a lengthy struggle in the hills around Mapao. Here, the Japanese, knowing they were virtually cut off and that they were unlikely to receive supplies or reinforcements, were determined to fight to the death. In increasingly difficult conditions 9 Brigade plodded on. The 2nd West Yorks – a fine and experienced battalion from an excellent county regiment – played a major role in this grim but unspectacular fighting. They spent weeks in unpleasant and isolated positions and their views do not always accord with the self-satisfied views expressed in some histories. They felt it was a platoon or Company war, and thought that even battalion headquarters was a bit cushy – as for brigade, division or corps headquarters, they were hardly in the fighting at all. While other units responded to Mountbatten's leadership, the West Yorks response was unethusiastic. They thought he was a bit too flashy, and when he talked to them about the advance to Rangoon and Singapore, one soldier grunted 'And we'll march every bloody mile.' Similarly, although Public Relations had done a good job in presenting Slim throughout Fourteenth Army, one day he visited the West Yorks and went quickly from one platoon to another. That evening one platoon commander asked a colleague, 'Who was that old chap you sent over to us this afternoon?'

In contrast to this impression of cynicism, there was an intense feeling for the unit. Professor Kenneth Ingham, who served in the battalion and won the MC in this fighting, has recalled the remarkable loyalty of Private Ike Burney. He had been wounded and was due to be posted to another Yorkshire regiment. The Duke of Wellington's. This meant he would be flown out of the siege to recuperate in India. He begged his platoon commander to fix things with the adjutant so that he did not have to leave his mates in 7 Platoon. This was done, and a few days later the officer walked past. Burney was in a slit trench, up to his knees in water, under a heavy Japanese bombardment, and he said 'Thank you Sir for fixing that up, I am so content to be back with my muckers.' Later the officer received an invitation, 'With the compliments of 7 platoon, would you please come and dine with us, but please bring your own mess tin.'

The real trial to everyone in this type of fighting was the continual slog, the severe physical pressure under the constant downpour, with everything soaking wet. Add to this the effect of a very poor diet over a long period, and the psychological effect of constantly losing old friends with whom you had lived for months or years. In the platoons the burial of a comrade became a regular routine. When a man was killed his section would quickly dig a trench, put the body in a blanket, an officer would say a few words, and a rough cross would be erected to mark the spot. Later the exact spot with full map reference and other details would be entered in Company records. Even these basic ceremonies were not always possible, and very few bodies lost out in the jungle were ever re-buried in the official cemeteries. In such conditions there was always some resentment among both officers and men about the staff at headquarters safely behind the lines. One officer dealing with a movement order said with some bitterness, 'I suppose the barons will go to Calcutta, while we serfs slog it out in Imphal.' This feeling was brilliantly parodied when Noël Coward flew into Imphal during the siege. Some people were slightly critical that his grand piano had to be flown in too, but the majority enjoyed his songs including

> 'He was dropped on his head,
> At the age of two,
> So now he's on the Staff,
> Up at GHQ.'

Or in similar vein, 'Sticking it out at the Cecil,*
> Doing our bit for the war,
> Going through hell,
> At Maiden's hotel,*
> Where they stop serving drinks prompt at four.'

Most units thought that Corps Headquarters, even though it was in the siege, had a much easier time than the fighting units. It was, rightly, blamed for things that went wrong – especially on the supply side. During prolonged periods in battle, under very difficult conditions, there would always be some criticism, but it was the spirit of a good unit that really kept men going.

For 5th Indian Division most of the fighting at this stage was patrolling in thick jungle under a monsoon downpour. Even in the best units this often resulted in complete confusion. On one occasion a patrol was fired on by its own artillery. The patrol leader got through on his wireless to the gunners at division HQ and said, 'Please tell the guns to stop because they are firing on us, but please give us the map reference because we are totally lost.' Each unit worked out its own techniques for attacking bunkers. There was always the closest support and co-operation with the RAF – one successful technique was for Hurricanes to come over three times to bomb or strafe, and then come a fourth time, without bombing or strafing, to make the enemy keep their heads down, while the infantry put in their attack.

*Two famous hotels frequently by senior officers.

In the struggle to defeat the Japanese in their defensive positions along the road going north to Kohima, 5th Indian Division was reinforced by 89 Brigade (2nd King's Own Scottish Borderers, 4/8th Gurkhas, 1/11th Sikhs) from 7th Indian Division, the remainder of which was still involved in the fighting at Kohima. The fighting centred on Sengmai, Kanglatongbi (then still held by the Japanese), and the formidable hill features around Molvom. 5th Indian Division commander (Briggs) ordered 123 Brigade to clear the road, while 89 Brigade cleared the enemy from the surrounding hills. This powerful attack by two brigades achieved some success after fierce jungle fighting, and the initial Japanese road-blocks and defensive posts were overcome, but the defenders merely retreated a short way to another good defensive position. In nearly a month's hard fighting throughout May, during which 9 Brigade (West Yorks, 3/9th Jats, 3/14th Punjabis) replaced 89 Brigade as the vanguard of 5th Division, the division advanced about fifteen miles.

Fairly soon after the victory of Nungshigum 20th Division, which had seen such very hard fighting at Shenam, was brought into the line in the area north of Nungshigum near Yangangpokpi. Here again a two-brigade attack was set up, hoping to destroy the remaining units of the Japanese 15th Division, and to advance far enough towards Litan and beyond in order to cut the line of retreat of Sato's 31st Division at Kohima. This major operation, carried out by 80 and 100 Brigades, who had fought so closely around Scraggy and Gibraltar, lasted from early June into July.

80 Brigade (1st Devons, 9/12th Frontier Force Regiment, 3/1st Gurkhas) set off on this long and arduous march on 7 June. The column had to hack its way through thick jungle, up steep slopes and under a constant downpour. Men climbed hills by hanging on to branches, while mules just slithered down in the mud. Small streams became dangerous torrents ready to sweep away men or mules. The conditions were bad enough, but the march was interrupted by occasional fierce clashes with the enemy rearguards. In spite of the appalling conditions, the brigade received effective support from the RAF who shot up enemy positions and, more importantly, dropped food and supplies.

While 80 Brigade trudged through the jungle, 100 Brigade stayed at Yangangpokpi and faced the final and desperate assault of Yamauchi's 15th Division. His forward units, though seriously depleted, put in strong attacks on 100 Brigade's defensive positions. One Japanese incursion advanced to within a couple of hundred yards of brigade headquarters, and held their ground for two days before being driven out. They showed this valour and determination, even though Yamauchi was now gravely ill, and was at complete loggerheads with Mutaguchi. Mutaguchi bombarded him with absurd orders such as, 'Seize Imphal!', or 'Seize the

Imphal airfields!', or 'Occupy Mission!' These orders were given when Yamauchi's total forces numbered little more than a battalion of troops fit to fight. It was remarkable that men in such a state could cause such serious problems to a full brigade, well dug-in and fully supplied.

20th Division held and extended the north-east front, while the West Yorks and Punjabis of 9 Brigade continued their slow and laborious struggle to push the enemy off the great hill mass of Molvom. The type of fighting in this phase of the battle can be illustrated by the fight for a hill which the West Yorks nicknamed 'The Hump'. Towards the end of May, as the monsoon increased in intensity, 9 Brigade made daily attacks. Sometimes a platoon would reach the summit of the Hump, only to be driven off again in a counter-attack. On 20 May a major attack was launched in which Hurricanes and massed artillery gave close support, but the Japanese resisted as resolutely as ever. While the infantry continued their attacks, a crucial role was played by the sappers in the supporting field companies. Using bulldozers and rock-blasting equipment, their most valuable contribution was to build jeep tracks so that supplies and ammunition could be carried up to the forward units, and the wounded brought down. The sappers also provided water cisterns, tarpaulin tanks and pumping-stations, and they were in constant demand to repair bridges and tracks and, during an advance, to remove booby-traps.

The Japanese still held on to the Hump and to Molvom throughout May, and Briggs then decided to attempt to by-pass these two strong positions, and to use both 9 and 123 Brigades to drive forward up the road to Kohima. So the Jats, Suffolks, Punjabis and West Yorks set out on another slow and difficult advance in unrelenting monsoon rain. The conditions suffered by 20th Division a few miles to the east were made more difficult by even steeper and harsher terrain. The sappers worked magnificently to build bridges over dangerous torrents only to have the whole thing washed away as the water rose unpredictably.

For these unfortunate battalions the main drive started on 6 June. They were to face another campaign as unpleasant as any they had already suffered. Approaching dim and unknown hills where many of their comrades were to die, they gave each hill a nickname. The West Yorks, Jats and Punjabis fought slowly forward, supported by 7th Cavalry and 3rd Carabiniers. The West Yorks took Zebra (this, like the succeeding nicknames, lay within a few miles of Safarmaina, on a hill feature just to the east of the road). In the sharp clash at Zebra, where the Stuart tanks were held up by mines, the West Yorks had 40 men wounded, but killed 26 of the enemy. After Zebra, the advance led to a feature with three small hills, nicknamed Pip, Squeak and Wilfrid (after a pre-war strip cartoon).

This became the scene of particularly severe fighting after a Company of the Punjabis was cut off on Squeak during a very heavy and prolonged rainstorm which made air activity almost impossible. Next, the Suffolks attacked two more hills called Isaac and James. The indefatigable sappers supported all these attacks, making up jeep and tank tracks as quickly as possible, but for all their care and effort sometimes tanks slid over the edge of a cliff, or the hill was so steep and slippery that the tanks had to be laboriously winched up the slopes.

On 7 June the Suffolks, in attacking Isaac, lost nine killed and nearly 30 wounded, but failed to take the hill. It was taken the next day, and the Jats resumed the lead, but then found that the enemy had evacuated the Isaac summit. By 12 June the Punjabis and West Yorks had made some hard-fought progress up the road. The list of quaint names continues. By 13 June the Jats had taken Wilfrid, and had captured two other hills, Eye and Button. These may sound light-hearted, but every hill was defended with the customary Japanese skill and determination. Another substantial feature called Liver appeared to offer little resistance, but when a platoon of Jats advanced towards one of the peaks on the side of Liver, the Japanese defenders suddenly opened fire. Out of a platoon of 27 men, only two were unscathed.

The slow and costly progress continued and the West Yorks reached the village of Safarmaina which they attacked with support from 3rd Carabiniers. On 15 June Liver still held out, but the Jats, supported by Hurricanes, tanks and artillery, pressed forward towards two other hills, Carter and Button, but as they reached the crests they were driven back by a shower of grenades and heavy small-arms fire. After a second company attack next day, Carter was recaptured, but it was so badly exposed to Japanese fire from Liver that it had to be abandoned.

The West Yorks continued their custom of giving Yorkshire names to the dim, nameless, dripping peaks which were costing so many lives. They had been held up at a tiny hamlet they called Driffield, surrounded as it was by three streams, which became Ouse, Swale and Avon. The colonel decided on a Company attack, but as the unit was crossing one of these streams the Japanese opened up with rifle and automatic fire and the usual shower of grenades. The company commander and second in command were both killed, and the Company had to withdraw in small groups through the jungle. Of 77 of the West Yorks who set out, 30 were killed and 20 wounded, and this severe defeat was inflicted by an enemy who had received no food or supplies for weeks, who was decimated by wounds and sickness, and was alleged to be running short of ammunition.

The continuing Japanese defence of Liver created a serious problem because it was holding up the advance of the whole of 5th Indian

Division, and delaying the efforts of IV Corps to open up the road to Kohima so that the huge air supply operation could be terminated. Briggs, after consulting the commanders of 9 and 123 Brigades, decided to send a full battalion, 3/14th Punjabis, on a detour to the west, to get behind the Japanese defenders on Liver. A second group of two battalions, 3/2nd Punjabis and 1/17th Dogras, were to go on an even wider detour to cut the road well behind the Japanese defences. The 3/14th Punjabis set off on 19 June, and were able to take their objective and hold it against Japanese counter-attacks. While these operations were proceeding 3/9th Jats prepared to make another effort to capture Liver, which involved an advance over Carter, Pill, Button and Milk Loaf. The attack started with a two-Company advance which successfully captured Pill. A further advance was supported by the 25-pounders of 4th and 28th Field Regiments and also by 8th Medium Regiment, but in spite of a formidable artillery bombardment the leading Jat platoons were unable to capture the summit of Liver and had to consolidate their positions overnight some way from the crest. At first light they sent out patrols and found that during the night the defenders had quietly slipped away from Milk Loaf and from Liver. In the week of fighting around Liver the Jats had lost 33 killed and 111 wounded.

Finally, on 22 June, before the two outflanking movements could be completed, the leading battalion of 123 Brigade, 1/17th Dogras, advanced up the Kohima road and at Milestone 109, just south of Kangpokpi, met the leading troops of 2nd Division. Imphal, which had been cut off from its supply base at Dimapur since the end of March, was relieved and soon convoys of trucks were heading south.

The Japanese soldiers of 15th Division on Liver had shown, even as late as 21 June, that they would defend their positions as bravely as ever, but the Japanese divisional commanders were facing grave problems which exacerbated their existing disagreements. As early as the beginning of May, reports about the poor condition of 15th, 31st, and 33rd Divisions had reached Mutaguchi's 15 Army Headquarters in Maymyo, and had been passed on to Kawabe, commanding Burma Area Army in Rangoon. At that same time, Mutaguchi, in a private message to a senior staff officer at GHQ in Tokyo, had written, 'Thinking of distant Tokyo, I am overwhelmed with shame.' (Louis Allen, p. 262.) Another staff officer returning to Tokyo from a visit to the three divisions, described the severe losses and the dangerous supply position. He suggested that there was some doubt about the success of the Imphal operation, but gave his opinion that in any event it must be completed before the end of May. Tojo, at Imperial General Headquarters in Tokyo, promised 30 additional aircraft, and sent a message to Kawabe that Burma Area Army must make every sacrifice to capture Imphal.

This message from the highest command in Tokyo only added to the problems faced by Kawabe in his headquarters in Rangoon. He was already well aware of the strong resistance put up by the British against Sato at Kohima, against Yamauchi and 15th Division north of Imphal, and against Yanagida and 33rd Division at Shenam and Bishenpur. He was aware too of the tensions which these reverses had caused between Mutaguchi and his divisional commanders. But Kawabe had other problems to plague him. Early in May, the Chinese had made an advance in the Salween area; in the north Stilwell's Chinese armies were advancing down the Hukawng valley; and the second Chindit expedition posed a major threat to the lines of communication for 18th Division facing Stilwell, and for the three divisions facing Imphal.

Kawabe felt he had to make some move to break this threatening impasse. On 21 May, therefore – when 214th and 215th Regiments were already hopelessly bogged down at Bishenpur – he sent a special order to Mutaguchi that Imphal must be captured immediately, even if that meant withdrawing forces from Kohima. This order achieved nothing and at the end of May Kawabe travelled north to see Mutaguchi himself. He reached Kalewa on 31 May and met Yanagida, whom Mutaguchi had just sacked from command of 33rd Division. Next he met Yamamoto, who was still pushing his troops into the attack in the Shenam area at a terrible cost, and finally, on 5 June, he met Mutaguchi. Kawabe himself was ill with dysentery, and he found Mutaguchi in an emotional state. He had just dismissed Yamauchi from command of 15th Division, and replaced him with Shibata. Mutaguchi could not bring himself to admit that he was unable to capture Imphal and both generals skirted around the issue. All the divisional commanders in the field promised success if they received more reinforcements, and Kawabe left for his headquarters saying he had confidence in them. Because Kawabe and Mutaguchi failed to face up to the reality of the situation that there was no possibility of capturing Imphal, and because they wanted to please their masters in Tokyo, they condemned thousands of brave Japanese soldiers to needless slaughter during the next dreadful weeks, during the whole of June and into July, until at last, in July, Mutaguchi gave the order to withdraw.

CHAPTER 9
ADVANCE TO RANGOON

FOURTEENTH ARMY, helped by the operations of the Chindits around Indaw, had inflicted a major defeat on Mutaguchi and his three divisions facing Imphal and Kohima. He and Kawabe, who refused to face up to the possiblity of defeat, had condemned their brave soldiers to needless slaughter and suffering, but by August 1944 the Japanese armies in all sectors of the Burma war were in retreat.

In that month many changes took place in the command structure of both the Allies and the Japanese armies. Mutaguchi, who had sacked his three divisional commanders, was now himself sacked and replaced by General Kimura. On the British side, although Slim was always loyal to Scoones, he was quite relieved when he was sent to a command in Central India, and replaced as GOC IV Corps by Messervy who had commanded 7th Indian Division so successfully. At about the same time, General Giffard – whose relationship with Mountbatten had always been very difficult – was replaced by General Oliver Leese, who had commanded the Eighth Army, and whom for many months Churchill had wanted to post to India to ginger-up what he saw as the slothful India Command.

In the aftermath of the mauling the three Japanese divisions had received at the hands of IV Corps, Fourteenth Army had to regroup ready to exploit their victory. From a number of possibilities, Operation 'Capital' emerged as the favourite, with its aim of advancing into Central and Southern Burma, on three main routes – XV Corps in the Arakan; IV Corps and XXXIII Corps in the centre; and the Northern Combat Area Command (NCAC) which was under Stilwell's command until he was replaced by General Sultan. As the NCAC moved forward, it had under its command 36th British Division under General Festing, which had replaced the Chindits after the Battle of Mogaung. Significantly, in view of Slim's attitude towards airborne forces, there were no airborne operations in the initial phases of Operation 'Capital'.

As soon as possible after the reorganization, 5th Indian Division – led by the Royal West Kents and the West Yorks, affectionately nicknamed The Western Brothers – began to harry Tanaka and 33rd Division as they retreated down the Tiddim road. Tiddim was captured after some stiff fighting and then the divisions joined forces with 11th East African Division which had had the unenviable task of advancing down the unhealthy Kabaw valley. In early December 1944 the divisions captured Kalewa where Slim had paused briefly in the final stages of the 1942 retreat. The forward planning of Fourteenth Army was excellent, and at the Chindwin crossing the longest Bailey Bridge in the world was assembled. Built in Britain, America and India, shipped to Calcutta, taken

The Advance to Rangoon, January to June 1945

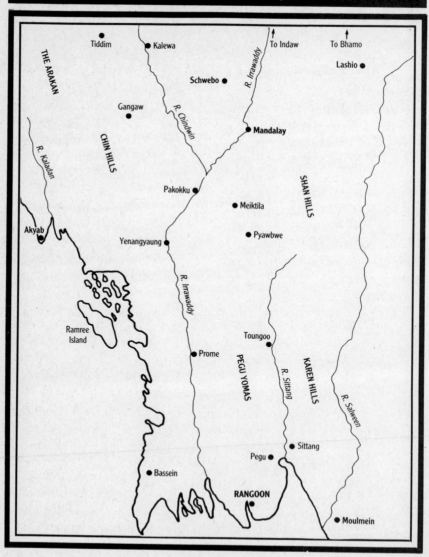

by rail to Dimapur, transferred by truck from there to Kalewa, it made a valuable contribution to the speed of the advance against the Japanese.

Before the end of 1944 the Japanese had realized that they could not hold all their positions in north Burma, and they were reconciled to the possiblity of losing their stranglehoid on the land route to China, but they still had formidable defensive forces at their disposal. Although 15th, 31st and 33rd Divisions were sadly depleted after Kohima and Imphal, there were still ten Japanese divisions in Burma altogether – numbering approximately 100,000 men – and some supplies were getting through. In addition, the Indian National Army and the Burma National Army were still operating, but as the tide turned against the Japanese these units became increasingly unreliable.

As a part of Operation 'Capital', while IV Corps and XXXIII Corps were advancing southwards towards Kalewa, XV Corps, which included 81st and 82nd West African Divisions and 25th Indian Division, was steadily pressing forward down the Kaladan valley in the Arakan, and preparing to make seaborne attacks down the coast towards Akyab and Ramree Island. On the eastern flank of Fourteenth Army, as a part of NCAC under Sultan, 36th British Division, after they had replaced the Chindits, were advancing fairly rapidly down to Indaw and beyond. Showing considerable ingenuity, they adapted a number of jeeps to run on the railway and to pull both wagons and carriages. In December 1944 they at last linked up with units of Fourteenth Army. Frank Owen, the editor of *SEAC* newspaper, described the conditions of this advance. 'It advanced through a wilderness, which had been rendered more savage by the Japanese. Burnt out villages, ruined pagodas, broken wagons, rotting equipment, rusting helmets stamped with the Japanese white dove of peace, unposted letters, and unburied corpses, such were the milestones along this march. Sweating and cursing, the eternal infantry-man slogged his way forward through the mud towards a ruined village with its garrison of death. (Owen, *The Campaign in Burma*, p. 116.)

Chiang Kai-shek had reneged on his agreement made at the Cairo Conference, but Chinese troops had been fighting for some time along the upper Salween valley in a harsh landscape more than 11,000 feet high, devoid of vegetation and shrouded in sleet, snow and fog. From this base they advanced farther and joined up with the Chinese divisions of NCAC under Sultan near Bhamo. They achieved at last what had always been the chief goal of American strategy, the re-opening of the land route to China. On 27 January 1945 Mountbatten, as Supreme Commander SEAC, signalled to Churchill and Roosevelt, 'The first part of the orders I received at Quebec has been carried out. The land route to China is open.' The next day the first convoy moved off with supplies for Chungking.

By the end of 1944 Slim's forces were powerfully poised on the edge of the central plain of Burma and the Japanese were retreating rapidly. Their speedy retreat posed him a new problem. The drier central plain would give added scope for his armour and motorized units and provide more open targets for the almost unchallenged air forces, but Slim needed – as he had done at Imphal – to draw the Japanese forces into battle and destroy them. He did not want to have to pursue them right through Burma and into Siam or Malaya. He therefore devised a plan which has been rightly praised as his most brilliant concept as a high-level commander. The plan centred on two important towns, Mandalay and Meiktila, and the railway, road and the River Irrawaddy that connected them. Clearly the Japanese would defend Mandalay as stoutly as possible. Slim's strategem was to have powerful forces advancing towards Mandalay from the north, doing everything possible – including a phoney Corps Headquarters sending real messages – to convince the Japanese that this was the main assault. Simultaneously he would send equally powerful forces on a lengthy detour to the west through the Chin Hills, to emerge from the jungle and the hills in the area of Pakokku and then to strike at Meiktila. From there his forces would wheel round to the north and east to intercept and destroy the main Japanese forces before they could retreat from Mandalay.

This, roughly, is what happened, but there is an interesting link back to the controversial Chindit issue. In *Defeat into Victory* (p. 393), Slim wrote, 'My new plan, the details of which were worked out in record time by my devoted staff . . . had as its intention the destruction of the main Japanese forces in the area of Mandalay.' He then added the details, that IV Corps would move secretly up the Gangaw valley, appear at Pakokku and strike violently at Meiktila. When questioned he later confirmed that this plan emerged in discussions with his staff.

At no stage, either in his book or in subsequent discussion, did Slim reveal that on 13 March 1944 he had received a memorandum from Wingate suggesting that the next major Chindit initiative after Broadway, assuming that IV Corps had made a substantial advance, would be to land a brigade at Pakokku, seize Meiktila and trap the Japanese forces before they could retreat from Mandalay. This lack of openness by Slim is well known to the Chindits, and is mentioned by Louis Allen (p. 398). This raises the gravest implications. Not only has Slim claimed the whole of the Meiktila plan as his own when in fact the idea originated with Wingate, but, having had this idea presented to him in March 1944, instead of withdrawing the Chindits after their success at Broadway in order to use them in another ideal situation at Meiktila, he handed them over to Stilwell to be used as normal infantry. The Chindits were never again used as Long Range Penetration Forces; instead, a few months later

– after sustaining more than 50 per cent casualties in the slaughter at Mogaung – they were disbanded. Here, clearly, is an added offshoot of the tragic death of Wingate. He would surely have succeeded in arguing his case when, after Broadway, he had Churchill's personal backing for the Chindits to be used again in the role for which they were armed and trained.

Before Operation 'Capital' got under way, skilful preparations were made by the Royal Engineers and other services – helped by bulldozers, elephants, boat-building operations and by the creation of airstrips – to prepare a route for IV Corps to move secretly on their 300-mile trek into the Chin Hills jungle, and then to emerge undetected near Pakokku. 17th Indian Division, still led by Cowan, and now extensively retrained and re-equipped, took the lead in this venture.

While IV Corps was setting off into the jungle in early January 1945, XXXIII Corps advanced rapidly and captured Shwebo from their old adversaries, 31st Division. From Shwebo 19th Division, under its successful and aggressive commander, Major-General Pete Rees, drove eastwards and crossed the Irrawaddy well to the north of Mandalay. 2nd Division and 20th Indian Division also made difficult and opposed crossings of the river which in places was over two miles wide, and provided a formidable obstacle when the far bank was held by determined defenders. Sensing their ultimate defeat, the Japanese soldiers did not give up, but rather fought on until every single defender was killed. For weeks these difficult battles continued until by early March, 19th Division was approaching Mandalay. This was a difficult obstacle, and included Fort Dufferin, built by the British in the 19th century, with a deep, wide moat and walls 30 feet thick. On 9 March Rees gave the first of several broadcasts for the BBC with a running commentary on the different actions he could see from his command post within sight of Fort Dufferin. The three divisions attacking Mandalay succeeded in deceiving Kimura into thinking that they were the major attacking force, and any units farther south just a feint.

The move by IV Corps via Pakokku to the fringe of Meiktila proceeded smoothly even though it involved crossing the Irrawaddy in the face of the enemy. All the divisions had hard-fought actions and several near disasters caused by ill-prepared boats, by outboard engines breaking down in the middle of a two-mile-wide river, and by tough Japanese opposition from the far bank.

On 28 February, when XXXIII Corps was already hammering at the suburbs of Mandalay, Cowan launched a well co-ordinated attack on Meiktila. He had 5th Indian Division and 255 Tank Brigade in support, together with motorized units from his division, and additional massed armour and artillery. Cowan surrounded the town and established road-blocks on the main exits. The battle for Meiktila lasted for four days of non-stop fighting with no quarter given. The Japanese had been ordered to defend the city to the last man, and they did virtually that. When they were finally overcome, more than 2,000 corpses were counted, but it was estimated that there were as many again in the bunkers, in the cellars, in the lakes or just blown to pieces by the aerial bombardment. Having been surrounded, the garrison was almost completely wiped out, and a very large stores area − the supply base for two Japanese armies − was captured. Slim, who was present at the battle, considered that, 'The capture of Meiktila was a magnificent feat of arms.' (*Defeat into Victory*, p. 452.)

Too late in the day the Japanese reacted to the loss of Meiktila, which was a disastrous blow to their whole position in central Burma, and they put in a series of strong counter-attacks during the following week (6−13 March). They assembled 18th Division from north Burma and a number of units from 53rd Division, 49th Division and the sorry survivors of 33rd Division which had just received another mauling at the hands of their old rivals, 17th Indian Division. With the Indian and British forces now defending Meiktila against a prolonged Japanese counter-attack, which lasted more than a week, the fighting was as close and severe as ever. For example, as units of 5th Indian Division flew into Meiktila airfield their Dakotas came under fire from Japanese automatic and small-arms fire. The Battle of Meiktila was one of Cowan's great victories, but he was under considerable stress because he had just heard that his son had been killed in the attack on Mandalay.

Because of their serious defeats and setbacks at Mandalay and Meiktila, the Japanese tried urgently to regroup their forces. General Honda was ordered to take over 18th and 49th Divisions − called 33rd Army − and to recapture Meiktila at all costs. He thought this plan was foolish, but loyally undertook the task, and on 22 March organized a two-division attack. The first attack was bloodily repulsed, with more than 200 men killed, though the Japanese gunners, skilfully sited and well camouflaged, did considerable damage and destroyed about 50 tanks. Overall, in an operation which lasted several days, while knocking out 50 tanks, they lost more than 50 guns and sustained 2,500 casualties. Honda realized that he could not continue to sustain losses at that level, and he pulled back ready to adopt delaying tactics as he moved south. At the same time, the Japanese 15th Army − made up of the devastated remnants of 31st and 33rd Divisions − were retreating rapidly towards Toungoo. As they fled they were ambushed and attacked by Gracey's 20th Division which had driven swiftly south from Mandalay. They wrought havoc on the so-called 15th Army − killing more than 3,000 men and capturing large quantities of guns and equipment. These decimated Japanese units, though partly reinforced, contained most of the survivors of the battles at Kohima, at Bishenpur, the Shenam Saddle and Mount Molvom.

In the Arakan XV Corps under General Christison, composed of 81st West African Division, 82nd West African Division, and 25th Indian Division, supported by Royal Navy, Royal Indian Navy, RAF and USAAF forces, drove south on a parallel course to the main advance in central Burma. They aimed to capture the airfields at Akyab and Ramree so that these could be used to give air support to IV Corps and XXXIII Corps as they approached Rangoon. After a series of spirited attacks by XV Corps, the Japanese evacuated Akyab in early January 1945 and then withdrew to Ramree. The Allies had been able to assemble some Combined Operations boats and equipment when they were no longer required in Normandy, and with this support the Indian and West African units, with strong air and naval cover, cleared the Japanese from Ramree and the surrounding mangrove swamps. Here too the Japanese suffered heavy casualties. On Ramree alone they lost more than 1,000 men and the survivors were driven into the mangrove swamps where many more died from sickness, starvation, drowning or being eaten by crocodiles. The Arakan as far south as Ramree, had been cleared of Japanese forces by the end of February 1945.

After the victories in the battles around Mandalay and Meiktila, Mountbatten and Slim had to consider their next move. The arrival of the monsoon – expected by 15 May – in many ways dictated their strategy. Slim could not afford to get his three corps held up short of Rangoon, with his communications stretching back hundreds of miles, and the monsoon weather making regular air support at such distances almost impossible. He had to bear in mind that the Japanese, ever since the battles at Kohima and the Aradura Spur, had shown that they were expert at causing delay to an enemy army. Therefore the Allied plan – hoping rather than expecting to capture Rangoon before the monsoon started – depended on four operations:

(a) XXXIII Corps (Stopford): 7th Indian Division, 20th Indian Division and 265 Tank Brigade, to advance south-west from Meiktila to overrun the oilfields around Yenangyaung, and to advance south to Prome.

(b) IV Corps (Messervy): 5th Indian Division, 17th Indian Division, 19th Indian Division and 255 Tank Brigade, to destroy the Japanese in the area of Meiktila and then to drive south to Pyawbwe and on to Toungoo and Pegu.

(c) XV Corps (Christison): 81st and 82nd West African Divisions and 25th Indian Division, to continue south from Ramree and prepare for combined operations.

(d) Operation 'Dracula': XV Corps with 26th Indian Division and a parachute battalion from 50 Indian Parachute Brigade (reformed after Sangshak) to make a combined operations assault on Rangoon with full air and naval support. Here too the start of the monsoon was vital.

The main operations around Meiktila were completed by the end of March, and on 30 March 17th Indian Division and 5th Indian Division started on the drive towards Rangoon down the Sittang valley. Nominally, two Japanese armies opposed their advance: Honda, commanding 33rd Army (18th and 49th Divisions), was still able to conduct some coherent defence, but 15th Army, which had preceded Honda, was now straggling eastwards into the Shan and Karen Hills where the relatively warlike tribes people were led by under-cover British officers, and now rose up to ambush, sabotage and destroy the retreating Japanese forces.

For the first two weeks of April serious fighting took place in the area between Meiktila and Pyawbwe, but increasingly Honda found himself conducting desperate defence, and then desperate retreat. On more than one occasion he was surrounded, and once even left a note, 'General Honda was here. Try harder next time.' After these battles he realized that the strength of his whole army amounted to less than a division, and he then began a controlled withdrawal towards Toungoo where he hoped to stand firm. In the battles around Pyawbwe British and Indian armour increasingly dominated the exchanges, and after 12 April they broke away from any major organized resistance and in ten hectic days reached Toungoo. Their advance became so swift that the leading tanks often passed disorganized Japanese stragglers plodding southwards, and in one town a Japanese traffic policeman held up his hand to stop an advancing tank and was immediately flattened.

Slim had sent XXXIII Corps to deal with the whole area around the Yenangyaung oilfields, the destruction of which during the retreat he had personally ordered. Here too, XXXIII Corps inflicted very heavy casualties on the enemy, and Gracey's 20th Indian Division, which took the left flank, destroyed any units that tried to cross the Prome road. 7th Indian Division and 20th Indian Division completed their tasks and on 2 May reached Prome where the main road and railway to Mandalay crossed the River Irrawaddy.

The Pegu Yomas, a range of small undulating hills, divide the Irrawaddy valley from the Sittang valley, and while XXXIII Corps was advancing towards Prome, IV Corps was speeding ahead of them down the Sittang valley. 17th Indian Division, leapfrogging with 5th Indian Division and 255 Tank Brigade, made such rapid progress that they outpaced Honda and reached Toungoo before the town could be properly defended. 17th Divison, still led by Cowan, and accompanied by armour, reached Pegu on 29 April. Pegu – a very large town and a place of bitter memory for Cowan who had passed through it during the 1942 retreat – controlled both the road and rail routes for any Japanese forces that left Rangoon to escape to Moulmein. In many ways it was more important strategically than Rangoon itself. Having reached Pegu on 29 April, 17th Division had three days of fierce fighting before they cleared the town. This, and the early arrival of the monsoon – not expected until the middle of May – proved doubly frustrating for Cowan because, naturally, he hoped that 17th Division would have the honour of recapturing Rangoon. This was not to be.

Mountbatten – at last given an opportunity to mount a combined operations attack – masterminded Operation 'Dracula' which aimed to capture Rangoon. He had relied on IV Corps to capture Toungoo airfield by 25 April to give air cover for the final assault on Rangoon. IV Corps achieved this by the 22nd. The forces involved in 'Dracula' included battleships, aircraft carriers, cruisers, destroyers, landing craft, troopships and minesweepers as well as overwhelming air power. The assault troops included 26th Indian Division and a Gurkha parachute battalion from 50 Indian Parachute Brigade.

On 1 May RAF reconnaissance aircraft flying over Rangoon saw a notice painted on the roof of Rangoon jail where prisoners of war were held, which said 'JAPS GONE'. The RAF at first thought that this might be a hoax, but were more convinced when 'EXTRACT DIGIT' appeared (the phrase 'Take your finger out' was RAF wartime slang). On 2 May an RAF Mosquito pilot landed at Rangoon airport and found it deserted, but the runway had been so badly bombed that he could not take off again. He therefore went to the docks, commandeered a sampan and sailed out to greet the armada of ships and landing craft as they sailed up the river with 26th Division ready to attack. The only casualties were suffered by the Gurkha paratroops from the ill-fated 50 Indian Parachute Brigade, who were hit by Allied bombs as they moved forward to attack. For the rest, the Japanese had fled.

As early as 22 April the Japanese commander, Kimura, had made up his mind that, with the rapid enemy advances towards Pegu, he must concentrate all available forces east of the River Sittang, and could not risk trying to hold Rangoon after Pegu had fallen. He was infuriated when he received orders from as far away as Saigon and Singapore, from people completely out of touch with the tactical situation, which told him to hold Rangoon to the death. He also had bitter clashes with commanders on the spot who disagreed with his orders to evacuate and thought that Rangoon should have been defended street by street. In fact the large majority of Japanese troops withdrew before the British arrived, and there was a phase of looting, pillaging and general mayhem before order was restored. During that period Subhas Chandra Bose with some of the Indian National Army bravely tried to quell the disturbance. Later, Japanese historians severely criticized Kimura for running away with his Headquarters to the safety of Moulmein.

Kimura evacuated Rangoon, but did nothing to help the still substantial forces trapped in the area of the Pegu Yomas. It fell to IV Corps and XXXIII Corps to destroy the remaining enemy forces there. During May and early June, when once again monsoon conditions returned, the Japanese soldiers who had survived the horrors of Kohima and Imphal were virtually annihilated. Even those who escaped over the River Sittang into the Karen Hills were attacked by Karen guerrillas. When the Japanese commanders signed the surrender document they referred to 153,000 of their forces. In fact they had fewer than 60,000.

Frank Owen, the distinguished editor of *SEAC* Newspaper, who went through the campaign and wrote his own account, considered that the reconquest of Burma from the north by Fourteenth Army was, 'A feat never before accomplished in history, and one worthy to rank with the most splendid military achievements.' (Frank Owen, *Campaign in Burma*, p. 147.)

The Japanese armies came to final and total defeat at the hands of Fourteenth Army which had fought them at Sangshak and Kohima, then held them in prolonged and bitter fighting around the Imphal perimeter, at Shenam, Bishenpur, Potsangbam, Nungshigum and Molvom. It was there, in the fighting which taken together makes up the great Battles of Kohima and Imphal, that the Japanese forces of Mutaguchi were fought and destroyed. What came after, notably the successful tactical battles of Mandalay and Meiktila, and the final victorious drive to Rangoon, were merely the aftermath of the two decisive Battles of Imphal and Kohima.

CHAPTER 10
VICTORY AND THE AFTERMATH

THE IMAGE of Fourteenth Army as 'The Forgotten Army' was too firmly established to be easily removed, and circumstance continued to keep the news of Burma off the headlines in Britain and America. The capture of Rangoon, the crowning achievement of Fourteenth Army, on 3 May 1945, took place one day before the surrender of Admiral Dönitz and all the German forces to General Montgomery on Luneburg Heath in Germany. The priority of the next day's headlines can be easily imagined. The euphoria of the victory in Europe lasted for a long time, and the interest of the people and the press had not fully transferred to the Far East when the atom bombs on Hiroshima and Nagasaki (6 and 9 August) brought the final Japanese surrender, so the achievements of Fourteenth Army never received the undivided attention and gratitude of the nation that it deserved.

The aftermath of the Burma victory was less than happy. In the final stage of the campaign, Mountbatten gained the support of the young Burmese leader, Aung San, even though he had to some extent co-operated with the Japanese, and Mountbatten felt that positive backing for Aung San by Britain would have kept Burma in the Commonwealth. This policy was opposed by the reactionary former Governor, Dorman-Smith, of whom it was said, 'His capacity for self-deception was almost infinite'. Then, before reconstruction could start, Aung San was murdered. Burma almost immediately left the Commonwealth (January 1948) and thereafter had a troubled history, with the northern hill people, notably the Karens and Kachins, openly opposing the government in Rangoon, and this led to decades of undemocratic military dictatorship. Many have asked if this was worth all the sacrifice and suffering of Fourteenth Army.

In Britain the national conception of the Burma campaign has changed substantially. Its shared suffering activated The Burma Star Association, one of the most effective ex-servicemen's organizations in the country, and this, over nearly 50 years, has done more than anything else to keep alive the memory and achievements of Fourteenth Army. Their efforts have been complemented by the image that has been built up of General Slim, later Field Marshal Viscount Slim, CIGS and Governor-General of Australia, who published *Defeat into Victory* in

1956. His reputation, supported by the respect and affection of the members of the Burma Star Association, has flourished ever since. That this was a considerable achievement is shown by two things – a video of the main events of 1944 (produced in 1990) which makes no mention at all of the Burma campaign, and the official film, 'Burma Victory', made in November 1945, which hardly mentions Slim.

The post-war build-up of Slim as the distinguished war leader, rightly considered by many to be one of the greatest Allied military leaders, has given a proper prominence to a seriously neglected campaign, but it has also masked one serious and lingering injustice. It is unfortunate that with the justifiable pride in the achievements of Slim and Fourteenth Army in Burma, there is still the shadow of the injustice which so many of the Chindits feel has been done to Wingate by the military establishment. The admiration for Slim of many Chindits has been tempered by their feeling that although he paid generous tribute to Wingate at his death in March 1944, he took a destructively critical view of him in *Defeat into Victory*, and this seems to have set the tone for other writers to follow. There is a strong body of opinion that this injustice should be rectified.

In looking back at the unfortunate controversy over Wingate and the Chindits and their contribution to the victory over Mutaguchi, it is significant that after the sincere and even fulsome tributes paid to Wingate at the time of his death by Slim, Mountbatten, Churchill and others, there was no open criticism of Wingate for more than ten years. Then *Defeat into Victory* was published in 1956, and the *Official History*, Volume Three, containing the attack by Kirby, in 1962. When Slim was writing his book he was already Governor-General of Australia. From Canberra, naturally, he had to contact colleagues back in London to refresh his memory and to remind him of necessary detail. There is no doubt that the man who would have had all the information he needed was the one engaged on the Official History of the campaign – none other than Kirby. So it is possible that, quite unwittingly, Slim absorbed some of the anti-Wingate prejudice from Kirby. After the publication of *Defeat into Victory* and the *Official History*, the majority of those who have written about the Burma Campaign have naturally turned to these books as their sources and have repeated or enlarged upon the criticism of Wingate.

The attack on Wingate by Kirby needs some elaboration. Kirby was a senior staff officer at GHQ Delhi in 1943, and clashed strongly with Wingate over the setting up of the Chindits. Years later he was asked to write the *Official History* and, as Bidwell wrote, 'He took his revenge', (Bidwell, p. 40) and set out to denigrate Wingate and all he had done.

Typical of Kirby's petty attempt to belittle the Chindits is his remark, referring to the first Chindit expedition, that Wavell, 'Allowed Wingate to try out his theories by making an incursion into Burma at a time when the operation could have little strategic value.' Yet that first Chindit operation changed the whole Japanese approach to the war in north Burma and led directly to Wingate's success at Quebec.

Kirby then tried to ridicule Wingate's colourful use of language, and the plan of 'Stronghold'. Continuing his attack on Stronghold, he wrote that Wingate, 'Used his formations as conventional forces – a role for which they were not equipped.' This is a preposterous comment, which seeks deliberately to falsify the whole concept of Stronghold, which was so successfully executed by Calvert at Broadway. Kirby continued his attack on Wingate by saying, 'He laid himself open to the charge of order, counterorder, disorder', and, 'He had neither the knowledge, stability nor balance [sic], to make a great commander.' Then comes the final disgraceful slur, 'Just as timing played a great part in his rise to prominence, so the moment of his death may perhaps have been equally propitious for him.' (Kirby, vol. 3, p. 223.)

Official histories do not normally put forward opinions of generals in a campaign, and Kirby's three-page attack on Wingate shows the intensity of his prejudice. His biased account brought a strong objection to the Cabinet Office from two former Chindits, Brigadier Mead and Sir Robert Thomson who, later, wrote, 'The whole assessment was no more than a hatchet job by little men who could not have competed with Wingate either in military argument or in battle.' (Thompson, *Make for the Hills*, p. 73.)

Another example of the dubious method used by the official historian is shown in a statement, which he quotes, from Mutaguchi, 'The Chindit invasion did not stop our plans to attack Kohima BUT they had a decisive effect on these operations, and they drew off the whole of 53rd Division and parts of 15th Division, one Regiment of which would have turned the scales at Kohima.' The real significance of this sentence is that the official historian omitted every word after BUT (Tulloch, p. 269). Further evidence comes from Air Marshal Sir Philip Joubert who stated that there was a deliberate policy to write down the Chindits.

Other examples abound of ex-Chindits being refused promotion, but perhaps Calvert, who suffered most from this prejudice and who received no recognition from Britain for his months of leadership and bravery up to and including the Battle of Mogaung, should be allowed a last word. He recalled that in an officers' club in Delhi in 1944, an elderly lieutenant-general said in a pompous way that the death of Wingate was the best thing that ever happened to the British Army. Later that night, a fully clothed general was hurled into the fountain – his assailants were never discovered.

It is right that, now, when more historical records are available for study, the issue of the injustice done to Wingate in the *Official History* should be openly and honestly pursued. Wingate was a difficult and sometimes an almost impossible colleague – as Mountbatten said, 'He was a pain in the neck to the generals above him' – but however difficult he may have been, he should have been accorded in the *Official History* the respect he deserved as a brave soldier and an outstanding leader, and not run down in a petty and vindictive way. This issue must be resolved before a final assessment of the Battles of Kohima and Imphal can be made, or the final chapter in the saga of the Burma Campaign can be written.

CHRONOLOGY
MARCH TO JUNE 1944

	Imphal area	Kohima area
3 March	Yamamoto Force attacks Tamu.	
5 March		Operation 'Thursday' launched.
8 March	33rd Division attacks Tiddim.	
14 March	17th Division leaves Tiddim.	
15 March	Japanese 15th and 31st Divisions cross the Chindwin.	
17 March	5th Indian Division to Imphal– starts	
19 March		Japanese 31st Division attacks Sangshak.
20 March		161 Brigade to Dimapur.
24 March	5th Indian Division to Imphal– ends Wingate killed.	
26 March		50 Brigade leaves Sangshak.
28 March	17th Division meets 23rd Division.	Jessami battle.
29 March	Imphal cut off.	
30 March		West Kents to Kohima.
31 March	20th Division destroy Moreh stores.	
1 April	20th Division reach Shenam.	2nd Division to Dimapur.
4 April	17th Division reach Bishenpur.	31st Division attacks Kohima.
5 April	Nungshigum battle starts.	West Kents back to Kohima.
6 April		Siege of Kohima begins.
13 April	Main Nungshigum battle.	
14 April	Nungshigum victory.	2nd Division reached Zubza.
18 April		Kohima siege raised.
19 April		Battle of Kohima begins.
21 April		Battles around 'Liver' and Molvom (continue until June).
11 May		Broadway abandoned.
13 May		31st Division driven out of Kohima.
17 May	NCAC capture Myitkyina airfield.	
19 May	33rd Division attacks Nungang (Imphal).	
31 May		31st Division ordered to leave Kohima.
2 June		Gurkhas capture Naga village.
9 June	Final Yamamoto attack on Shenam.	
16 June		Battles around Molvom continue.

22 June	Imphal siege ends, 2nd Division meets 5th Indian Division.	
27 June		Chindits capture Mogaung.
7 July	Japanese retreat from Bishenpur.	
8 July	Mutaguchi orders general retreat.	
1945		
27 January	Burma Road re-opened.	
28 February	17th Division attacks Meiktila.	XV Corps capture Ramree
9 March	19th Division attacks Mandalay.	
22 April	IV Corps captures Toungoo.	
29 April	17th Division captures Pegu.	
1 May	Capture of Rangoon.	
2 May	XXXIII Corps captures Prome.	

BIOGRAPHICAL NOTES

Alexander, General Sir Harold. Commanded British forces during the 1942 retreat.

Archer, Wing Commander in 221 Group RAF.

Arnold, General. Commanded USAAF, and was a strong supporter of Wingate.

Auchinleck, General. Succeeded Wavell as Commander-in-Chief in India.

Baldwin, Air Marshal Sir John. Commanded Third Tactical Airforce.

Boatner, General. Stilwell's chief of staff, who followed Stilwell's anti-British lead.

Bose, Subhas Chandra. Leader of the Indian National Army supporting the Japanese in Burma.

Bower, Ursula Graham. The remarkable woman who worked with the Naga people before and during the war.

Briggs, Major-General. Commanded 5th Indian Division.

Brodie, Brigadier. Commanded 14 Chindit Brigade which flew into Aberdeen.

Brooke, General Sir Alan. Chief of the Imperial General Staff.

Burney, Private I., a fighting soldier of 2nd Battalion, West Yorks.

Burton, Brigadier. Commanded 63 Brigade in 17th Division.

Cairns, Lieutenant. Won the VC at White City.

Calvert, Brigadier. Commanded 77 Brigade at the Chindit Stronghold at Broadway – the most successful Chindit commander.

Cameron, Brigadier. Commanded 48 Brigade in 17th Division.

Chiang Kai-shek. Commander-in-Chief of the Kuomintang forces in China.

Cochrane, Colonel. Leader of Number One Air Commando, which took part in Operation 'Thursday' with the Chindits.

Collins, Mr L., with the Devonshire Regiment at Shenam.

Cowan, Major-General 'Punch'. Took over 17th Division during the retreat and commanded it until victory at Rangoon.

Coward, Noël. Entertainer, flew into Imphal during the siege.

Craddock, Squadron Sergeant-Major in 3rd Carabiniers at Nungshigum.

Crowther, Brigadier. Commanded 89 Brigade in 7th Indian Division.

Dewey, Phil., signaller in the Royal Norfolk Regiment at Kohima.

Esse, Brigadier. Commanded 49 Brigade in 23rd Indian Division.

Evans, Major-General. Commanded 123 Brigade and later, 5th Indian Division.

Fergusson, Brigadier. Leader of 16 Chindit Brigade which marched from Ledo to Indaw.

Formby, George. Entertainer, flew into Imphal during the siege.

Fukunaga, Colonel. Commanded Japanese 58th Regiment at Sangshak.

Gandhi, Mahatma. Indian leader in the campaign for Britain to 'Quit India'.

Giffard, General. Commanded the Eastern Army in India at the time of Imphal and Kohima.

Gillian, Noel. Member of American Field Ambulance.

Goschen, Brigadier. Commanded 4 Brigade in 2nd Division, killed at Kohima.

Gracey, Major-General. Commanded 20th Indian Division throughout the campaign.

Greeves, Brigadier. Commanded 80 Brigade in 20th Indian Division at Shenam.

Grover, Major-General. Commanded 2nd Division, and was relieved of command after the battle of Kohima.

Hafiz, Jemadar. Won the VC at Imphal.

Hanaya, Major-General. Commanded Japanese 55th Division in the Arakan.

Harman, Lance-Corporal John, Royal West Kents. Won VC at Kohima.

Hawkins, Brigadier. Commanded 5 Brigade in 2nd Division at Kohima.

Hirakubo, Masao. Japanese officer at Kohima.

Honda, General. In charge of 33rd Army after the defeat of Meiktila.

Hope Thomson, Brigadier. Commanded 50 Indian Parachute Brigade at Sangshak.

Horsford, Lieutenant-Colonel. Commanded 4/1st Gurkhas in final attack at Kohima.

Horwood, Lieutenant, Northamptonshire Regiment. Won VC on the Chindwin.

Hunter, Colonel. Commanded Merrill's Marauders.

Ingham, Professor Kenneth. With 2nd West Yorks at Imphal.

Irwin, General. Commanded Eastern Army in India during the 1942 retreat and clashed with Slim.

James, Brigader. Commanded 100 Brigade in 20th Indian Division.

Kawabe, General. Commanded Japanese Burma Area Army at Rangoon.

Kelly, Sergeant, Northamptonshire Regiment, on the Silchar Track.

Kimura, General. Commanded the Japanese forces in Rangoon prior to their defeat.

King, Brigadier. Commanded 1 Brigade in 23rd Indian Division, succeeding McCoy.

King, Sergeant, Royal West Kents. In charge of 3in mortars at Kohima.

Kirby, Major-General. Staff Officer at GHQ Delhi, and later author of the *Official History of the War in Burma,* in which he denigrates Wingate.

Lama, Ganju. Won VC and MM at Imphal.

Laverty, Lieutenant-Colonel. Commanded Royal West Kent Regiment at Kohima.

Leech, Sergeant. In Devonshire Regiment in Shenam.

Leese, General. Succeeded Giffard in November 1944.

Lentaigne, Major-General. Commanded 111 Chindit Brigade, and succeeded Wingate.

Lloyd, Major-General. Commanded 14th Division during 1943 reverse in the Arakan.

Loftus-Tottenham, Major-General. Commanded 33 Brigade at Kohima, and later 81st West African Division.

Lomax, Major-General. Commanded 14th Division in the Arakan, succeeding Lloyd.

MacKenzie, Brigadier. Commanded 32 Brigade in 20th Indian Division.

Mao Tse-tung. Leader of Chinese Communist forces, who defeated Chiang Kai-shek in 1949.

Marindin, Brigadier. Commanded 37 Brigade in 23rd Indian Division.

Matsumura, Colonel. Commanded Japanese 60th Regiment in 15th Division.

May, H. Bugler in Royal Norfolk Regiment at Kohima.

McCoy, Brigadier. Commanded 1 Brigade in 23rd Indian Division.

Merrill, Brigadier. Stilwell's son-in-law, who commanded Merrill's Marauders.

Messervy, Major-General. Commanded 7th Indian Division and, later, IV Corps.

Miyazaki, Major-General. Commanded the Japanese Infantry Group of 31st Division which attacked Sangshak.

Morris, Brigadier. Chindit leader who commanded Morris Force in the Bhamo area.

Mountbatten, Admiral. Supreme Commander SEAC.

Murata, Major-General. Chief of Staff of Japanese 33rd Division attacking Imphal.

Mutaguchi, General. Commanded Japanese 15th Army in the assault on Kohima and Imphal.

Netradahadur, Subadar. Won the VC at Imphal.

Nishida, Captain. Intelligence Officer with Japanese 31st Division at Kohima.

Omoto, Colonel. Commanded Japanese 51st Regiment at Nungshigum.

Pawsey, Charles. Deputy Commissioner at Kohima, who stayed throughout the siege.

Pearson, Squadron Leader 'Fatty Pearson'. Founded 194 Squadron in 1942.

Perowne, Brigadier. Commanded 23 Brigade which had Chindit training but was not used in that role, and operated north of Kohima as part of XXXIII Corps.

Randle, Captain, The Royal Norfolk Regiment. Won the VC on Norfolk Ridge at Kohima.

Randolph, Padre with the Royal West Kents at Kohima.

Ranking, Major-General. Area Commander at the beginning of the Kohima siege.

Rambir Singh, Subadar. Won the VC at Imphal.

Rees, Major-General Pete. Commanded 19th Division in the advance to Rangoon.

Richards, Colonel. Garrison Commander at Kohima.

Roberts, Major-General Ouvry. Commanded 23rd Indian Division at Imphal.

Rome, Colonel. Chindit leader, second in command to Calvert at Broadway.

Roosevelt, F. D., US President. Led the Allies during the war.

Russhon, Major, USAAF. The officer who delivered the photographs of logs on Piccadilly at the start of Operation 'Thursday'.

Sakuma, Colonel. Commanded Japanese 214th Infantry Regiment in 33rd Division, in attack on Bishenpur.

Salomons, Brigadier. Commanded 9 Brigade in 5th Indian Division.

Sasahara, Colonel. Commanded Japanese 215th Infantry Regiment in 33rd Division, in attack on Bishenpur.

Sato, General. Commanded Japanese 31st Division, in the advance from the Chindwin, in the attack on Kohima, and in its final defeat.

Scoones, Lieutenant-General G. A. P. Commanded IV Corps during the siege of Imphal.

Scoones, Brigadier. Brother of the Corps Commander, he commanded 254 Tank Brigade, and developed tank tactics for jungle fighting.

Scott, Lieutenant-Colonel. Commanding Officer of 2nd Battalion The Royal Norfolk Regiment at Kohima.

Shapland, Brigadier. Commanded 6 Brigade in the fighting around Kohima.

Shibata, General. Took over command of Japanese 15th Division after Mutaguchi sacked Yamauchi.

Slim, General. Flew into Burma when the retreat had started and commanded

Burma Corps. He built up Fourteenth Army and led it to victory in the battles of Imphal and Kohima and in the advance to Rangoon.

Snelling, Major-General. Responsible for administration in Fourteenth Army, particularly supplies and transport.

Stalin, Joseph. Leader of USSR, who met Roosevelt and Churchill at Teheran.

Stilwell, General. Commanded the Chinese forces in north Burma, and was Deputy Supreme Commander SEAC.

Stopford, General. Commmanded XXXIII Corps when it advanced to break the sieges of Kohima and Imphal.

Sultan, General. Succeeded Stilwell in command of American/Chinese forces in north Burma.

Sun, General. Commanded Chinese 38th Division, during the retreat, then retrained it, and joined Stilwell's forces in north Burma. The most successful Chinese general in the campaign.

Suzuki, Colonel. Chief Japanese agent in Burma before the Japanese invasion.

Symes, Major-General. Commanded 70th Division, and accepted position as second in command to Wingate; resigned after Wingate's death.

Tanaka, General. A strong leader who took over command of Japanese 33rd Division after Mutaguchi dismissed Yanagida.

Tazoe, General. Commanded Japanese Air Force in Burma, and clashed with Mutaguchi over the Chindit attack.

Thompson, Flight Lieutenant. The RAF officer attached to 77 Brigade at Broadway and after. Author of *Take to the Hills.*

Tojo. Japanese Prime Minister and Chief of Army Staff, 1942–4.

Trim, Lieutenant-Colonel. Commanded 4/5th Mahrattas at Sangshak.

Tulloch, Brigadier. Second in command to Wingate. Author of *Wingate in Peace and War.*

Turner, Sergeant in The West Yorks Regiment who won the VC at Ningthoukhong.

Vincent, Air Vice Marshal. Commanded 221 Group RAF.

Warren, Brigadier. Commanded 161 Brigade, which included the Royal West Kents, during the siege and battle of Kohima.

Waterhouse, Sergeant in 149 Squadron Royal Armoured Corps at the Kohima Tennis Court.

Wavell, General. Commander-in-Chief in India and subsequently Viceroy of India.

Williams, Lieutenant-Colonel. Known as 'Elephant Bill' for his remarkable work with elephants, he took part in operations when 20th Division withdrew to Shenam.

Wingate, Major-General. Founder and leader of the Chindits, who was killed soon after the start of Operation 'Thursday'.

Wingfield, Lieutenant-Colonel. Commanded 3/1st Gurkha Rifles at Shenam.

Yanagida, General. Commanded Japanese 33rd Division until he was replaced by Tanaka.

Yamamoto, General. Commanded the Japanese Infantry Group of 33rd Division in the main attack on Shenam.

Yamauchi, General. Commanded Japanese 15th Division which attacked Imphal from the east.

Yeo, Major. The brilliant gunner observation officer, who was in the siege of Kohima, and directed the guns from the 161 Brigade Box.

Young, Captain. Commanded a unit of the Assam Regiment and gave his life rather than surrender.

Young, Lieutenant-Colonel. The doctor in charge of the medical arrangements during the siege of Kohima.

GLOSSARY OF MILITARY TERMS

This is a very simple outline for readers who may not be familiar with military terminology, and is not intended to be specific. Nearly every sentence should contain that valuable word 'usually'.

British Army
UNITS AND RANKS

A **battalion,** commanded by a lieutenant-colonel, was made up of four **companies** each commanded by a major, and each company had three **platoons** commanded by a captain or a lieutenant. The battalion had a regimental sergeant-major, each company a company sergeant-major (Warrant Officers) and each platoon a sergeant. Each platoon had three sections, each commanded by a Corporal or Lance-Corporal.

Each platoon numbered about thirty men armed with rifles; each **section** had a Bren gun; and the platoon had a 2in mortar. The battalion had 3in mortars in a headquarters company.

Each **brigade,** commanded by a brigadier, was made up of three **battalions**, and three brigades made up a **division,** commanded by a major-general. A **corps** was composed of two or more divisions commanded by a lieutenant-general, one rank higher than a major-general. Two or more corps made up an **army.**

In the **Royal Artillery,** the equivalent of an infantry battalion was the field regiment, commanded by a lieutenant-colonel, and made up of four batteries, each commanded by a major. There was one field regiment per division, and it was armed with 25-pounders. Each corps had one medium regiment armed wih 5.5in howitzers.

Indian Army
The Indian Army coincided fairly closely with the British Army in terms of rank and structure. In an Indian division, a brigade would, usually, have two Indian battalions to one British battalion.

The majority of officers were British, but there were viceroy commissioned officers approximating to senior warrant officers, and their ranks were subadar-major, subadar and jemadar. NCOs' ranks included havildar (sergeant) and naik (corporal).

The designation of the Indian Army regiments can be illustrated from the Gurkhas. There were ten Gurkha regiments, and each regiment had several battalions, so reference is made, e.g., to 3/8th Gurkhas, meaning the Third Battalion of the 8th Gurkha Rifles, or, similarly, 9/14th Punjabis.

The Indian Army artillery included a jungle field regiment armed wih 25-pounders, 3.7in howitzers and 4.2in mortars, and a mountain regiment specializing in anti-aircraft and anti-tank guns.

Japanese Army
The Japanese Army had similar names and ranks, except that a unit of three battalions was called a regiment, not a brigade, and was commanded by a colonel. Each Japanese division was commanded by a lieutenant-general, with a major-general in command of the Infantry Group, e.g., Yamamoto Force from 33rd Division.

BIBLIOGRAPHY

This is a selection of books that give readable further detail on different aspects of the Battles of Imphal and Kohima, and on the Chindit issue.

General Books

Allen, Louis. *Burma The Longest War.* Dent, 1984 (paperback 1986). This excellent book gives admirable detail on every aspect of the Burma campaign, including remarkable information on the Japanese forces.

Calvert, Michael. *Fighting Mad.* Jarrolds, 1964. An excellent account of the Burma campaign by a brave fighting soldier.

— Slim. Ballantine, 1973. A sound brief account (paperback).

Kirby, S. W. *The War Against Japan.* vol. 3, 1962. The Official History, but it contains a disgraceful attack on Wingate.

Slim, Field Marshal Viscount. *Defeat into Victory.* Cassell, 1956. Slim's highly respected and detailed account of the campaign, but it contains ungenerous criticism of Wingate.

Smith, E. D. *Battle for Burma.* Batsford, 1979. A good general account.

Most of these books contain substantial detail on the battles of Imphal and Kohima.

Imphal

Atkins, D. *The Forgotten Major.* Toat Press, 1989 (also *The Reluctant Major*). Two excellent books written by the commander of a small unit. They catch the whole atmosphere very well.

Cooper, Raymond. *B Company, 9 Border Regiment.* Dobson, 1978. A good account, written soon after the war by a young infantry officer.

Evans, Geoffrey and **Brett-James,** Anthony. *Imphal.* Macmillan, 1961. A full and detailed study by two officers who took part in the battle.

Kohima

Campbell, Arthur. *The Siege.* Allen & Unwin, 1956. An excellent novel based very closely on actual events.

Phillips, Lucas. *Springboard to Victory.* Heinemann, 1966. A good general account of the Battle of Kohima.

Seaman, Harry. *The Battle at Sangshak.* Leo Cooper, 1989. A very good description of the critical battle, and the unjust treatment of 50 Indian Parachute Brigade.

Swinson, Arthur. *Kohima.* Cassell, 1966. A detailed and thorough study of the battle.

The Air Factor

Franks, N. L. R. *The Air Battle of Imphal.* 1985. A good and detailed account of this important aspect of the battle.

Williams, Douglas. *194 Squadron, The Friendly Firm.* Merlin Books, 1987. A vivid account of the operations of this Dakota squadron which flew into Imphal and Kohima and took part in Operation 'Thursday'.

The Chindit Issue

Calvert, Michael. *Prisoners of Hope.* Cape, 1952. A moving description of the battles at Broadway and Mogaung by the most successful of the Chindit leaders.

Fergusson, Bernard. *Beyond the Chindwin*. Collins, 1945 (also *The Wild Green Earth*). Interesting descriptions of the author's experiences as leader of a Chindit column.

Masters, John. *The Road Past Mandalay*. Joseph, 1961. Another good description of the actions of a Chindit column.

Mead, Peter. *Orde Wingate and the Historians*. Merlin Books, 1987. An exposé of the injustices done to Wingate and the Chindits.

Sykes, Christopher. *Orde Wingate*. Collins, 1959. A full and sympathtic biography.

Thompson, Sir Robert. *Make For The Hills*. Leo Cooper, 1989. Contains a vital section on Operation 'Thursday', and gives trenchant views on the Chindits.

Tulloch, Derek. *Wingate in Peace and War*. Macdonald, 1972. Written by Wingate's second in command, it highlights many of the injustices of which he was a victim.

INDEX

Units involved in the campaign are mentioned at the beginning of each chapter.